CW01184194

The Roadhouse Comes to Britain

The Roadhouse Comes to Britain

Drinking, Driving and Dancing, 1925–1955

David W. Gutzke and Michael John Law

Bloomsbury Academic
An imprint of Bloomsbury Publishing Plc

BLOOMSBURY
LONDON • OXFORD • NEW YORK • NEW DELHI • SYDNEY

Bloomsbury Academic
An imprint of Bloomsbury Publishing Plc

50 Bedford Square
London
WC1B 3DP
UK

1385 Broadway
New York
NY 10018
USA

www.bloomsbury.com

BLOOMSBURY and the Diana logo are trademarks of Bloomsbury Publishing Plc

First published 2017

© David W. Gutzke and Michael John Law, 2017

David W. Gutzke and Michael John Law have asserted their right under the Copyright, Designs and Patents Act, 1988, to be identified as Authors of this work.

All rights reserved. No part of this publication may be reproduced or transmitted in any form or by any means, electronic or mechanical, including photocopying, recording, or any information storage or retrieval system, without prior permission in writing from the publishers.

No responsibility for loss caused to any individual or organization acting on or refraining from action as a result of the material in this publication can be accepted by Bloomsbury or the authors.

British Library Cataloguing-in-Publication Data
A catalogue record for this book is available from the British Library.

ISBN: HB: 978-1-4742-9450-8
ePDF: 978-1-4742-9449-2
eBook: 978-1-4742-9451-5

Library of Congress Cataloging-in-Publication Data
Names: Gutzke, David W., 1949- author. | Law, Michael John, 1956- co-author.
Title: The roadhouse comes to Britain : drinking, driving and dancing, 1925-1955 / David W. Gutzke and Michael John Law.
Description: London ; New York : Bloomsbury Academic, an imprint of Bloomsbury Publishing Plc, 2017. | Includes bibliographical references and index.
Identifiers: LCCN 2016041964 (print) | LCCN 2016043345 (ebook) | ISBN 9781474294508 (hardback) | ISBN 9781474294515 (epub) | ISBN 9781474294492 (epdf)
Subjects: LCSH: Roadhouses–Great Britain–History–20th century. | Leisure–Great Britain–History–20th century. | Automobile travel–Social aspects–Great Britain–History–20th century. | Drinking of alcoholic beverages–Social aspects–Great Britain–History–20th century. | Dance–Social aspects–Great Britain–History–20th century. | Great Britain–Social life and customs–20th century. | Great Britain–Civilization–American influences. | BISAC: HISTORY / Europe / Great Britain. | HISTORY / Modern / 20th Century. | HISTORY / Social History.
Classification: LCC TX910.G7 G88 2017 (print) | LCC TX910.G7 (ebook) | DDC 647.9541/0904–dc23
LC record available at https://lccn.loc.gov/2016041964

Cover design: Adriana Brioso
Cover image © British Motor Industry Heritage Trust

Typeset by Integra Software Services Pvt. Ltd.
Printed and bound in Great Britain

Contents

List of Illustrations		vi
Acknowledgements		vii
1	Introduction	1
2	Gaudy Shacks and Palaces	15
3	Transatlantic Transgressions	31
4	Driving to the Roadhouse	53
5	Negotiating Class	65
6	Americanization and Modernity	81
7	The Roadhouse in the Public Imagination	95
8	Death of the Roadhouse?	111
9	Conclusion	123
Appendix – Catalogue of Interwar British Roadhouses		131
Notes		135
Bibliography		161
Index		176

List of Illustrations

Figures

2.1	Summary of Daniel Russell's American roadhouse typology	16
2.2	British roadhouses – proposed typology, development and influences	18
2.3	Hungaria River Club, 1925	22
2.4	Ace of Spades, Great West Road from the air, 1934	24
2.5	Thatched Barn, Barnet Bypass, late 1930s	25
2.6	Showboat, Bray, Maidenhead, 1934	26
3.1	Ace of Spades, Kingston Bypass, clubroom, 1933	38
3.2	Gymnastics at the Thatched Barn, 1938	47
4.1	Opening night of the Ace of Spades, Kingston Bypass, 1931	63
5.1	Spider's Web, 1935	74
6.1	Ace of Spades, Kingston Bypass, cocktail bar, 1933	86
6.2	Thatched Barn swimming pool, late 1930s	90
7.1	Monica Ewer in 1930, aged 41	99
8.1	Rawlin's garage and roadhouse, 1945	118
9.1	Roadhouse openings, 1927–39	125

Map

4.1	Major London roadhouses	57

Tables

4.1	Car adoption in the United States and Britain	54
4.2	Major London roadhouses	57

Acknowledgements

David Gutzke

The shared writing between John Law and me – a historical geographer and a historian – has produced a book reflecting the synthesis of our thinking. We brought different experiences, skills and perspectives to the topic, which made the final outcome a truly joint venture in our effort to write comparative history.

Many people contributed to this book's completion. Two close friends in particular warrant recognition. Trevor Lloyd read carefully every draft, making shrewd comments about style, substance and interpretation that elevated the book's quality to a much higher level. I have met few scholars as selfless, generous and knowledgeable as Trevor, for whose help I am forever grateful. Another friend, David Fahey, likewise read and commented on numerous drafts, from which I benefitted enormously. Unrivalled as a database searcher, he too gave unstinted time to locating sources, books and recently published material. I also want to thank Chris Waters who advised on sources and the concept of Americanization at an early stage in the project, which helped shaped our thinking, approach and understanding of roadhouses. Both David Kyvig and Thomas R. Pegram guided us about sources on prohibition in America, especially recent literature on drinking.

I am grateful to Missouri State University for its generous financial support, and to Dean Victor Matthew and Professor Kathleen Kennedy, who grasped the scholarly importance of what I was researching and facilitated writing with teaching schedules giving me blocks of time in which to write. Support came also in other forms. I received a faculty research grant to spend a summer in England; a subsidy for purchasing the copyright and reproduction fees for photographs; and, near the end when still teaching, an international travel grant to England to deliver a paper on roadhouses at a Bristol conference and to confer with my co-author, John Law, about final revisions to the manuscript.

I have much enjoyed working with John, and the cross-disciplinary exchange which immeasurably improved the framework, quality and argument of our book. In this process, I also acquired a good friend and fellow drinker of real ale.

So far at times from crucial sources, I learned to exploit the remarkable skills of Shannon Conlon and Deborah Williams, the University's two specialists at Interlibrary Loan. Their familiarity with database searches, peculiar regulations of lending libraries and obscure locations of materials made my research unexpectedly enjoyable and fulfilling. I am indebted to them for their kindness, insight and professionalism.

John Law

This book is the result of a long collaboration. For my part, it started in 2006 when my PhD supervisor, David Gilbert, suggested that some material I had produced for my Master's on the Ace of Spades roadhouse looked promising and more interesting than other ideas I was putting forward for my thesis. This led to my writing an article on roadhouses for the *Journal of Historical Geography*. I thought, at this point, that I was the only person interested in this obscure interwar leisure resort. An email from the United States from David Gutzke showed me that I was way off the mark. Here was someone who knew a lot about roadhouses and their American cousins. David had read my article and liked it enough to arrange a meeting on his next visit to Britain. So, we very slowly mapped out the idea for this book, where David brought his great depth of scholarship on the history of alcohol in the UK, and I brought what I knew about interwar cultures of motoring, Americanization, suburbanization and roadhouses (of course). Only ten years later, we had a book manuscript.

In the course of writing this book, I have been the recipient of much kind help from colleagues. Mark Clapson, the mentor of my late-blooming academic career, has always supported my efforts and whenever I need a clue where to look next, unfailingly delivers the goods. Geoff Levett has provided me with encouragement for this project throughout, discussed over many lunches, some of which David Gutzke has attended. I would also like to thank Martin Doherty and the University of Westminster for providing the financial support needed to license the photographs for this book.

Closer to home, my wife Katie and my daughters Lizzie, Charlie and Pippa have all been incredibly supportive of my late in life change of career and seem to have found the chapters of this book that they have read interesting, which I take as a good sign.

1

Introduction

Racy Roadhouse

Chorus

He	I'll run you to a racy roadhouse.
	It's really quite exclusive in its way
	There's whoopee in that little racy roadhouse
	until the break of day
She	I'd love to see this racy little roadhouse,
	you'd better get your Riley right away
	And run me to that racy little roadhouse
	until the break of day
He	I know that you'll adore the perfect dancing floor
	And if you're feeling thirsty there's a bar
	And when it's after time and alcohol's a crime
	'mums' the word, we can wangle a 'blinder'
She	There's rapture in my heart at your proposal
	And when we're tired of dancing, we can stay romancing
	in that racy little roadhouse
	until the break of day.[1]

'Racy Roadhouse', a song published just after the height of roadhouse popularity, alludes to many themes of this book, encapsulating transgression, class, automobility, illegal drinking, dancing and illicit sexual conduct. In the 1930s, roadhouses were famous and infamous, but today, if mentioned at all, roadhouses are perceived as merely another type of drinking establishment owned by the brewing industry. But they had little in common in fact with brewers' improved public houses or inns along bypass roads. Years ago, A.J.P. Taylor posed a central question about the 1930s: What was more significant for the future – over a million unemployed or over a million private cars? The automobile looms large in this book because roadhouse patrons arrived with friends in chauffeur-driven automobiles, took taxis or most often drove themselves.[2]

Roadhouses became popular in Britain in the 1930s, with dining, dancing, cabaret, swimming and other entertainments around the clock as key activities. They appealed to the type of privileged customer who went to West End nightclubs. Roadhouses, placed on newly built fast roads on the outskirts of cities, could only be reached by car, so they at first attracted wealthy and stylish customers. As time passed, they became more notorious than glamorous and their appeal to high society faded.

Emerging late in the 1920s around suburban London, roadhouses became fashionable early in the following decade, reaching their widest appeal in the years 1933–37. By the decade's end, they totalled around 200, spread throughout Britain, though disproportionate numbers surrounded London, the country's most prosperous region in the depressed 1930s.[3]

This introductory chapter explains why the roadhouse is an important but overlooked aspect of British leisure in the 1930s and beyond. It positions the roadhouse as a vital way of understanding the impact of new mobilities on the leisure habits of at first a metropolitan elite, and then an increasingly suburbanized middle-class clientele. How the concept itself travelled across the Atlantic, and became transformed into something distinctly British, though still showing signs of its American parent, is a recurring theme.

Americanization was a major influence on British society in the 1930s, as in the whole of the twentieth century. The roadhouse's story is partly about the influence of America on British interwar culture. Americanization can be viewed as a consequence of and response to the US economic and political hegemony maintained throughout the twentieth century, and it was evidenced, in part, through the consumption of American cultural products in Britain. In this context, Peter Taylor defines Americanization as a 'process of emulation and adaptation under the condition of consumer modernity'.[4] The adaptive aspect of Americanization is one of its distinctive qualities. Adaptations occurred through mediation, undertaken either for commercial or policy reasons or through the actions of ordinary people enjoying American culture in their own way. This mediation is often explained via the metaphors of hybridization or creolization.

Hybridization proposes a deliberate act of mixing two original sources to yield a new output, which suggests the actions of British commercial producers of Americanized material. Creolization better describes the actions of individual recipients who rearrange the semantic structure of a foreign source, mixing it with their own culture to create new meanings. In an influential contribution, Rob

Kroes proposes that these processes could be seen as a 'semiotic black box'.[5] As its name implies, the inputs and outputs of a transformational process can be known without understanding the nature of the mechanism that made the changes.

Theoretical concerns inform this book insofar as they help identify the receipt and adaptation of American cultural sources.[6] This is appropriate not just because American companies made no direct investment in British roadhouses, but because the latter's owners undertook no visits to understand how American country clubs and roadhouses operated. American influence on British roadhouses was principally mediated through Hollywood films and to a lesser extent newspapers, American literature and music.

Contemporary literature associated with the roadhouse explains how Americanization projected the image of the British roadhouse as a site of glamour, transgression and danger. A constant diet of American films, music and fiction promoted roadhouses as part of an imaginary America in suburban London (and elsewhere in Britain). Roadhouses were not so much a hybridization of the American original but rather a pastiche of the scenes of American country clubs shown in films. They were not, in fact, merely US imports, but developed from old-fashioned British petrol stations and roadside tearooms. In literature, roadhouses were popular settings for fast action as a secret hideout for gun-toting gangsters or in more grown-up writing as a seedy example of a corrupt, materialistic society.

Anglo-American transatlantic connections promoted Americanization in diverse ways. Marriages between British aristocrats and American heiresses, their upbringing imbuing them with greater freedom and autonomy than females in British landed society, encouraged new attitudes about women's conduct.[7] Easily overlooked, too, in this parallel were bartenders who as refugees from prohibitionist America would often be found serving in British roadhouses, blurring distinctions still further. Having relocated to Britain as a result of prohibition, American bartenders, the best qualified employed in London's West End and roadhouses, resisted offers to return to their homeland once prohibition ended because British salaries were higher than anything paid in the United States.[8] Given the transatlantic travel of many of the wealthy, drinking in unlicensed British roadhouses engendered a similar degree of satisfaction as they had experienced in the United States in thwarting police authorities, drinking alcohol illegally in speakeasies, cabarets and roadhouses, and frequenting establishments promising sexual intrigue.[9]

In examining how the American roadhouse came to influence its namesake in Britain, similarities as well as differences are recurring themes. However close the resemblance between the two countries, it was never of course entirely exact. London's Soho might have contained in a microcosm many of the traits – illegal drinking, gambling, prostitution, violence, shakedowns and gunfire – so readily evident in prohibitionist Chicago, but here the likeness ends.

Much academic and popular historical attention has been devoted to examining the world of semi-legal Soho night clubs of the 1920s and 1930s, while its more modern competitor, the roadhouse, has been mostly ignored. Roadhouses were synonymous with fast driving, anonymity, vulgarity and Americanization, thus producing a fulcrum in this book for our analysis of how new forms of leisure changed Britain in the 1930s and beyond.

In adopting a comparative approach, we analyse first the context in which roadhouses rose to popularity in dry America, considering the extent to which they signified changes in women's education, employment, use of public space, courtship and drinking habits, ultimately producing the iconic symbol of the 1920s, the flapper. We then consider how these ideas were inculcated into a British context in the late 1920s.

Long before the United States enacted prohibition in 1919, courtship rituals had fundamentally altered. New female drinking habits had emerged as a result of desegregated public drinking. A sense of individualism arising from working outside the home, together with growing white-collar employment, contributed to an entirely new image for young women. No longer would a woman's parents impose their rules as the basis for dating. Free of parental supervision and chaperones, they gained greater freedom but lost control of the dynamics of dating to young men who dictated how relationships developed.

In destroying the saloon and its masculine environment, prohibition accelerated this shift, reconfiguring drinking habits. Speakeasies, cabarets, roadhouses and nightclubs soared in numbers creating new public drinking space: for the first time drinking, hitherto segregated by gender, class, race and ethnicity, became egalitarian. Diverse factors prompted US females to embrace new drinking habits, notably college educations and inexpensive automobiles. Money, mobility and sense of adventure drove women to embrace new forms of leisure, entertainment and even jobs, such as bootlegging.

One new destination for courting couples was the roadhouse, located in American suburbs outside municipal authority. Eating, drinking and dancing drew vast numbers of juveniles and young adults whose patronage fuelled the expansion of such establishments in the 1920s. Much of this new drinking culture was harmless, but still attacked because of its lack of parental supervision, practising of new controversial dances (such as the erotic shimmy), jazz music ('jazz' was slang for sexual intercourse), late-night revelry, alcohol consumption and association with prostitution.

Roadhouses, of course, ran the full gamut from the respectable to the disreputable. Those with seedy reputations provoked the ire of authorities anxious about prostitution, drugs, gambling, vice and alcohol, an illegal beverage which many patrons enjoyed from their own hip flasks.

As a term in Britain, 'roadhouse' was used in varied ways in the 1930s, ranging from small roadside tearooms to enormous establishments on the outskirts of major cities. The most famous version was the 'super' roadhouse, at the height of elite fashion in 1933 and made known to a wider audience by being featured in many newsreels, newspaper articles, films, stage plays, songs, and popular and more serious literature.[10] These roadhouses were a significant component in the transformation of leisure in the 1930s and beyond, reflecting the greater levels of social and physical mobility brought about by new technologies, suburbanization and the influence of American culture.

Super roadhouses such as the twin Ace of Spades, the Spider's Web and the Thatched Barn were built on new arterial roads leading from central London. Initially, they drew wealthy Londoners excited by the prospect of a high speed run into what then was open countryside. At night, roadhouses delivered all the fun the West End could supply with dancing, classy restaurants, cabaret and added swimsuit parades, dance demonstrations and the like; roadhouses subverted the licensing laws to offer all night drinking.[11] Other pleasures may well have been offered; rumours abounded of prostitution and transgressive behaviour in the car park. During the day, a family atmosphere reigned with the emphasis on sport. This included tennis and archery and, at some establishments, horse riding, but for most it meant swimming in or lounging around an oversized pool, which as the day drew on was floodlit.

Roadhouses were designed to afford the 'smart set' an exclusive forum in which their activities pivoted around display, spectacle and consumption. According to Viscountess Rhondda, this social grouping

> spends its time playing bridge in the afternoons, motoring round to see its friends, plays a little tennis, dances a good deal, keeps the most fashionable kind of dog it can afford, spends a large proportion of its time … at its dressmaker, [and] spends all it can squeeze on jewellery.[12]

Leisure among Britain's smart set has until recently been ignored as a subject of scholarly interest. In exploring these elite drinking establishments, which emerged late in the 1920s, other important topics, such as the interaction between the traditional landed classes and the *nouveau riche*, are equally illuminated. Roadhouses served as the venue for desegregated leisure with the swimming pool as an ideal setting for the sexes to mix and socialize. Women participated equally with men as roadhouse patrons, but were also involved more directly as managers and sometimes even as owners, whose class background spanned the social spectrum of those with capital, from the middle classes to the gentry and even aristocracy. Owing to the exclusive image of roadhouses and the people who ran them, the smart set turned to this new venue as a setting for wedding receptions, parties and other functions.

Roadhouses became astonishingly popular because of the sweltering summers of the mid-1930s, late-night hours, popular entertainment, floodlit swimming pools and sumptuous food. Here patrons could escape London and venture into the countryside, a short journey of well under an hour. Given their meteoric rise in the public consciousness, roadhouses naturally acquired an enviable reputation as lucrative ventures. Like roadhouses themselves, this image proved to be transitory, with their heyday over long before the war's onset. Already losing a reputation for elite recreation and dining, the roadhouse found war-time conditions ill-suited for carefree leisure, especially with petrol rationing.

Analysis of social class, gender, clientele and desegregated leisure places the roadhouse in a broad context as a basis for understanding why they became chic, attracted thousands of admirers and established a name for catering to the wealthy and mobile of interwar Britain.

For Britons, drinking for middle- and upper-class males in the late Victorian and Edwardian years had been remarkably restricted. For decades, gentlemen's social clubs had proven home for propertied men seeking a refuge from the drudgeries of domestic life in the company of other males, especially in London where the concept had become most fully developed. As unlicensed purveyors of alcohol and enjoying unrestricted hours as well as virtual immunity to legal oversight, such clubs exploited the borderline between respectable and disreputable premises in which class acted as the critical delineator. Drunkenness drew an indulgent eye from the police, who connived at enforcing the law primarily against the working class.[13]

By examining how the culture of drinking became transformed amid the First World War, the roadhouse's emergence as a new venue for alcohol consumption and leisure for the smart set comes into sharper focus. Within this context, the clientele of various drinking places and, critically, their modification over time affords a greater understanding of the roadhouse's evolutionary history.

British drinking habits began changing from 1916 when vast numbers of respectable upper working- and middle-class women patronized pubs in unprecedented numbers, the first decisive shift in popular drinking habits in over a century. Women responded to diverse motivations: government policies, rising numbers of females entering the workforce and earning money, loss of male companionship (with men serving abroad), loneliness and bereavement – all these made pubs a sanctuary for those seeking solace.[14] Fears of a conservative backlash against women encroaching on hitherto masculine space led Lord D'Aberdon, Chairman of the Liquor Traffic Central Control Board (CCB), to act on his Progressive principles, embracing a new policy of gender equality in public drinking.[15]

Post-war life made this new drinking regime difficult to sustain without the CCB's active support. Anxious about a renewed attack on women's drinking to reassert traditional gender boundaries which had excluded all but the most impoverished and disreputable from frequenting pubs and beer houses, some prominent brewers asserted their new-found Progressive beliefs in championing a public house improvement movement. Over the course of the interwar years, the brewing industry built, rebuilt or renovated some 6,000 public houses, aimed at reclaiming public drinking premises as irreproachable venues for upper-working and middle-class men and women. Its expenditure on public house improvement overall reached some £100 million as the base of public house drinkers expanded, with about 40 per cent of all women frequenting pubs by the late 1930s.[16]

Improved public houses gave patrons wider amenities than traditional boozers, from tables and chairs, hot food and non-alcoholic beverages to indoor and outdoor games and gardens. Much money was spent on uplifting the environment with flowers, tablecloths, expensive panelling and tasteful décor. New or rebuilt interwar pubs might be had for as little as £3,200, but brewers, wanting the old, disreputable image of drinking establishments as boozers banished, laid out lavishly, with new or rebuilt pubs averaging £7,800. At the apex stood superpubs, those eighty premises representing the top 3.5 per cent of new improved pubs that cost at least £20,000.[17]

Central to the improved pub was the lounge, an entirely new room in which gender-neutral drinking prevailed. Here, brewers created a new subculture of drinking, closely 'resembling the smoking room of a club'.[18] Women and men sat at tables, ordered from waiters or waitresses and displayed typical bourgeois traits – discipline, restraint, orderly behaviour and efficiency. The lounge pre-eminently projected genteel culture: carpeted floors, cloakrooms rather than lavatories or water closets, upholstered chairs, stylish prints, green plants, fresh flowers, pleasing décor and non-intoxicating drinks. In this morally uplifted ambience, spittoons, stone floors, stand-up drinking, draught beer drunk from pint glasses, outdoor conveniences and long service counters – all hallmarks of traditional masculine pubs – vanished. Beverages consumed likewise denoted the class status of respectable drinkers. Men drank bottled beer or whisky, while women wine, cocktails or stout. Whether in cost, planning, layout or design, brewers went to great lengths to foster an atmosphere where the masses could meet their betters to receive instruction in order and discipline as part of a process of moral uplift. Ultimately, brewers saw improved pubs, the lounge the centrepiece of their gentrification, as an experiment in interclass mixing. Too long the site of what critics called the masculine republic, the pub underwent a process of social engineering with all classes interacting, at least in the lounge, to foster a more integrated society.[19]

Downward diffusion of amenities generally associated with select hotels and sizable urban inns became part of brewers' marketing strategy. At superpubs, patrons often encountered chefs preparing tasty cuisine, spacious dance and assembly halls, letting rooms, cocktail bars and orchestras. Sport too lured the athletic – golf, tennis, squash, bowling and swimming. In this social repositioning of the gentrified public house, brewers went one step further, renaming their improved establishments as hotels which duly appeared in county directories in this more exclusive category.[20]

To these improved pubs with their wider amenities, costly ambiances, more spacious layouts and tasty meals, motorists from the propertied classes would be drawn. Roadhouse proprietors also recognized these possibilities, but, significantly, did not set out to be respectable. They offered instead both unrestricted drinking hours and even more sophisticated forms of entertainment.

Differences in age, mobility and class powerfully shaped how and where females drank in Britain. Roadhouses generally attracted an older, up-market segment of the population. By the late 1920s, just 2.3 per cent of Britons possessed automobiles, a small amount compared to America. Physical immobility in Britain restricted class access to nightclubs, cabarets and roadhouses. Courtship rituals remained tightly circumscribed for most women, with chaperones required for female university students and debutantes. Nevertheless, Steve Humphries notes that nearly 40 per cent of women had premarital sex, with chances of pregnancy for them of about 50 per cent.[21]

Outside London and big cities, rural social venues were not much better. Country clubs, their attractive amenities of tennis, golf, dining and drinking, provided an alternative, though here guests needed to be prepared for staying overnight as part of a lengthy holiday. W. G. McMinnies, a well-known sportsman, aviator and motorist, first published his motorists' guide, *Signpost*, in 1935. He identified the club owner's dilemma: admit the 'hoi polloi' as a strategy for bolstering membership or restrict members to the better class. 'One thing is certain', he cautioned, 'you cannot mix the two'.[22] Central to attracting individuals was possession of a club licence, in which members enjoyed all the privileges of being a subscriber. Roadhouses therefore emerged late in the 1920s when few commercial rivals catered to the smart set, residents of suburbs in bigger cities and of smaller provincial towns.

How the roadhouse crossed the Atlantic and, in an entirely different milieu, became cleansed of its more risqué traits, modified to fit different drinking laws and broadened to encompass patrons of a more exclusive social status, comprises one main theme for investigation.

British roadhouses, like their US cousins, had risqué reputations, but what united them was the reality – or at least perception among some Britons – of illicit sex. In assessing the validity of lewd behaviour at British roadhouses, the reputation of their American counterparts undoubtedly predisposed critics to view Anglo-American roadhouses as mirror images of each other. Even taking this into account, sufficient evidence has been uncovered to support our thesis that the British roadhouse served as a venue for sexual liaisons and rendezvous. That more extensive evidence never appeared in the press owed undoubtedly much to libel laws, social influence of elite patrons who served as the mainstay of the clientele, reticence about discussing publicly a taboo topic and police oversight as restricted at roadhouses as at West End gentlemen's social clubs.

Roadhouse clientele changed over the period. In the years 1929 until 1933, the height of roadhouse fashion, the typical roadhouse customer was part of an elite metropolitan group of highly mobile people. Their interest in roadhouses reached a high point when its most senior member, the Prince of Wales, visited the Ace of Spades.

Going to a roadhouse was a modern alternative to frequenting a night club in London's West End, but was undertaken by driving a car rather than by taking a cab. In this way, the glamour and modernity of speed met with the glamour of wealth and privilege. These activities were documented and parodied by Evelyn Waugh in *Vile Bodies* (1930), and this trope has been reproduced in present-day representations of the interwar period in Britain, where every car is a red two-seater and all the girls wear cloche hats or short skirts.[23] Of course, this *demi-monde* was atypical of normal life in the early 1930s, but their modernity prefigures aspects of life in Britain after the Second World War when these pleasures were more widely available to all.

This group of high rollers has attracted some attention from historians examining the relationships between leisure and transgression. The most direct coverage is found in David Taylor's *Bright Young People: The Rise and Fall of a Generation, 1918–1940* (2007), which tracks the self-destructive aspects and extensive drug use of this elite group.[24] It concentrates on the central London scene and records no visits to roadhouses. There was, in one leading roadhouse at least, a crossover of ownership and interest between the suburban roadhouses and the seedy nightclubs of central London. These latter establishments are a central aspect of Judith Walkowitz's superb work on the Soho nightclub scene, *Nights Out: Life in Cosmopolitan London* (2012), which she explores with great deftness.[25]

The next generation of roadhouse customers moved in when the elite moved out from around 1934. As car ownership grew rapidly in London's suburbs and the Home Counties, widening groups of motorized middle-class clientele adopted the roadhouse habit. This change in roadhouse patronage during the course of the decade reflected three interrelated demographic themes. First is class, a topic which inevitably requires close consideration in any study of British life. The interwar period was an important period of class formation, where changes to Britain's industrial structure connected with a population movement away from the countryside and outer regions towards major cities fuelling an increase in the ranks of the lower-middle classes. These were the people who rented or bought inexpensive houses on new estates and found work in light industries and in offices and had more time to spend on leisure than their parents' generation. Immediately 'above' them in class terms were the more established middle classes, who by the middle of the 1930s had increased disposable income to spend on cars and leisure.[26] The key text for this topic is Ross McKibbin's *Classes and Cultures: England, 1918–51* (1998), which provides a comprehensive scholarly analysis of the forces in play in this period. It is accompanied by a wide range of work that helps position the changes and frailties of the class structure in Britain for this book.[27]

Second is suburbanization, which is closely related to class change in the 1930s. For British cities the effects of suburbanization were dramatic. For example, London's suburban population grew by 1.9 million people between the wars.[28] These new citizens were those most keen to adopt the benefits of a middle-class lifestyle, enjoying their leisure time, sometimes in the private domain of their recently acquired back gardens, but also in going out to the new improved pubs that spread throughout suburbia. Towards the end of the 1930s, this group began to go to suburban roadhouses for the first time. The most well known of the texts on British interwar suburbia is Alan Jackson's *Semi-Detached London: Suburban Development, Life and Transport, 1900–39* (1973). Although written many years ago and eschewing discussions of regional suburbanization, its insights are still widely applicable. Jackson's book was followed by more recent studies on which this book has also relied.[29]

The third demographic change relates to increased mobilities. During the 1930s, car use increased rapidly as the effects of recession were set aside. This provided middle-class Britons with an autonomous mobility that changed their capacity to spontaneously move through city and suburb. No longer were they constrained by the rigidity of the railway network and its timetables. Roadhouses became increasingly dependent on this phenomenon as wider usage required access to a car. This book relies on the groundbreaking work of Sean O'Connell's *The Car and British Society: Class, Gender and Motoring 1896–1939* (1998) and others writing for a more general audience.[30] It also reflects Michael John Law's work on the car's relationship with mobility and suburbia in interwar London.[31]

The effects of changes to class, suburbia and mobilities were all seen in how leisure developed in the 1930s. Academic examination of this topic has often focused on working-class experiences. This valuable project was triggered by the Marxist turn of the 1970s that emphasized the agency of Britain's working classes, which had been so often portrayed as an indistinguishable passive mass, who spent its leisure time in vertical drinking at the corner pub.[32] Less work has been done on middle-class leisure, perhaps due to their connection with suburbia's supposed homogeneity and boredom. Neither glamorous or powerful, nor oppressed and worthy, the interwar middle classes have escaped a single comprehensive review of their leisure pursuits.[33]

Some key individual aspects of middle-class leisure have been investigated. Attending the cinema, an almost universal interwar activity, has received much attention.[34] This is rightly so, as it was such a dominant practice; going to the cinema was the most popular leisure activity, very closely followed by reading books and magazines. Alison Light's influential *Forever England* (1991) repositioned middle-class women's reading material as a surprising generator of suburban modernity.[35] Holidaymaking was popular among the newly mobile middle classes and their choices have attracted studies.[36]

This book adds to the canon of work that studies a specific middle-class leisure activity. For the *bourgeoisie*, going to a roadhouse became an alternative or adjunct to other leisure activities such as golf, tennis and bridge. It is too late now to undertake oral history exercises on visits to roadhouses in the 1930s, so it has become necessary to assemble its history from a diverse selection of archival materials and popular representations of the period. The nature of British roadhouse ownership, primarily in the hands of small companies or often eccentric individuals, has meant that very little archival material survives. A few architectural plans of smaller roadhouses can be found in county archives, but that is all.

The roadhouse phenomenon was quite brief. After 1935, roadhouse proprietors battled against changing tastes, increased competition and then the impact of the Second World War. The effect of changing fashion, demographics and competition diminished markedly the attractiveness of roadhouses as a business. To provide swimming pools and West End orchestras was extremely expensive, and when demand tapered off, many roadhouses struggled to make a profit. The late 1930s saw many advertisements for roadhouses for sale at knock-down prices.

The decline from intense fashionability and concentrated media attention was abrupt, and so merits examination. First, this small group of thrill-seeking metropolitan types had a short attention span, flitting from one fashion to the next. Second, as motoring became more available, access to a car allowed people from below the 'top drawer' to patronize roadhouses, permitting middle-class revellers to infiltrate what had been a private club atmosphere. Third, Britain's major brewers, grasping the demand for middle-class motorized drinking, built many enormous competing roadhouse-style pubs and hotels to cater for their needs.

Arrival of the war and restrictions on private travel killed off many roadhouses. Petrol rationing and austerity that followed also limited the likelihood of revival. Nevertheless, one or two roadhouses prospered after the war; the Spider's Web in North London was popular with tourists and *nouveau riche* customers well into the late 1950s.

One fascinating dimension of the British roadhouse is the way in which it became a frequent setting in literature in the 1930s. This initially reflected the roadhouses' short-lived reputation as the fashionable destination for London's elite, a romantic and glamorous place of encounter. From the early 1920s onwards, the British press, imported short story books and Hollywood movies linked American roadhouses with disorder, juveniles, violence, bloodshed and murder. These narratives insinuated into the mind of the British public an image of novel drinking norms which predisposed how many Britons came to view the local version of the roadhouse. In this manner, British roadhouses assumed some of the trappings ascribed to roadhouses in American literature and movies.

Roadhouses began appearing in British detective fiction, the most typical genre of the decade, and, in a less sophisticated medium, in boys' story papers such as the Sexton Blake series. Novelists such as Graham Greene and Anthony Powell also set plots at roadhouses. Both authors positioned the roadhouse car park as a centre of illicit sexual encounter; in Powell's case from a distance of thirty years.[37] One curious characteristic of this topic is how the roadhouse lived longer in the literary imagination than in real life.

Our study establishes roadhouses for the first time as resorts for the motorized interested in romance, courtship and, sometimes, sexual intrigue. Roadhouses and the automobile were inseparable. Our thesis is that at their peak in the mid-1930s, roadhouses, powered by increasingly extensive automobility, delivered a new form of leisure that combined a contemporary obsession with exercise, the outdoors and the exotic with West End entertainment. Their remote situation provided the locus for actual and literary transgressions as well as societal concerns about anonymity and wider class mixing. Although loosely based on an American archetype, roadhouses combined English architectural manners with the Americanized popular culture prevalent in Britain in the decade before the Second World War.

The Roadhouse Comes to Britain has an explanatory opening based around the pre-history of the roadhouse, and will describe in the penultimate chapter how the roadhouse declined, but remained in the national imagination for many years. In between these chronological bookends we organize the remaining chapters thematically.

2

Gaudy Shacks and Palaces

It is very difficult to say what is and what is not a Road House.[1]

British roadhouses were an interwar phenomenon. They began in the mid-1920s as an exclusive and low-key offering for the wealthiest, grew to represent the height of fashion in about 1933 and were then imitated by both brewers and independent entrepreneurs that widened their customer base until they became increasingly *déclassé*. Roadhouses were mostly put paid to by the impact of the Second World War. Throughout this cycle of development, the roadhouse was particularly associated with the motor car and the wider mobilities that its introduction and adoption generated.

The term 'roadhouse' has antecedents from long before the commercial production of the car began in the first decade of the twentieth century. The *Oxford English Dictionary* (OED) traces the word back to 1806 where its meaning was simply that of a pub or lodging house with a roadside location for travellers who needed refreshment and accommodation.[2] It would seem likely that this definition preceded this particular dating by many decades. The OED first sees the introduction of the term in relation to cars and motoring in an American context in 1924. It portrays the American roadhouse as 'A restaurant, bar, or nightclub located on a major road, usually in a rural area or on the outskirts of a town or city, typically providing entertainment such as music and dancing, and often allowing gambling.' The quotation cited: 'Hitting it out for a roadhouse in a low-slung roadster at 100 miles an hour' is more specific in its linking of car-borne automobility, transgression and modernity.[3] References to roadhouses in American newspapers can be found from as early as 1917.[4]

Two critical factors fostered the American roadhouse's rise to prominence. The first was the widespread adoption of the car in the years after the First World War. Automobile ownership grew from 6.7 million in 1919 to 27 million by 1929, reaching a level of almost one car per household.[5] Second, prohibition in the United States from 1919 to 1933 encouraged the development of out of town, unregulated establishments. The American roadhouse has been well described as 'A drinking establishment offering dining and dancing to a diverse and fluid patronage that flourished with the spread of the automobile'.[6]

American roadhouses were, from their inception, associated with transgression and crime. Warren Belasco reports in *Americans on the Road* (1979) that hoteliers considered these roadhouses to be 'centres of debauchery'.[7] In 1931, researcher Daniel Russell identified six different types of roadhouses that were based on the following services: prostitution; gambling; saloon facilities; dancing; eating; and drinking and picnics.[8] Russell divided roadhouses into two main groups by how transgressive they were, although all these services could sometimes be found within a single establishment. Russell shows that illegal drinking, gambling and prostitution were central to the function of many roadhouses. Some were less transgressive, but almost all attempted to subvert prohibition restrictions. Russell's typology is shown below (see Figure 2.1).

Some writers commenting on the rise of British roadhouses proposed that they directly derived from an American source. For example,

> They [the road-houses] have supplied a modern need which the Londoner did not know until New York impregnated him with it, the need of some place to go.[9]

> We now find gaudy shacks working under the American title of 'road-houses'.[10]

> Road-House is an American expression, dating from the 'dry' period.[11]

This 'impregnation' was cultural rather than managerial or architectural. No evidence exists of American ownership in British roadhouses, inspection of American roadhouses by British owners or even the influence of American vernacular styles of roadhouse architecture on their British counterparts.[12] In contrast, American cultural impact on British roadhouses was predominantly

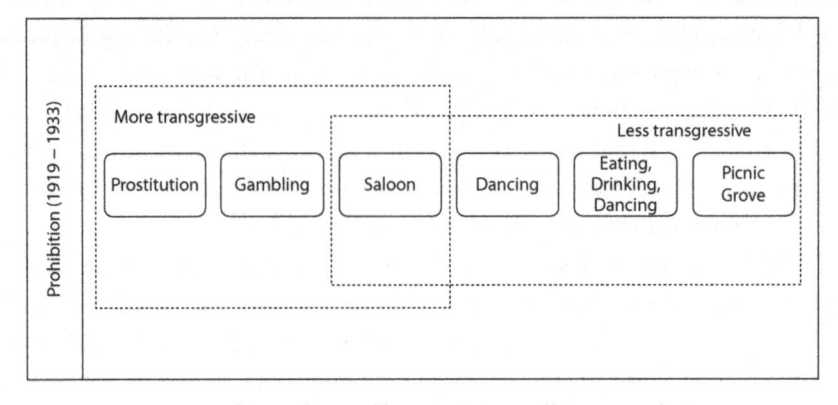

Figure 2.1 Summary of Daniel Russell's American roadhouse typology.

seen in the presentation of entertainment, the design of cocktail bars and in their somewhat transgressive atmosphere and liminal positioning on the edge of town. The sources of this cultural influence were American films, plays and literature.

British roadhouses were elusive to define, and a number of attempts were made to pin them down. George Long pronounced that roadhouses were 'large and expensively equipped establishments for the well to do.... Swim – Dine – Dance is the usual slogan'.[13] The newly formed Roadhouse Association thought that a 'thoroughbred roadhouse has petrol in its veins', that is, had come from a filling station archetype although this principle was undermined by the inclusion of some conventional hotels in its listings.[14] That well-known traveller around England S. P. B Mais commented that 'the coming of the Lido-Tea-House-Swimming-Pool-Dance-Hall-Roadhouse has drawn away some of those people from the river, who now motor to these centres in the country where they can have all the delights that they could have had if they had stayed in town'.[15] Mais was referring here to an indirect antecedent to the roadhouse, the river club, which combined entertainment and leisurely travel by boat.[16]

To qualify as an interwar roadhouse therefore required, as a minimum, an establishment on a roadside location providing food, drink and some form of diversion or entertainment to motoring customers. Entertainment varied considerably from a small zoo to super roadhouses that offered dancing, swimming, outdoor sports and flying fields. The one exception to this overall rule is the smaller pub roadhouse, discussed later in this chapter.

This book's typology of British roadhouses of the interwar period is divided into three periods and organized by archetype: tearoom; garage; river club; improved pub; and hotel (see Figure 2.2). By the end of the 1930s, each archetype developed into a particular and distinctive form of roadhouse. In the years between 1927 and 1933, involving the greatest change in the development of roadhouses, a process of cultural adaptation produced these types. The resulting set of fully developed roadhouses – rural roadhouse; super roadhouse; hybrid pub-roadhouse; pub roadhouse; and hotel roadhouse – goes some way to explaining the confusion over definition of roadhouses then and subsequently.

In summary, tearoom proprietors adapted their establishments by adding extra facilities for motorists. Garages added tearooms to their premises and, using examples from earlier river clubs, eventually developed into full-fledged super roadhouses. Hotels, also under the influence of the sophisticated river club, changed their marketing to attract drivers, and finally some major brewers,

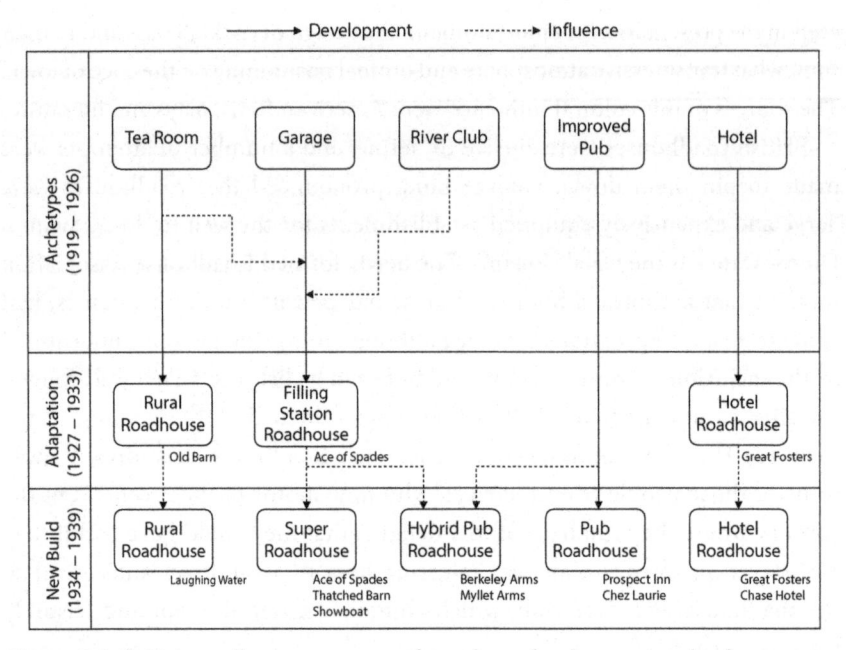

Figure 2.2 British roadhouses – proposed typology, development and influences.

keen to recruit middle-class customers to their improved pubs, provided extra levels of sophistication for their motorized patrons to form pub roadhouses. Of these varied forms, this book will concentrate on the best-known and most fully developed offering, the super roadhouse.

By the mid-1920s, Britain's wealthier households had started buying motor cars in large numbers. This was particularly so in the south and south-east of England, where 134,000 cars travelled the roads in London and the Home Counties by 1926.[17] In these days before mass-production factories in Britain, most cars were open-topped and with hand-built coachwork. These cars were bought by the wealthy, who would usually have a chauffeur to do the driving or if they were male and adventurous would do the driving themselves. New motorists saw the motor car as a vehicle for exploration and their destination was, typically, the English countryside with its beauty spots. In response, hoteliers developed their former stables into garage accommodation for these new motorists. Entrepreneurs, who recognized this newly mobilized wealthy clientele as potential customers, developed or adapted facilities catering to them. These new practices became a cause for concern for the protean British environmentalist movement, led by town planner Patrick Abercrombie and architect Clough Williams-Ellis.[18]

An early offering for motorists was the provision of a cup of tea, food and toilet facilities. Such tearooms were often converted old barns and other suitable rural accommodation that reinforced the idea of touring 'Olde England' by motor car. Some of these establishments would, eventually, be expanded into a type of roadhouse. New cafes and restaurants were also developed, aimed specifically at the motorized population. Many of these were, in turn, developed into much grander places, so it is difficult to see the original intentions behind the designs of these very first British roadhouses.

Williams-Ellis's plans, drawn up in 1924, for a roadhouse serves as one interesting source. He had a flourishing practice between the wars and specialized in 'largish South of England houses and in purpose-built roadhouses which looked rather like them, serving the new car-owners'.[19] In the 1930s, he was also the architect of a well regarded modernist roadhouse, Laughing Water. Although most well known by the public today for his romantic Italianate design for a village at Portmeirion in north Wales, Williams-Ellis was in the interwar period the influential author and editor, respectively, of those early environmental calls to action, *England and the Octopus* (1928) and *Britain and the Beast* (1937).[20]

His design, costing £14,000, a substantial sum for the period, was either unexecuted or if built was short-lived. This roadhouse took the form of a huge thatched cottage, and was defined specifically for the motorist.[21] Williams-Ellis set out the appeal: 'The road ... [has] something utterly new in the history of the world, and that is a perpetually hurrying horde of pleasure-seekers'.[22] This purpose-built establishment came with a car park, a quite early use of the idea in Britain. The car's working-class chauffeurs were accommodated in a separate building that also housed the roadhouse staff. This segregation of the classes was typical, but a further separation also appeared in the choice of lounge.[23] Two were available to the motorist, one associated with a café and beer store and the other with a restaurant and wine cellar. So, the more formally dressed motorists of Britain's upper classes would be drawn to the restaurant, and those more informally dressed or less certain about their class credentials could opt for the more informal café.[24]

Williams-Ellis included a photo of what he saw as an elegant and appropriate 'roadside tearoom' in *England and the Octopus*. He contrasted it with an example of an ugly tearoom with a new extension and vulgar advertising for tobacco into which 'cars may pull in'. Williams-Ellis's exemplar tearoom is very similar in style though smaller than the example above; it is likely that he was its architect.[25]

A good example of the rural tearoom roadhouse is the Old Barn, located on the London to Hastings road near Tonbridge in Kent. Its owner, Commander Tomlinson (RN, retired), recalled that 'As motoring for pleasure began to increase, a demand sprang up for meals, especially teas, in more open spaces where cars could be left without blocking a street where the owner and his family could sit in sunshine and fresh air.'[26] Tomlinson, whose adjacent malthouse had a white-painted slogan 'Oceans of Cream', would not have been popular with Williams-Ellis and the Council for the Preservation of Rural England (CPRE). The Old Barn had a grand tearoom, a swimming pool, a private landing field and a small zoo with penguins and a monkey, thus fulfilling S. P. B. Mais' definition of a roadhouse. On Saturdays, patrons were encouraged to 'bring a tail coat and white tie and dance', hoping to attract more up-market customers than the suburban roadhouses such as the Ace of Spades, where photographs showed dinner jackets rather than white tie as the dress code.[27]

One further addition to the stock of rural roadhouses was Williams-Ellis's 1933 Laughing Water at Cobham in Kent. Despite his preservationist inclinations, Williams-Ellis was, then, a keen exponent for modernism, which his design for Laughing Water reflected.[28] He used a simple timber structure, referencing many nautical themes typifying the period. One enthusiastic architectural writer thought that it was 'what our roadhouses and roadside cafes could be like if we took more trouble over them'.[29] That 'the pond is utilized to the upmost for rowing and swimming' suggests a roadhouse atmosphere.[30] So did the weekend when 'a London orchestra plays till midnight, evening dress or uniform being essential on these occasions'.[31]

Another antecedent of the modern roadhouse was the river club. This creature of the first two decades of the twentieth century emerged owing to the Edwardian obsession with boating and the river.[32] One of its key locations, Maidenhead, on the Thames thirty miles from London, was portrayed in a 1933 newsreel as 'almost the home of river-clubs for London's enjoyment brigade'.[33] Here, the urbane and urban could disport themselves in fashionable style. Michael Arlen, one of the most popular authors of the 1920s, wrote about a river club in his 1924 best seller *The Green Hat* (1924). One of his Bright Young Things says 'I've heard there's a River-Night-Club arrangement about here', although his companions doubt whether it was sufficiently exclusive for them.[34]

Established in 1913 in Maidenhead and surviving into the 1930s, Murray's River Club was the summer residence of its sister West End club. One remarkable feature was an illuminated glass dance floor that encouraged outdoor night-time dancing.[35] In the 1920s, Murray's River Club attracted the same type of clientele as roadhouses would pursue a few years later that included

> stars of the musical comedy world, leading members of beauty choruses, and originals of picture postcards.... Heads of 'big business' too; stockbrokers in striped trousers; undergraduates in loose ones; and Guards subalterns by the dozen.[36]

One history of British films contains a more transgressive memory of Murray's: 'Cocaine was what people came for... It was slipped to you in packets, very quietly, when you coughed up the loot'.[37] Given the origins of super roadhouses in river clubs and their similar clientele, the prevalence of cocaine in both is highly likely.

One sophisticated destination was the Hungaria River Club, located where the Bath Road crossed the Thames just outside Maidenhead. In 1929, this club presented a mock-up of a Parisian street scene and nightclub. Restaurateur Joseph Vecchi set up the Hungaria with funding from the patrons of his fashionable like-named establishment in London.[38] Historian D. J. Taylor notes that the club was 'packed with Society and Bohemia every week-end'.[39]

A newsreel film featuring the Hungaria showed some smart young people arriving at the club by boat, already dressed in swimming costumes, whom a smiling *maître 'd* (incongruously kitted out in full evening dress) greeted. The party began the fun by swimming in a small pool (by later roadhouse standards) and then enjoying dancing, dining and cabaret: 'inside the club, fast moving feet are dancing to Maurice and the boys'.[40] The river club was positioned as an elite and carefree fashion for its lower middle-class and working-class newsreel audience. Those at the cinema living much harder lives, however, must have reacted with raised eyebrows. Photographs of the terrace at the Hungaria revealed its beautiful outdoor restaurant set out under a flower-strewn pergola with seating for eighty customers at tables with white tablecloths.[41] Such images of river clubs amply demonstrate both sophistication and widened scope of entertainment (see Figure 2.3).[42]

Entrepreneurs of the first roadhouses were mindful of this type of entertainment when they imagined what possibilities these new arterial roads created. Super roadhouses, the elite of the genre, offered facilities very similar to those at river clubs, notably swimming, dancing, visiting celebrities and cabarets. It is intriguing that the Pathé newsreel series of 'Outer London Clubs and Cabarets' made no distinction between river clubs and roadhouses and set the Hungaria next to the Ace of Spades. Murray's club and the Hungaria were both examples of clubs with an established presence in London's West End. This town and country relationship can also be seen in the Thatched Barn roadhouse, owned by a less than respectable Soho club owner, Jack Isow.[43] When it became apparent that wealthy Londoners would use the car to expand their leisure opportunities, entrepreneurs offered similar facilities on London's new arteries, the bypasses and roads of outer suburbia.

Figure 2.3 Hungaria River Club, 1925. Copyright The Francis Frith Collection.

To this expansion, the government contributed enormously. In the late 1920s, it funded the development of a large-scale project to build fast arterial roads and bypasses around Britain's major cities. There was a particular concentration of road building in London, which had suffered more than most from traffic congestion in its Victorian outer suburbs and the small towns that surrounded it.[44] These spreading networks had a pointed cultural impact in the late 1920s and early 1930s when they became associated in the public mind with fast, elite driving. This was particularly so on the Western arterial roads: the Kingston Bypass, the Great West Road and Western Avenue. This reinforced a centuries-old link between fashion and the western side of London; the Kingston Bypass led to Brooklands, the home of interwar motor racing; the Great West Road led to Maidenhead and Ascot; and Western Avenue sped traffic to Oxford. It was hardly surprising, therefore, that super roadhouses catering for wealthy motorists appeared on these new highways. Hence the bypass had replaced the river as the conduit for delivering London's *demi-monde* to the countryside for swimming, dining and dancing.

Alongside the early tearoom could be found another progenitor of the 1930s roadhouse, the petrol or filling station, one of the most provocative 'uglifications' of Britain's countryside with former smithies and other roadside buildings being converted into ramshackle garages with a few petrol pumps outside. Williams-Ellis urged the building of attractive filling stations in a vernacular style that fitted into a countryside setting. One such example was set alongside the new Kingston Bypass in suburban south-west London. This type of new garage characterized those that added tearooms and restaurants to become full-fledged roadhouses, mixing a tiled-roofed, white-walled, country-cottage styled garage with modern petrol pumps.[45]

The original filling station roadhouse was the Ace of Spades, first built on the Great West Road, closely followed by its twin on the Kingston Bypass.[46] Although each had a restaurant and a swimming pool, the Kingston roadhouse received almost all of the popular attention in newsreels, newspaper articles and books. Both of the Ace of Spades roadhouses originated from filling stations. The Ace of Spades Petroleum Company developed them in a series of stages that exemplify the development route in our proposed typology (see Figure 2.2).[47] It opened its garage and tearoom on the Kingston Bypass in 1927, which were pictured in a motoring magazine in 1929 but not for their social interest.[48] It formed the accidental background of a picture of the latest motoring safety improvement, the roundabout, needed because of the volume and speed of traffic already using the new arterial roads. Wherever they crossed a major road, regular car accidents ensued, particularly at night. This is suggestive of the number of cars passing the Ace of Spades' front door, travelling to the countryside and seaside or driving into town for a special occasion. The admittedly murky photograph captured the Ace of Spades in its earliest stage as a petrol station, with several pumps facing the road. Hidden from view was its tearoom.[49]

Within two years, the Ace of Spades had been transformed from this humble beginning into one of the first sophisticated super roadhouses in Britain. At its opening on 20 July 1931, a staid looking crowd examined their party balloons rather gloomily. This seems a long way from the 'Bright Young People' and royalty that formed its customer base within a couple of years attracted by additions of a restaurant, dancing and cabaret.[50] Expansion came on 30 June 1933, with a clubroom and swimming pool added to its facilities.[51] The clubroom enabled members to circumvent licensing laws that prevented alcohol being served in the afternoon and late at night in public houses. Easily visible from the air, the open-air swimming pool was very large with a diving board, a poolside bar and an Ace of Spades motif in the centre of its tiling (see Figure 2.4). Introduction of an outsized pool was a significant nod to the obsession for all things outdoor that characterized the 1930s, an idea also seen in the public lidos built to cater for a social group of swimmers much wider than at the Ace of Spades.[52]

The Ace of Spades also attracted patrons with its outdoor facilities in the fields alongside the roadhouse. These would prove short-lived, its fields soon

Figure 2.4 Ace of Spades, Great West Road from the air, 1934. Reproduced by permission of Historic England Archive.

covered in houses in the rapid ribbon development along main roads that was so troubling in the 1930s. Customers could take advantage of its riding school, polo ground and its new flying field. The numbers that arrived by plane would surely have been quite few, but allowed the roadhouse to be seen as being at the forefront of modern life. This was reported in the biography of an early pilot, Eric Starling, who

> also availed himself of a similar facility on 23rd July 1933 at a road house called 'The Ace of Spades' at Kingston. These road houses considered a pilot's meal to be a good investment since they drew additional patrons attracted by the presence of the parked aircraft.[53]

The success of the Ace of Spades did not go unnoticed. Its clientele, elite and wealthy, provided an example to other entrepreneurs who wished to make money from the roadhouse habit. Taking their model from the fully developed filling station roadhouses, adventurous businessmen replicated the full suite of roadhouse offerings but in new, purpose-built buildings. This allowed them to build roadhouses in a coherent single design, in sharp contrast to the rather heuristic outcome to the Ace of Spades. The two biggest and most fashionable of these new super roadhouses were the Thatched Barn and the Showboat.

The largest roadhouse in Britain, the Thatched Barn, was situated on the Barnet Bypass, another of London's new arterial roads. This purpose-built Elizabethan-style creation was designed to catch the attention of passing motorists heading to the Great North Road and to pull in a London-based audience to its members' Barn Club. By being placed to the north of London, the Thatched Barn could attract customers for whom the Ace of Spades would be too distant for a casual drive. Massive in scale, it sported a thatched roof and half-timbered elevations (see Figure 2.5). It had a huge swimming pool and a car park that could accommodate 1,000 vehicles, while its restaurant could seat 400. Tennis and squash courts, a gymnasium and a golf school also beckoned members. In effect, the Thatched Barn was an early country club in the American sense. As a guidebook put it, 'there is dancing every evening to a well-known band and a cabaret every Saturday evening. The place's position, half an hour's run from town, makes it an ideal object for an evening's expedition'.[54] Harold Clunn portrayed the Barn Club as 'another palatial new roadhouse with a swimming pool, tennis and squash courts and billiard rooms. Here one may dance to the tunes of the Barnstormers' Orchestra every afternoon and evening'.[55]

The Thatched Barn was probably the greatest tudorbethan structure ever built, fascinating and grotesque in turn. The cost of construction of this monument to metropolitan leisure and wealth was estimated as £80,000.[56] This was an enormous sum, considering that the price of a smart, well-sized suburban house of the period was about £1,650.[57] The Thatched Barn was approximately four

Figure 2.5 Thatched Barn, Barnet Bypass, late 1930s. Author's collection.

times the cost of the more glamorous improved pub roadhouses that were built in this period for a 'staggering' £20,000 or more.[58]

Maidenhead's Showboat roadhouse was also purpose-built as a fashionable motoring destination. As the road came to the fore in the interwar period, it was appropriate that Maidenhead should be the location for a grand roadhouse with the river replaced by the London to Bath road. The Showboat, which opened in April 1933, was, in contrast to the Thatched Barn, of *moderne* design, mixing aspects of modernist architecture and deco styling, the whole resembling the bridge of an ocean liner. Its architect, Eric Norman Bailey, had established his reputation in designing cinemas using similar themes.[59]

This was a highly ambitious development (see Figure 2.6). Praise came from the local paper which promptly dubbed it '"The Palm Beach of Maidenhead" displaying the latest innovation' in roadhouses.[60] W. G. McMinnies described the Showboat as

> A very modern building containing a fine sprung oak floored ballroom and restaurant decorated in two shades of green, chromium and black and a magnificent pool surrounded by built-up terraces and cubicles which effectively screen the bathers from the wind. The American bar has a club room, which resembles the deck of a ship, [and is] also ultra-modern in furnishing and decoration.[61]

Figure 2.6 Showboat, Bray, Maidenhead, 1934. Author's collection.

The presence of nearby Edwardian buildings restricted the Showboat's size of operations; it offered fewer outdoor sports than advertised at some roadhouses. Its range of indoor facilities, however, was probably the widest in the country.

The weekly newsreels featured this strikingly new roadhouse, showing young couples and families enjoying the sun deck, sunbathers in their swimming costumes and variety acts performing in the ballroom.[62] Owners of the Showboat recognized that the wealth and leisure time of residents of the Home Counties ensured steady patronage day and night throughout the year. By allowing women and children to use its facilities, the Showboat distanced itself from the gendered Edwardian atmosphere of the golf club and created an updated version of Victorian domestic bliss.

Emergence of the hotel roadhouse, however, arose in quite different circumstances. Early in the 1930s, several longstanding Home Counties hotels changed their branding and offerings, effectively repositioning themselves as roadhouses.[63] As with all roadhouses, qualifying as such venues in the public eye required a decent-sized swimming pool and dance band in the evenings as amenities.

Great Fosters, a Tudor house in Egham, Surrey, was converted into a hotel in the 1930s in response to the booming roadhouse craze.[64] For additional authenticity its owners transported a medieval barn from nearby Ewell re-erecting it at Great Fosters to provide ample space for dancing.[65] Other hotels – Oatlands Park (Weybridge), Birch Hotel (Haywards Heath) and Chase Hotel (Ingatestone) – followed Great Fosters in this scramble to join the ever expanding ranks of roadhouses.[66]

Pub roadhouses likewise had distinctive origins. In promoting reform of the public house immediately following the First World War, brewers asserted their progressive beliefs with some 6,000 new, rebuilt or reconstructed premises as part of a massive effort at reconfiguring the culture of drinking. Enlightened progressive brewers had ambitious goals: expanding the customer base with respectable drinkers from the upper working and middle classes, incorporating women in a desegregated room called the lounge, fostering an environment antithetical to drunkenness and inculcating bourgeois cultural norms. They emphasized the provision of food, games, gardens and a morally uplifting atmosphere as a strategy to reduce drunkenness.[67]

Some improved pubs had many of the trappings of what the public came to see as roadhouses. Adopting the term 'roadhouse' allowed brewers and pub owners to further blur the social distinctions between various types of roadside provision. David Gutzke has argued: 'In appealing to motorists dining out, improved roadside pubs projected an image as refined as the type of customer they sought'.[68] This mimesis has resulted in a confusion with a long history that roadhouses were solely a development of the improved pub. This idea has been uncritically accepted by many, even scholars. Clive Aslet, an architectural historian, asserts that roadhouses 'were the improved public house at its most typical and best' but fails to note the famous super roadhouses of the 1930s that had nothing to do with the world of the pub.[69]

Prominent brewers and a handful of independent entrepreneurs built some small modernist roadside pubs (using the terms 'public house' and 'roadhouse' interchangeably) in south-eastern England. Prominent examples were the Comet (Great North Road at Hatfield), Chez Laurie (Thanet Way, Herne Bay, Kent) and a few miles further down the road to Canterbury, the Prospect Inn by renowned modernist architect Oliver Hill. Spanning the social divide, with their commitment to a modern style of building they attracted both private motorists and parties of charabanc customers.[70] No one style dominated – mock-Tudor, neo-Georgian, Modernist and French chateau style premises appeared, all rather incongruously thinking of themselves as roadhouses. The most luxurious pub roadhouses represented a mixing of the superpub and the super roadhouse, each sharing stylish restaurants and dancing to West End bands. Brewers enticed wealthy and sophisticated roadhouse customers with new pubs built on a palatial scale. These resulting buildings comprised a hybrid in which they possessed the imposing physical size, layout and architectural style of the elite improved public houses on the one hand with an imitation of the wide assortment of leisure activities, alcoholic beverages, food and cabaret of the super roadhouse, on the other. One well-known example of the hybrid pub roadhouse was the Berkeley Arms (Cranford) located directly on the Bath Road and built for Benskin's, a major regional brewery based in Watford. Travel writer Harold Clunn described it as a 'hostel rebuilt on a much grander scale and is now a favourite stopping place for teas and luncheons. In appearance it resembles some palatial French chateau and is noted for its Florentine restaurant and dance floor'; its architect, E. B. Musman, also worked on the Ace of Spades clubroom.[71]

Characteristically, the roadhouse pub segregated customers by class reflecting the time-honoured practice in public houses. Entering the Berkeley Arms through its main front door, customers moved into the saloon bar. Along the main frontage to the Bath Road was a separate entrance to a huge restaurant and saloon lounge. More upmarket clients sat in a loggia for summer evenings evoking 'the delicate sophistication of a Mayfair restaurant, complete with jazz band, skilful chef and noiseless long-tailed waiters'. On a side road, away from the junction with the Bath Road, two public bars served working-class customers 'where one may play darts in the company of the local lads'.[72] The brusquely named 'Meal Room' promising simple fare for the wealthier customers' chauffeurs completed the class segregation.[73] Interestingly, one authority on such matters, W. G. McMinnies, unlike other commentators, viewed the Berkeley Arms as a hotel rather than a roadhouse, because no legitimate respectable roadhouse offered accommodation: 'at some time or other the last twelve miles into London may seem too tiring and you will stay the night at this delightful place, and will find the bedrooms ultra-comfortable and as modern as the rest of the hotel'.[74]

The roadhouse originated neither as a brewer's improved pub, nor did its gestation involve, however short, a period as a mere drinking establishment. Brewers built a small number of hybrid pub roadhouses, and converted just several inns. No one agency accounted for most of the money fuelling the explosion of roadhouse establishments; brewers came late into the field and spent quite modest amounts. Brewers were just as likely to purchase existing roadhouses as to build the premises themselves.

The abstract concept, though not the broader meaning, of the roadhouse arrived in Britain from the United States. Admittedly, the practices of the British roadhouse were highly susceptible to the import and adoption of American cultural sources, but more important in its evolution were earlier archetypes that powerfully influenced how Britons conceptualized their own version of this 'transplant'. Super roadhouses led the fashion, and to them this book devotes much of its attention and analysis. Each of these pre-eminent roadhouses derived its origins from earlier forms of suburbanized leisure. Critical was the influence of the river club, remarkably similar to super roadhouses, in which the car and the arterial road replaced the boat and the river. In their provision of dancing, music and restaurants to mobile, affluent middle-class leisure seekers, the roadhouse can trace its lineage back to the late Victorian period. Thus, this particular middle-class leisure activity existed in its various guises from about 1880 to 1955. One can extend the idea of suburban leisure gardens to even earlier times. Arriving by boat to the suburban pleasure gardens at the late eighteenth-century Vauxhall for pleasure and assignation has many similarities to roadhouse life of a later age, which this book explores.

3

Transatlantic Transgressions

Writing in the early 1960s, columnist Raymond Postgate declared that 'the era when America altered the whole landscape of British drinking was, paradoxically enough, … when they themselves were officially prevented from drinking – the years of Prohibition'.[1] Given this intriguing reciprocity, it is imperative to understand how and why women's drinking patterns changed in the first quarter of the twentieth century. In examining how the American roadhouse came to influence its namesake in Britain, the pivotal role of the American roadhouse therefore must be investigated.

Long before the First World War and the roaring twenties 'a revolution in manners and morals' had ensued in the United States, with profound consequences for the emergence of roadhouses. Automobiles, telephones and increased numbers of work partners promoted unprecedented privacy and personal freedom between men and women in the early 1900s. Women gained a sense of individualism, spending greater amounts of time outside their homes. Their white-collar employment soared, while technological developments expanded leisure time, especially after 1914. These changes together would foster a new type of young women, the 'flapper', based in urban areas, drawn from the middle and upper classes, self-confident and independent. In her dancing, public behaviour, casual courtships and affairs, the flapper exhibited her zeal for experimenting with new-found freedoms.[2]

Courtship rituals also fundamentally altered. Young women, formerly supervised by parents within the confines of the home where they greeted young men calling on their daughters, began practising what was now called dating without parental guidance. With more time and leisure than the classes beneath them, middle- and upper-class women explored urban life, enjoying the privacy and anonymity conferred by working-class street life.[3]

Women's greater latitude in interacting with males contributed to the emergence of new drinking habits. Desegregation of public drinking began in big US cities such as New York from the early 1900s, a process that accelerated with the saloon's long-drawn out death, begun even before prohibition. During the roaring twenties, vast numbers of women were drawn into public drinking spaces hitherto unavailable to them, significantly reconfiguring drinking habits.[4]

When prohibition destroyed the disreputable masculine saloon, females, formerly averse to entering these dens of iniquity, became emancipated.[5] Prohibition reconfigured drinking habits, with considerable scope for women to participate in illegal activities such as liquor manufacturing, bootlegging and retailing as well as consumption. Creating public drinking space for women in the burgeoning new drinking culture, speakeasies, cabarets, roadhouses and nightclubs enabled women's entry into what became a more egalitarian world. Drinking among college students most clearly revealed the new democratic regime.[6] Prohibition in a sense turned class attitudes on their head. According to historian Thomas Pegram,

> Whereas saloons had offended middle-class sensibilities before prohibition, prohibition-era speakeasies furnished enjoyment and a hint of illegal adventure to the self-indulgent new middle class of the 1920s.[7]

Diverse factors shaped female drinking habits. Almost equal numbers of men and women went to colleges in the United States, where roadhouses drew patrons across the class spectrum, with juveniles a particularly common demographic group. Mobility critically defined drinking habits. Ownership of mass-produced, relatively inexpensive automobiles led to their diffusion downwards into the working class. Given widespread ownership of automobiles, the modest outlay on an evening out and the almost even gender division, roadhouses overall had an egalitarian ambiance. Flappers and consuming alcohol, especially of cocktails, were synonymous in the United States.[8] Americans' wider mobility thus profoundly affected courtship and sexual conduct. Drinking became the passport to social acceptance for single women in prohibition America. There was simply no alternative: if a male suitor was prohibited from bringing a bottle or flask along with him to the woman's house, 'he won't call again'.[9]

As a term, the flapper signified that the sexes were for the first time interacting without chaperones on dance floors and in cabarets and nightclubs as well as in automobiles. Virtually unfettered dating freedom owed much to the rapid spread of cars, with 20 per cent of Americans owning one by 1927. To the automobile must be ascribed a new sexual practice, 'petting', in which hitherto forbidden sexual contact flourished amid the privacy of the 'brothel on wheels'. First publicized as a practice in 1916, petting – and its attendant petting parties – gained notoriety in F. Scott Fitzgerald's *This Side of Paradise* (1920).[10] Babs, a fifteen-year-old high school student residing in a borough contiguous to Manhattan, had been introduced into the practices of her precocious peers, becoming an expert at petting parties in which rendezvous at roadhouses played a central role. 'I had come to look on them', she reflected, 'rather as necessary penalties, paid for a rather precarious footing on the social ladder of the younger set'.[11]

On the outskirts of cities or small villages along major highways, roadhouses escalated in numbers throughout the 1920s. North of Chicago on Dempster Road, roadhouses were literally situated side by side, each with 'its syncopated orchestra' where 'dancing continues there well past midnight'. Noted criminologist A. G. Barry, who had devoted years to investigating US roadhouses, knew that 'old residences had been turned into dance halls and numerous barns into roadhouses'. In exploring such establishments near a sizable city, Professor William McKinley Robinson noted their interiors were typically small, with stale air and semi-darkened rooms.[12] Having studied over one hundred roadhouses in Cook County, Chicago, two other authors offered a portrait of the typical roadhouse:

> One or two-storey, queerly-named frame structures containing an improvised old-fashioned bar and a medium sized, dimly lit, ill ventilated and smoky dining room filled with decrepit chairs and tables covered with soiled linen, an automatic instrument and radio or jazz band, a rough dance floor, and decorated with twisted streamers of brightly-colored, gaudy crepe paper.[13]

Roadhouses attracted a mobile clientele interested in eating, drinking and dancing. 'Dancing is only an incidental service, the major functions being the dispensing of refreshments, food, and the provision of vaudeville entertainments similar to that offered by cabarets', observed one investigator for the Juvenile Protective Association. Although roadhouses drew customers of all ages from all classes, access to automobiles and high prices established a formidable threshold for some potential patrons. Flappers were commonplace customers at many roadhouses, especially in suburbs of large cities. In fact, when a Connecticut woman planned on visiting such establishments alone, experienced garage proprietors supplied a list of companions from which to choose as an unofficial male escort.[14]

In selling alcohol illegally, roadhouses predictably became involved with burgeoning organized crime. Knowledgeable of where the wealthy dined and relaxed, the 'six robber barons' hit the Palm Gardens Roadhouse, southwest of Chicago at 3 am in October 1929, netting some $10,000, all but $2,500 in jewellery. Either Chicago roadhouse proprietors paid tribute money to appease the barons or faced repeated robberies, in this case the fifth in three months.[15] Several months earlier, six bandits armed with machine guns had robbed the Ridgeland Farm Roadhouse, located in an exclusive South Shore district, and extracted $20,000 from affluent Chicago businessmen.[16]

The least respectable of these places offered not only bootlegging, but also illegal activities – gambling, prostitution and vice. Nearly one-fifth of Cook County roadhouses, near Chicago, were equipped for accommodating prostitutes and their clients, with rooms rented at nominal prices.[17]

That some roadhouses were no more than well-known fronts for prostitution engendered their disreputable reputations. Located in lower-class villages, their streets seedy, rough and poorly patronized, suburban Chicago roadhouses catering to working-class men wanting prostitutes needed accessibility and privacy – transportation facilities had to be nearby as many clients, sometimes homeless, lacked automobiles. Indicative of their lower-class status, patrons of prostitutes who could afford transportation came in old Fords and second-hand cars. Prostitutes were mostly whites, but one black female ran a house with black women. In either case, the prostitutes were working class, and whatever money they earned their pimps appropriated at week's end. To this establishment, 'unmarried couples also came ... and spent the night with the permission and knowledge of the house'. Many other roadhouses had women available for prostitution, and sometimes entertainers did double-duty when demand arose.[18] Criminal gangs organized white slavery rings in which mobsters provided names of women to roadhouse proprietors running brothels, cabarets and tearooms in seven north-eastern states.[19] 'Hundreds of girls in their teens', commented the *Atlantic News-Telegraph*, 'are revolving slowly around a huge roadhouse circuit of vice'. Narcotics trapped young women into prostitution. Brothel keepers received a percentage of the profits, usually one-half of the prostitute's earnings, but the well-oiled operation, functioning much like a theatre circuit, netted her nothing more than a miniscule income after she paid for accommodation and her man's upkeep. So extensive was the far-flung nature of the business that the slave ring operated 'on the outskirts of virtually every town of any size in the east'. Prostitution was often linked with drugs and aliens. Charges of Mexicans supplying marijuana to some teenagers at Kansas roadhouses for holding 'marijuana parties' appeared in newspapers in August 1929. In a survey of twenty-five states, the US Children's Bureau reported the common sentiment that 'liquor and narcotics keep the road houses running'.[20]

US roadhouses overwhelmingly catered to juveniles and adolescents, fostering what one authority called a 'delinquency found in the night life of roadhouses'.[21] Cruikshant Hotel (Pennsylvania), 'the most notorious roadhouse in the county', served high school girls with alcohol, for which the proprietor was sentenced to two years in prison and fined $2,000. High school students participating in petting parties at roadhouses, thought one newspaper, were 'almost a national institution'.[22]

Roadhouses were popular places for sexual liaisons, enacted not just in unlit, discrete parking lots but in the premises themselves, their privacy affording opportunity to drink from a flask between dances. A survey of Kokomo, Indiana, revealed that seven of the nine roadhouses catered to those seeking booze as an accompaniment to petting parties. For couples eager to explore romantic feelings, roadhouse parking lots represented 'the only safe havens for necking couples', declared one newspaper.[23] Outside city limits and vigilant municipal control, roadhouses enticed couples with car parks shrouded in darkness. Despite packed car parking lots, Seattle roadhouse proprietors grumbled about dismal business.[24]

Automobiles, so critics charged, loomed large as contributors to this immorality. 'A young couple, a bottle of moonshine and an automobile are the most dangerous quartet that can be concocted for the destruction of human society', avowed the Superintendent of Chicago's Cook County Schools.[25] One clerk attested that 'if he had [access to] a car, there would not be a single virgin left in town'.[26] Dallas county Sheriff Dan Harston felt compelled to inaugurate an attack on what he described as the 'pet and parking' system which he knew 'accompanies the roadhouse dances'.[27] Soon, the YMCA as well as leaders of Women Reform took up the crusade, declaring 'war' on the flapper and 'her petting parties'.[28]

The collapse of relationships based on common ages excited criticism. At roadhouses middle-aged or elderly men danced with younger women, sometimes forming liaisons. 'I am private secretary to a man who takes me out to luncheon now and then, and when his wife is out of town we motor out to some nifty roadhouse and have dinner and dance', wrote a correspondent to the popular columnist, Dorothy Dix. 'There is no harm in it', she reassured Dix.[29]

Critics of US roadhouses so strenuously objected to roadhouses in large part because of their alleged immorality. Moonlight dances, body dancing, hip flasks, evocative music and curtained booths – all these shocked moralists. Some states, such as Massachusetts, enacted laws regulating curtained booths and 'immoral dancing'.[30] Even American roadhouses with unblemished reputations aroused mistrust. As unlawful, unlicensed and unsupervised drinking venues outside municipal areas, they sold banned alcohol, sometimes to juveniles, and played jazz, a music played in minor keys and so associated with prostitutes and sexual intercourse. Central to public distrust was the erotic shimmy, an entirely new dance performed at cabarets in white/black border areas that required dancers (crammed into limited dancing areas) to shift their focus from feet to torso.[31]

American writers unconsciously created an enduring image of US roadhouses. Eleanor Early, in her novel *Whirlwind* (1928), portrays a Boston society girl surprising her husband and sister-in-law at a roadhouse, downing cocktails and making love.[32] In a series entitled 'Flapper Fanny', an anonymous author gives her fictional roadhouse a name, 'Ye Blue Moon Inn', reminiscent of English public houses. Eager to avoid public attention and notoriety, her two main characters decide to use a backroom for privacy, only barely escaping detection in a raid.[33] Maud Radford Warren, in contrast, depicts her female character as balking at patronizing roadhouses because she associated them with 'petting' parties. Yet another popular author, Vina Delmar, depicts her characters as engaging in sexual conduct that stops short of sexual intercourse, a view that some historians have accepted. But more recent studies have disputed this portrayal, documenting that premarital intercourse among women soared to almost 50 per cent early in the 1920s.[34]

American fiction likewise powerfully shaped British public perceptions of the United States. Dashiell Hammett's novel *Red Harvest* (1929), which featured the Silver Arrow, with its illegal booze and violence, helped popularize the image of the American roadhouse as disreputable. The sleazy reputation was given wider currency when Paramount turned his novel into a movie, 'Roadhouse Nights', which opened in London in 1930.[35] Morality loomed large, however, in other films. In Colleen Moore's *Why Be Good?* (1929), an impecunious heroine is deemed worthy of marrying an affluent man because she steadfastly refuses to degrade herself by frequenting a roadhouse. Chastity in fact was a recurring theme of roaring twenties films.[36]

Guardians of the moral order naturally sought to impose their standards on roadhouse customers. Jessie F. Binford, Director of the Juvenile Protective Association in Chicago (Cook County), argued that roadhouses were objectionable for countenancing 'suggestive' dancing which 'would never be allowed in our public ballrooms'; permitting adolescents to rent rooms without scrutiny or inspection; and allowing their cars to be parked in secluded areas. Of particular concern was the breakdown of moral controls hitherto exercised by parents, teachers or other well-known adults. Patrons, miles away from home and thus assured of anonymity, were exposed to unfamiliar people and places, depriving them of guidance as well as constraints vital for their own protection.[37]

Critics registered disapproval of roadhouses on other grounds. Waukesha's State Supervisor of Rural Schools, George S. Dick, deemed women who had to be specifically instructed to avoid roadhouses as 'not fit to be teachers'.[38] Periodic raids on roadhouses imperilled careers. Billed as an 'authority on the Problems of Love and Marriage', Beatrice Fairfax recounted in her newspaper column, 'Advice to the Lovelorn', how a couple explored a roadhouse of dubious repute, and barely escaped arrest, which in the man's case would have 'ruined his career with a big insurance company'.[39] Dancing likewise aroused moralists' ire.

Amid escalating gang rivalry for control of illegal activities, violence became endemic, giving US roadhouses an image of bloodshed and murder in the early 1920s. Sir Basil Thomson, former director of Britain's CID (Criminal Investigation Department), returned from two visits to the United States in 1924 with the stark observation of prohibition's impact: 'Americans had grown accustomed to this murder'. He carefully noted the differences between the two countries: one in every 12,000 Americans was murdered each year, whereas one in every 635,000 Britons faced the same fate.[40] New York's Chief of Police attributed some 10,000 unexplained murders to the automobile, many of them connected with roadhouses. In suburban Chicago, one minister complained of being 'surrounded on all hands by road-houses'. British newspapers dutifully disseminated these commentaries.[41]

Sensational newspaper stories about US roadhouses successfully insinuated an image of novel drinking norms in prohibition America in the mind of the British public early in the 1920s. Returning from the United States, Margot Asquith, wife of former Liberal Prime Minister H. H. Asquith, accused young women of drinking heavily. Another Briton travelling abroad to the United States, Clare Sheridan, an English sculptress, learned that many Britons agreed, and 'seem to think American youth is composed entirely of immoral, drunken flappers, lounge lizards and roadhouse rogues'. British newspapers, she knew, were instrumental in creating this fallacious stereotype. Based on her reading of the press, one 'would think that the only things which happen in the United States are holdups, murders and divorces'.[42]

Britons saw a direct parallel between themselves and the United States for other compelling reasons. Illegal drinkers, gamblers, gangsters, robbers, gunmen, burglars, bootleggers, dope peddlers and users, prostitutes as well as blackmailers – all pervasive most conspicuously in Chicago – also characterized parts of West London and Soho in the 1920s and 1930s. Violence, gangland rivalries, police raids and unlawful consumption of booze made each seemingly the carbon copy of the other, though in the West End of London obviously on a much smaller

Figure 3.1 Ace of Spades, Kingston Bypass, clubroom, 1933. Architectural Press Archive/RIBA Collections.

scale. Owner of numerous nightclubs in these districts, Mrs Kate Meyrick, heralded as the 'Queen of Nightclubs', required little convincing that 'in those days London was just as bad as Chicago, if not worse'. Transatlantic visitors must have found the similarity striking, almost as if Chicago had been transported across the Atlantic to thrive in London's shadier nightclubs.[43] Everywhere, the process of Americanization was equally discernible.[44] Proprietor of the '43' nightclub on Gerrard Street where prostitutes and dope peddlers roamed freely and often profitably, Meyrick excelled at creating a transnational ambience. According to Judith Walkowitz, she imported underground Chicago to Soho, giving London dives a 'transatlantic flavour': nightclubs borrowed heavily from speakeasies in some cases down to an American name, such as the Florida or the Manhattan; physical and structural layouts were copied (notably basement dwellings as in Meyrick's case of the 43); elaborate rituals were instituted for gaining entrance (peepholes, barred locked doors and formidable doormen); and American jazz bands with their distinctive tunes, rhythms and cross-class as well as erotic sexual appeal were recruited, hired and promoted.

At the centre of the 43 and so much else in clubland stood Mrs Meyrick, personifying rebellious flappers who consumed cocktails, smoked publicly, varnished nails and wore lipstick, rouge and mascara, as well as flouted unreasonably restrictive licensing laws. Walkowitz suggests that Meyrick provided a 'modernized, "Americanized" variant of elite heterosexuality' in which a distinctive 'culture of speed' supplanted traditional divisions of night and day. Literally overturning time allotted for work and leisure, patrons participated in a new timeframe with the moment now ascendant in a world distorting class customs, social hierarchy and sexual boundaries. Risk, speed and disguise, Walkowitz argues, became the hallmarks of this nether world. Hence, patrons from diverse and indeed incongruous backgrounds intermixed – the respectable with the disreputable; debutantes with drug users, thieves and crooks; heterosexuals with homosexuals; the 'Bright Young Things' with the fast crowd; and married couples with prostitutes and bohemians. In Walkowitz's words, London's clubland became a 'hedonistic action environment', intent on undertaking activities, such as dining, breakfasting and dancing, well into the early morning hours, long after the rest of working society had retired. Nightclubs, explains historian Heather Shore, had 'a veneer of danger and excitement that proved attractive to the "bright young things" and later to roadhouse customers'.[45]

In patronizing London's vibrant nightclubs, Britain's smart set had become accustomed to an ambience which British roadhouses replicated but which they also carefully sanitized, retaining the risqué drinking after hours, gambling and nocturnal dancing, and dining (see Figure 3.1). British roadhouses were redolent of nightlife in prohibition America, but tamer, members of the smart set confronting the loss of carefree fun if authorities intervened but little else – jewellery, personal safety and money were all secure. Risk but not the danger of Soho nightclubs was part of the adventure. Participating in roadhouse nightlife enabled the well-heeled to inhabit safely a specially created twilight zone, something not quite thoroughly respectable but still protected from rubbing shoulders with those of either far more limited financial means or dubious characters.

Given the process of Americanization, British roadhouses did not escape the stigma of their more lurid American counterparts. 'As at present conducted', one proprietor conceded, 'many road houses are not viewed with favour by the Authorities'. Immoderate drinking naturally provoked criticism. Having met a woman at a roadhouse and been smitten, novelist Sir Max Pemberton anticipated her needs – dancing and drinking, perhaps excessively. Inevitably, he thought, 'some Road Houses had to be merely the Haymarket night club over again with licenses refused to them and perhaps an early if undeserved reputation for naughtiness'.[46]

Those who thought they knew the roadhouse best felt compelled as a result to defend it in print. W. G. McMinnies, for example, expressed scepticism at the pervasive perception of roadhouses as 'rather naughty'. Reassuring his motorist readers that roadhouses listed in his travel guides were impeccably respectable, he devoted a separate section in the inaugural issue in 1935 to outlining their attractions and praising their prices as outstanding value.[47] Commander Tomlinson also denied the validity of the strictures against roadhouses: 'cases of young people too merry to drive a car are very rare'.[48]

Both men's assessments warrant closer examination. McMinnies' popular annual guides, begun in 1935, identified roadhouses with irreproachable reputations, thereby requiring him to differentiate implicitly between acceptable and risqué establishments. In the light of this distinction, Tomlinson's own denial of youth's excessive drinking becomes questionable. McMinnies provided entries for both of Tomlinson's roadhouses, the Old Barn and Tudor House, from the very first edition. Lacking a liquor licence, Tomlinson turned to nearby accommodating publicans to apply for a licence extending licensing hours when a special dance was booked at the Old Barn. Drinking, he admitted, continued well beyond the special permit by several hours, but Tomlinson nevertheless upheld the Old Barn's reputation as an establishment in which he as the proprietor never (directly) served drinks outside licensing hours.[49]

A liquor licence was emblematic of respectability, the stamp of approval from licensing magistrates. Monica Ewer writes about this topic in her novel, *Roadhouse* (1935). Both its managing director and another employee tell Alison

Reed, recently hired as the new personal secretary, to remove her cosmetics, the pre-war attire of prostitutes. 'A place like this has to keep a good name – if it can', remarks her colleague, Hope Wilson. 'You have to be very careful or you can lose your [liquor] licence', she adds.[50]

Proprietors of 'a new type of roadside non-licensed refreshment house know that so long as they do not actually sell alcoholic beverages, consumption can take place on these premises the round of the clock', commented the *Caterer and Hotel-Keepers' Gazette* in June 1932.[51] Often the vehicle for obtaining alcohol was literally the automobile, transformed into a portable off-licence with champagne and whisky bottles 'peeping coyly out of capacious overcoat pockets'. Some roadhouse proprietors had few scruples about acting as intermediaries, promising to obtain alcohol for patrons in as little as five minutes.[52]

Curiously, this evoked images of American practices. Opened in 1931, the Spider's Web, lacking a licence, acquired the alcohol ordered by patrons from a pub three-quarters of a mile away. 'Business proved so good that motor bicycles had to be maintained to keep up a constant service'. Newspapers, commented J. Williams, 'christened them "The Rum Runners" and gave invaluable publicity'.[53]

Both playwrights and filmmakers were instrumental in ensuring the term acquired a pejorative meaning. Ideally placed to foster a transatlantic connection, Walter Hackett, an American playwright, spent his interwar years writing plays in London. One of them, *Road House*, written early in the 1930s, pivots on the metamorphosis of a Victorian inn, the Angel, located on the Portsmouth Road in suburban Surrey, into the Angel Face roadhouse immediately following the First World War. With its swimming pool, cocktail lounge and amenities targeted specifically at the wealthier sections of the middle classes, the British roadhouse ranked as a more refined establishment than its American counterpart. But Hackett did not entirely escape his American background. Frequenting his Angel Face was a heterogeneous group of aristocrats, the nouveau rich and criminals. As with writers in the United States, he made the roadhouse the rendezvous for extramarital affairs. 'So many of our clients don't care about their husbands', remarks the proprietress. Not even the established social elite were immune. Lady Chetwynd engages not only in adultery, but also robbery. Several young women strip off all their clothing, and dive into the swimming pool to rescue a man befuddled with champagne.[54] By the time Gaumont Studios transformed the play into a film of the same name in 1934, the roadhouse had become the venue for an American-style racket in which Lady Chetwynd, together with two confederates, burgle the homes of customers who were drinking, swimming and committing adultery at the Angel Face. Nor did the owner, Kitty Tout, escape scandal in the screen version of the play. Tout has her own questionable past of mixed lineage, being the product of a brief liaison between a barmaid-cum music hall performer and a member of the local gentry.[55]

Fictional roadhouses also found dubious opportunities for their male employees:

> The tea-dance that afternoon therefore saw Jeremy starting forth on another calling that of a 'gentlemen instructor' with a salary of three pounds a week – 'but you can earn five times as much as that if you are not really squeamish' ... [together with] free board in an annexe to this yellow-fronted, blue-doored, green-windowed, morally crimson roadhouse.[56]

Critical fictional portrayals likewise inculcated in the public mind an image of the British roadhouse as obviously popular but distinctly sordid. In *Thou Shall of Death* (1936), Nicholas Blake creates the imaginary Fizz-and-Frolic Club, near the Kingston Bypass, site of the real-life Ace of Spades, the archetypal roadhouse, which Lord Marlinworth describes as 'very posh and popular'. He derides its owner, Cyril Knott-Sloman, however, 'as just the sort of dago to make a success of a thing like that'. Lady Marlinworth, who lives with her husband at his family's country house, dismisses Knott-Sloman as 'proprietor of a brothel'. One of his female associates, Lucilla, is described by another character euphemistically as a 'sort of high-class decoy' for the roadhouse. Philip Starling, an Oxford Don, shares this loathing. The club owner, he observes, 'was a brass hat in the war and runs a road-house in the peace, and if you can tell me a more nauseating combination of activities I'll eat my hat'. Both the Frolic and its proprietor evidently justify this prejudice: the roadhouse has barely escaped police prosecution on several occasions, and rumour has it that both Knott-Sloman and his companion, Lucilla, are blackmailers. Befittingly, the cigar smoking, female-bottom slapping, silken roadhouse owner gets murdered for conniving at extortion.[57]

The following year Margery Allingham reinforced this unsavoury image in *The Case of the Late Pig* (1937). R. I. P. Peters, nicknamed 'Pig' by those who knew him well, is universally loathed. Having made money, he uses underhanded tactics to buy a beloved country club, Halt Knight, as well as several contiguous East Anglian country estates. He then proposes to despoil the picturesque setting with a roadhouse, featuring a swimming pool, dog-racing track, cinema and dance hall. Appalled local residents are up in arms, and the much detested Pig meets an abrupt end, murdered by a hefty geranium urn dropped from a nearby roof on his head.[58]

In that same year, the roadhouse's alleged reputation for unlicensed drinking, sexual escapades and uninhibited partying acquired more scandalous connections – prostitution, sleazy Soho nightclubs, dope peddling and white slave trafficking. In mystery writer Valentine Williams' short story, 'The Dot-and-Carry Case' (1937), two people are found dead, apparent suicides – married stockbroker Dudley Frohawk and his amour, Leila Trent – at a car park of a disreputable roadhouse on the Great North Road. She had performed as an entertainer at the roadhouse, has numerous 'gentlemen friends', and is described as 'a little guttersnipe ... picking a precarious livelihood between her "gentlemen friends" and the lower class of Soho nightclubs'. Her close associate, 'Malay Joe' Long Brady, is involved with a 'dope-peddling crowd', often frequenters of roadhouses. Born in Malta in 1899 and known as a jewel thief and himself a morphine addict, Brady had served time in French prisons for dope selling, and is a 'white-slave trafficker, narcotic smuggler'. Manderton, the detective, suspects Trent of distributing narcotics at the roadhouse and elsewhere. The case climaxes with the respectable stockbroker acquitted of wrongdoing, having been impersonated by Malay Joe. In the tradition of gangland killings in Chicago so well publicized in Britain, an interloper from a Belgian syndicate wanting to muscle-in on Malay Joe's activities is ultimately found dead outside London, 'his smart clothes smeared with mud and blood, his hands tied behind him, three bullets in his head'.[59]

One year later, in *Brighton Rock* (1938), Graham Greene uses the Queen of Hearts roadhouse on the London to Brighton road as a suitable night out for his anti-hero Pinky and his racecourse gang. Here they enjoy the usual roadhouse facilities with the addition of sex in the car park with a roadhouse good time girl.[60]

Such images in the media and fiction may suggest why McMinnies became disenchanted with roadhouses as a respectable retreat for motorists after 1937 for inclusion in his touring guide. Having faithfully listed and fulsomely praised leading establishments – Ace of Spades, Thatched Barn, Clock, Laughing Water, Old Barn and Spider's Web – from his initial 1935 issue, he unceremoniously abandoned this practice, slashing his roadhouse entries by two-thirds. By 1939, just two establishments in McMinnies' inaugural list of forty had survived; no explanation was ever offered for this purge.[61]

By any reckoning, McMinnies' entries seem peculiar when regarded as a whole. Why were so few roadhouses added to his original list, even those that had appeared after 1934? Constraints of space, of course, limited his freedom, but some of these establishments clearly deserved recognition. Consider three conspicuous omissions – the Houseboat (1935), Stewponey (1936) and Willow

Barn (1938) – that cumulatively cost nearly £80,000. Why were some of the most expensive roadhouses deemed unfit for McMinnies' guides? Two other roadhouses, the Finchdale Abbey (1936, £30,000) and the Nautical William (1937, £30,000), did find their way into his guide, but just briefly for one year after opening. Unquestionably, the most expensive roadhouse, the Thatched Barn earned his accolades until 1937 when abruptly dropped, never to reappear. McMinnies explained neither his criteria for listing roadhouses nor his reason for losing faith in the concept.[62]

Fiction certainly served as one source of the roadhouse's risqué image, but so did reality. Some, perhaps many, of the roadhouses excluded from McMinnies' guide were those which equally contributed to their unsavoury image. In the southeast – the Gay Adventure, Monkey Puzzle, Chez Laurie, Havering Court and Sugar Bowl – fell into this group. Reporters covered the opening of the Monkey Puzzle (West Sussex) in 1933, featuring a swimming pool as well as outdoor sports, but ignored it thereafter.[63] This certainly qualified as one of the popular but anonymous roadhouses criticized for its drunken motorists in the *Manchester Guardian*:

> Unfortunately, only a small minority of motorists grasp these facts. The staffs of garages adjoining popular roadhouses tell really appalling stories of the drinking habits of the wilder motorists. In the dining rooms of roadside hotels sedate parties of reputable motorists may be seen every day consuming far more liquor than is rational.[64]

The writer then proposed that a more attractive form of non-alcoholic refreshment should be found for roadhouse customers. This sentiment, however, was not widely shared. It was quite normal to think of drinking beer as a way of refreshing oneself and only excessive drinking of spirits was considered anti-social.[65]

Later that year Arthur E. Bennett intimated in another newspaper article that much criticism of disreputable behaviour at roadhouses was fully warranted.[66] He might have pointed to illegal sales of alcohol in the previous year at Fleetwood, Lancashire, where two women were fined £70. These two distributors had the misfortune to be charged, but the practice of retrieving alcohol for patrons was widespread at many roadhouses.[67] In this instance, the alcohol was purchased before patrons placed the order, thus the intermediators transacted the sale before purchase.

Other factors clearly motivated McMinnies to exclude increasing numbers of roadhouses from his guide. Insight into his thinking had appeared in a newspaper exposé published in the summer of 1932 in which it claimed that roadhouses with the most dubious reputations were not the most luxurious, but those well down into the second, or even third, tier masquerading as unlicensed tearooms.[68] Some commentators were incapable of appreciating these distinctions. Writing in a 1935 travelogue of England, Ivor Brown derided roadhouses as a homogenous group for their 'garishness' and catering to the low-end customers, what he called 'the new paganism in its flashiest form'. Outraged at one roadhouse's advertisement featuring its 'Super-Super-Barmaids', he dismissed outright roadhouses in general as inferior to country clubs.[69] Liquor was nevertheless obtainable to resourceful patrons and shady roadhouse proprietors. According to one investigator, 'some of these cafés rival the notorious "roadhouse" of America, which cater for wild parties'. At such gatherings, the reporter added, 'petting parties' may be seen indulging in wines and liquor until the small hours of the morning.[70] Elsa Dundas's Kentish roadhouse specializing in 'dainty teas and cakes' fits remarkably well into this description. A former typist, Dundas and her brother invested her inheritance of £700 in this new venture, which became quite successful. Her roadhouse became a retreat for bosses and their typists. One elderly man accompanied a woman young enough to be mistaken as his daughter but called her 'darling', and she responded by addressing him as 'sir'.[71]

Britons' prejudice against these new watering holes originated in these establishments' lack of respectability. Consider the history of the Chez Laurie. Thomas Warrington had retired as a metal merchant and served as a publican of several different hotels. With cash from the former and experience from the latter, he bought several acres near Herne Bay as the site for his conception of a roadhouse, soon called Chez Laurie. Undaunted by his failure to obtain a liquor licence, he built the premises and opened for business early in 1938. Having spent some £13,500 on an establishment that featured 'a very excellent high class meal' and dancing, Warrington was chagrined when magistrates again rebuffed his application for a licence. He had several difficulties, notably his rivalry with three nearby new improved pubs. But what unsettled magistrates and in no way advanced the merits of his case was his risqué décor that adorned the walls: cocktail and playing cards decorated with nude figures.[72]

Warrington felt astonished at his rejection, partly because of the select clientele for whom he catered on a quite considerable scale: 8,000 had purchased meals in his first year of business.[73] Warrington, his barrister argued, aimed at patrons who wanted 'a place where they could get a first-class cuisine and find those facilities, comforts and luxuries that one got in the modern high-class restaurant'. What neither he sought nor they wanted was the public house trade, especially the plebeian element which invaded coastal pubs in charabancs. The

Roman Galley, one of the three nearby new improved pubs, had cornered this end of the market, its pull-in during the summer months 'chock-a-block with charabancs', his barrister noted derisively. No one, he urged, would define them as 'the really high-class trade', the customers whom Warrington thought his establishment ideally suited. Warrington had invested a substantial sum on his roadhouse, slightly less than what the brewery had spent on the Roman Galley. Ironically, though he believed the Chez Laurie to be superior, what separated it from the nearby pubs was not so much the cost of the premises as the type of customers who frequented each. His customers comprised the elite: 'the private motor car people', socially middle class and above.[74] But Warrington found that his risqué establishment proved too embarrassing to appear in McMinnies' annual guides aimed at the smart set.

In denying Warrington a licence, magistrates reaffirmed the view that the Chez Laurie was *déclassé*. Roadhouse proprietors themselves, however, did not necessarily agree with this perspective. Reminiscent of Haymarket nightclubs, such as the Embassy, Chez Victor and Ciro's, that applied repeatedly but unavailingly for liquor licences, thereby incurring a stigma in the eyes of legal authorities, roadhouses such as Chez Laurie, lacking a licence either through choice or legal rejection, likewise attained an image as establishments of ill-repute or possibly mere naughtiness, depending upon the proclivities of the observer. That many Soho licensed nightclubs in serving liquor well beyond licensing hours of 12.30 am provoked police raids, most famously on Mrs Meyrick's clubs, may have simply elevated the appeal of those roadhouses which emulated them. Besides, the Prince of Wales dined in the exclusive and expensive Kit-Kat in the Haymarket the day before a raid, an unofficial endorsement of the establishment. Police raids never seemed to discourage patrons of Mrs Meyrick's nightclubs, which temporarily closed only to reopen under a different name.[75]

Class habits crucially shaped divergent attitudes towards recreation. Quite simply, leisure habits of the well-to-do did not conform to society in general. This social elite ate dinner later than the rest of Britain, and hence wanted to drink, swim and dance later into the evening and early morning. Most importantly, they had money to afford this lifestyle. Such a regime sat oddly with licensing laws, but not with accommodating roadhouse proprietors. Attacks on Soho nightclubs were so successful late in the 1920s in part because patrons, deprived of other viable alternatives, turned to roadhouses as the best option. There was, too, the fact that liquor prices at nightclubs, as at roadhouses, were sufficiently high to deter undesirable interlopers. Super roadhouses also featured the most

Figure 3.2 Gymnastics at the Thatched Barn, 1938. From *The Order of the Bath*. Copyright British Pathé.

fashionable black American jazz bands, dancing to the latest crazes and the opportunity to combine two irresistible pursuits – dancing and swimming – at the same venue (see Figure 3.2). This same combination had proven extremely successfully at a swimming-pool party at St. George's Baths, where guests danced in swimming costumes.[76]

In allowing alcohol consumption on public premises without a liquor licence, roadhouse managers cleverly exploited a legal loophole. In this sense, there was indeed a similarity at least between establishments in this category and roadhouses in America. Once Britons grasped this point, the British roadhouse came to be viewed as having acquired some of the disrepute associated with its US cousin. For British patrons of unlicensed roadhouses, the intrigue of drinking alcohol was accentuated with 'bottle parties' in which participants brought their own booze as well as food. Such parties were reminiscent of amusing distractions that Loelia (later Duchess of Westminster) and Gaspard Ponsonby, her brother, had introduced into their smart circle in the 1920s.[77]

To a large extent, class underlay Anglo-American attitudes to drinking. According to the *Manchester Guardian* in 1928, there was 'one law for the rich and another for the poor', 'Indeed', the paper continued, restraint on drinking in prohibition America 'hardly touches the rich at all if they choose to ignore the law'. Otho W. Nicholson MP likewise knew that in the United States 'on every hand the law is broken ... with the satisfaction of having overcome some stupid obstacle standing in the way of rational enjoyment'. Britons, nocturnal celebrators of carefree leisure at roadhouses, fully empathized.[78]

Roadhouses certainly had no monopoly on late-night drinking, dining and dancing. Their proprietors understood the London's nightclubs against which they had to compete to draw the clientele they sought. With drink available (with food) legally until 2 am and illegally until the wee morning hours, patrons drank prodigiously and spent profligately, the same as in popular West End nightclubs of Mrs Meyrick. Virtually any alcohol could be had at a price, usually double what pubs charged.[79]

Britain's social elite followed a schedule suited to late-night entertainment and eating. One reporter, who arrived at a roadhouse after 11 pm, encountered burgeoning crowds that, he learned, diminished only after 1 am, with food still available for another hour. The peak of patrons came at midnight, 'when fashionably dressed crowds drive down from the heart of London'. In one two-hour period (11 pm–1 am), not quite 400 swimmers swelled the aggregate numbers.[80] Emulating West End nightclubs, some roadhouses catered to these nocturnal patrons, offering breakfasts of bacon, eggs and kippers. The Ace of Spades, the recognized roadhouse pioneer, for instance, promised meals 'at any hour of the day or night', and dancing on weekends until 3 am. This may explain why five years elapsed before the Ace applied for a liquor licence.[81] Drinkers not violently drunk could consume alcohol whenever they wanted, which sharply contrasted with pubs and nightclubs with their shorter licensing hours. This, together with roadhouses' relative isolation, also meant that loud music, singing and intoxication would draw no attention from authorities.

Competition was certainly not the only reason why some roadhouse proprietors shunned a liquor licence. Part of the allure of roadhouses was precisely their differences with public houses, which the propertied linked with a plebeian clientele. All licensed premises were subject to police supervision, and this intrusive scrutiny would have circumscribed patrons' conduct.

The unlicensed British roadhouse promised patrons the privacy they cherished during leisure, while creating a risqué environment in which they carried (or ordered) and consumed liquor of their own choice, much like drinkers at US speakeasies and roadhouses. In this context, roadhouses were vastly superior to nightclubs, which sold alcohol after licensing hours and hence faced periodic raids. Behaviour to which patrons had grown accustomed – complete privacy, unsupervised observation and guaranteed anonymity – would be lost once premises became licensed. Such roadhouses would no longer possess, moreover, a racy reputation, conveying something equally quite naughty, associated with their US counterpart. It was surely no accident that Warrington's Chez Laurie had six bedrooms for overnight accommodation on its second floor. Four other unlicensed establishments excluded from McMinnies' guides – the Aldermaston Mill, the Mill Stream, the Monkey Puzzle and the Popular Road House – all had similar accommodation. McMinnies listed the Finchdale Abbey Hotel, costing £30,000, after its initial opening in 1936 for just one year. Overnight accommodation was here well provided with nine bedrooms.[82] Some extraordinarily costly premises, such as the Myllet Arms, had a licence but also overnight accommodation, but still failed to meet McMinnies' exacting standards.[83]

Given sensitivity of the topic, general English reticence about discussing sex and legal issues of libel, critics withdrew discreetly into innuendo. H. W. Dawson, representative of William Whittaker & Co., brewers, disclosed to the *Yorkshire Evening Post* that 'there has been a great deal of talk ... about roadhouses that have fallen into a considerable amount of disrepute, especially in this district [Otley, Yorkshire]'. In their interwar survey penned at the outset of the Second World War, *The Long Week-End* (1941), Robert Graves and Alan Hodge remarked that roadhouses 'provided ... a night's lodging and no awkward questions asked'. On the Great West Road, they added, 'one or two of them had a reputation of being "bagnios" in the Italian sense'.[84]

Marriage for the 'smart set', wrote historian Pamela Horn, 'offered freedom to engage in an independent life away from parental supervision, and to enjoy agreeable flirtation with eligible young men when the opportunity offered, in a way that was impossible for a single woman who valued her reputation'.[85] Unmarried women of the smart set with enough income, in contrast, though still tightly controlled by chaperones in town, could own a motor car and drive themselves, entirely free of a chauffeur's supervision. Socially beneath this exclusive group, 'fashionable young women' had been 'allowed to attend [formal gatherings] unaccompanied by chaperones' in growing numbers in the early 1900s, argued Earl Mayo who pointed to the 'American influence on English social customs' as the chief explanation. Roadhouses proved to be one place that commonly beckoned these different social strata of women, save for debutantes who endured as rigid control over their conduct in the 1930s as in the 1920s.[86] Unmarried women, too, incurred a stigma as a result of such a visit. 'The ensemble seemed far too attractive and seductive to some observers', thought historian Graham Robson, 'so they were labelled as "fast" – any girl visiting a road-house with her boyfriend in his sports car immediately gained something of a reputation'.[87] Britons traveling to roadhouses would thus come chiefly from the generally well-heeled middle- and upper-middle classes, together with those socially above them, to consume legal alcoholic beverages.[88]

For some patrons, roadhouses became a splendid retreat from publicity, and rendezvous of sexual intrigue. For instance, an immoral affair developed between Mrs Muriel Phillips (36), manager of Havering Court (Harlow, Essex), and Sidney J. Furze (65), with whom she became intimate in 1932. For £6 per week, a very tidy sum, Phillips became Furze's 'secretary'. When the affair came before the Court, it was deemed one grounded on 'immoral considerations' with sex exchanged for money as the basis.[89]

Illicit roadhouse affairs were by no means confined to this single instance.[90] 'If one compiled a list of Sunday golfers based on information gleaned from golf club secretaries and officials, and then deducted the total number of golfers who actually made that day sacrosanct for golf, it would be possible to find out exactly how many two-timing alibi-hounds were playing their golf in roadhouses', smirked the *Daily Mail*.[91] One of the first roadhouses, the Ace of Spades (Kingston Bypass), received publicity with a newsreel shot in 1934, and in one segment a patron seated at a table with a female companion held up a dinner plate to hide his face as the camera panned the audience.[92]

Sensitivity of the Spider's Web to a suggestive drawing, published in *Men Only*, a pornographic magazine, in 1952, raises pertinent questions. On entering the Web's cocktail bar, a patron is introduced to an outlandish woman, lewdly dressed with heavy makeup. In suing for libel, the Web contended that the picture insinuated that the roadhouse 'employed women of loose morals to frequent their premises, that male customers visiting the premises were introduced to such women by the management for immoral purposes, and the premises were a bawdy lair and a place of resort of prostitutes'. Concluding that the drawing misrepresented the Web's respectable clientele, the Court fined the periodical £500 in damages.[93]

Of the unaddressed questions, one in particular warrants comment: What motivated the Web's complaint? Winning what can only be regarded as a nominal sum was surely a pyrrhic victory. If the Web really possessed an irreproachably unblemished reputation, the lawsuit was wholly unnecessary. In fact, *Men Only*'s picture satirizing the Web's problematic morals inevitably raised questions about what actually transpired at this private, exclusive venue on a regular basis. Was this challenge to a pornographic magazine deliberately intended to publicize to its readers what they might well expect when frequenting the Web's cocktail bar but could not, for reasons of libel, say in print? Certainly, those familiar with the Web's early history in which it circumvented liquor laws by arranging for alcohol to be supplied to patrons, despite the roadhouse's lack of a licence, indicated how the roadhouse saw itself as occupying a borderland between legal and illegal behaviour.

One can only speculate whether roadhouses sometimes also served other purposes. English divorce laws might have led to collusive divorces in which (usually) the husband went to a hotel and provided plausible evidence of adultery to enable his wife to sue. Roadhouses certainly were preferable to questionable hotels, but the overwhelming desire to suppress undesirable publicity would explain why newspapers published no sensational stories.[94]

Close connections between some Soho nightclubs and suburban roadhouses underlined the widening web of nightlife in the 1930s, and contributed to the roadhouse's unsavoury reputation. Throughout the 1920s and 1930s, Jack Isow ran a series of unlicensed clubs – notably the Roxy Club, Windmill Club and the Majestic Billiard Hall – repeatedly raided for illegal drinking and gambling. His last venture in 1935 proved the most successful, establishing the Shim Sham club in Soho on Wardour Street, the familiar haunt of prostitutes who prowled in the numerous sleazy nightclubs. The Majestic Billiard Hall, located below the Shim Sham, drew the attention of the Sabini gang, with the premises vandalized and employees attacked. Months later in 1936, unlicensed dancing and music provoked a police raid on the Shim Sham. Apparently infuriated at being refused entry to the Thatched Barn roadhouse because he was a Jew, Isow acted on his threat to take it over and sack the doorman. He soon regretted this business venture. Raided for running a gambling house and permitting unlicensed drinking, dancing, singing and music, Isow was arrested, convicted and imprisoned. Illicit sex was never mooted as an attendant problem, but he certainly created a context conducive to it.[95]

Roadhouse car parks had assumed new possibilities late in the 1920s when manufacturers introduced closed roofed cars that further encouraged unconventional sexual behaviour. This novel form of the car offered a warm, secure and heated location for lovers to enjoy themselves, at a time when it was quite difficult for unmarried couples to use hotel rooms. Some roadhouses advertised overnight accommodation, but the roadhouse car park was an important location for both straight and homosexual encounters. Aimed at this guarded group of society was a list of possible all-night destinations on a coach-trip poster that named the Ace of Spades.[96] Coded words – 'bohemian' and 'unconventional' – disclose the poster's purpose. Homosexuality was strongly punished, and so was forced out of public gaze into private clubs and London's 'cottages' and parks. Given the seclusion both legal and physical of roadhouse car parks, it is hardly surprising that homosexuals turned to them as relatively safe romantic venues.[97]

Americanization assumed a critical role in the roadhouses' history. From US newspaper stories reprinted in Britain and comments of British visitors returning from the US also publicized in the press, Britons acquired an image of US roadhouses as sites of violence, lawlessness, bloodshed and murder. When the roadhouse as a venue in turn crossed the ocean, Britons naturally presumed that many of the trappings of this US invader would be inevitably transposed to a British setting. Thus, it came about that Britons were predisposed to view distinctive cultural norms in US and British roadhouses as virtually identical. Early critical press coverage of 'Bright Young Things' publicized their escapades of sex, drink and drunkenness, some of them at roadhouses that acquired a pejorative reputation.[98]

However, much leisure in the smart set in America and Britain came to resemble each other, they were still distinctly different. McMinnies was especially sensitive to this issue when compiling his guide to motorists' pleasure grounds, which he thought qualified as thoroughly respectable following his personal inspection.[99]

Our study establishes roadhouses for the first time as resorts for the motorized social elite interested in romance, courtship and, sometimes, sexual intrigue. Roadhouses and the automobile were inseparable. Sean O'Connell's research on the automobile in interwar Britain is quite suggestive in linking increased youth sexual activity among the middle classes with growing car ownership.[100] Given the huge disparity between automobile ownership in Anglo-America, not to mention other pertinent factors, Britons would never fully replicate the extent of sexual conduct in the United States. Access to automobiles shaped differences between them in terms of class, wealth, age, courtship patterns and standard amenities available at the ultimate destination. Roadhouses in Britain were never plebeian, never a site of mass entertainment, never an adolescent retreat and never linked with violence, organized mobs or sex rings. Nevertheless, some of the popular perceptions of American roadhouses influenced how many Britons came to see their own version of the roadhouse.

Did some roadhouses afford more opportunities for sex than had existed previously, or simply displace sexual conduct that had gone on elsewhere? The evidence is inconclusive for any confident generalization, a conclusion not surprising given the secrecy enveloping private affairs.

4

Driving to the Roadhouse

In 1938, Graham Greene described the journey from Brighton along the London Road, where a group of racecourse gangsters were planning to visit the Queen of Hearts roadhouse:

> 'It's the best roadhouse this side of London' ... They drove out in the old Morris into the country ... Advertisements trailed along the arterial road: bungalows and a broken farm, short chalky grass where a hoarding had been pulled down. The Queen of Hearts was floodlit behind the petrol pumps: a Tudor barn converted, a vestige of a farmyard left in the arrangement of the restaurant and bars: a swimming pool where the paddock had been.[1]

As well as reinforcing the public perception of roadhouses as transgressive, Greene caught in his writing the excitement of driving a car along an arterial road for a *déclassé*, raucous night out. In the 1930s, the roadhouse was closely associated with driving a car, just as in previous generations roadside inns and tearooms were associated with cyclists. Interwar roadhouses were developed specifically to service the ever-increasing number of car drivers in Britain; it is no coincidence that most roadhouses were to be found in the Home Counties, the part of the country where car usage was at its highest.

Country roadhouses were able to adapt themselves to the car by letting them park in a nearby field. Suburban super roadhouses, often located on arterial roads, had to provide their customers with well laid out car parking. The largest roadhouses paid particular attention to this aspect of their offering making sure that customers could always find somewhere to leave their car. The largest roadhouse in the country, the Thatched Barn, was able to accommodate as many as 1,000 cars.[2] The Showboat in Maidenhead advertised on its opening that it offered a 'large free car park', which can be seen in an aerial photo of the building (see Figure 2.6). It is intriguing that even as early as 1933 the competition for parking a car was such that drivers had become accustomed to pay for this convenience and that to get it for free was an attractive proposition.[3]

Roadhouses, in the general sense of entertainment destinations based around the car, arrived in the United States twenty years before Britain. America's experience was dissimilar to Britain in many ways. Car adoption was earlier and more rapid than in Britain because of greater net incomes, less public transport and lower prices through greater economies of scale as well as earlier adoption of mass production techniques. Although delayed in comparison to the United States, motoring culture in Britain between the wars was transformed as cars became more numerous and were adopted by wider social groups. The differences were dramatic in both absolute and relative terms and are shown in Table 4.1.

Relatively slow adoption of the car in Britain compared to the United States and the absence of prohibition meant that roadhouses did not begin to emerge until the late 1920s. The pattern of adoption in Britain was very different across its regions, reflecting the widely varying rates of economic growth across the country in the fifteen years after the First World War. Demobbed servicemen found on their return that the staple industries that Britain had relied on for decades, such as cotton, shipbuilding, coal and steel had seriously declined in market demand and profitability, a consequence of both world economic conditions and underinvestment compared to the country's main competitors.[4] Consequently, many formerly prosperous areas now faced deep economic recession. These areas were mostly located on the country's peripheries, for instance in Scotland, Yorkshire and Lancashire, South Wales and Cornwall.

During the 1920s, new business opportunities emerged primarily in the south, which only heightened differences in regional incomes. These new industries were based around light engineering, consumer products and early electronics. Some of this economic growth was due to the arrival of American companies wishing to jump Britain's tariff barrier that was designed to penalize American imports of cars, vacuum cleaners, sewing machines and the like. American companies were

Table 4.1 Car adoption in the United States and Britain

	United States (thousands)	Great Britain (thousands)
Total number of motor vehicles, 1920	9,239	650
Total number of motor vehicles, 1930	26,750	2,273
Ratio of population to motor vehicles, 1920	11	63.9
Ratio of population to motor vehicles, 1930	4.6	19.7

Note: Figures derived from (United States) David Blanke, *Hell on Wheels: The Promise and Peril of America's Car Culture, 1900–1940* (Lawrence: University Press of Kansas, 2007), 56; (UK) William Plowden, *The Motor Car and Politics, 1896–1970* (London: Bodley Head, 1971), Appendices and 1921 and 1931 Census, visionofbritain.org.uk.

attracted to locations in and around London, because of its prosperity, familiarity, good road infrastructure, young workforce and stable electricity supplies.[5] As the outer regions of Britain stagnated and many of their families experienced extreme poverty, London's new suburbs and its Home Counties grew in wealth and in car acquisition. North East England was particularly poor, having five times fewer cars per head of population than Surrey, part of the prosperous South.[6]

One factor differentiating growth in car ownership in south-eastern England was the impact of suburbanization, an important aspect of demographic change in the 1920s and 1930s. In the first two decades of the twentieth century, cars were owned by the very wealthy, who were found, firstly in large houses in the countryside; secondly in the wealthy established suburbs in the leafier parts of suburban London such as, notably, Esher or Hampstead; and thirdly in the centre of town. The County of London accounted for just less than 100,000 cars in 1931, and these were, even at this late date, often chauffeur driven and owned by the wealthiest families.[7] Because of the high population density of an area where the poorest lived alongside the wealthiest, London appears not to be in the forefront of car ownership, but, in truth, Westminster was an epicentre of car usage, while nearby Fulham was not. Central London was the national home of car retailing, centred around manufacturers' glamorous showrooms in Great Portland Street, Berkeley Square and Piccadilly.[8] One illustration of the use of cars by the very wealthy can be seen in the behaviour of Lord Londonderry, one of London's richest men, who not only kept four chauffeurs for his family, but also drove himself.[9]

Interwar London underwent a massive suburbanization that formed a new layer of lower middle-class residents. In the 1930s, many of them became car owners for the first time. About 1.9 million people moved to suburban London in the period between 1921 and 1938, which amounted to a growth of 52 per cent, but some boroughs more than doubled in size during this period.[10] Some of these suburbanites would become roadhouse customers.

While car ownership in central London increased slowly after the initial boom in the 1920s, suburban car ownership grew as rapidly as its population. This is, for some, a surprising thought as in many accounts London's suburbs in the 1930s were considered to be highly dependent on public transport. In reality, car usage varied greatly from suburb to suburb. Predictably, the old established suburbs, with many wealthy residents, were likely to own cars. In Esher, home to the Gay Adventure roadhouse, almost one household in two had the use of a car by the end of the 1930s. The next group down likely to buy cars were residents of newly established suburbs like Hendon, who were a short run from the Thatched Barn and the Spider's Web. In boroughs like these, display and status were very important, and if cars could not be purchased with cash then they could be bought using instalment credit 'hire-purchase'. Some thought this shameful, but social embarrassment could be avoided if one bought a car at an anonymous car dealer in central London.[11]

In the late 1920s and 1930s, the British Government established a new network of arterial and bypass roads around Britain's major cities, with a special emphasis on London. 'Arterial' roads were those that led from London as the 'heart' of the country to outlying cities. Bypasses, designed to avoid or bypass busy towns that had formed around eighteenth-century arterial roads, were the location of some of Britain's most important roadhouses, such as the Ace of Spades and the Thatched Barn.

For all their association with interwar modernization, arterial roads originated in the busy streets of Edwardian London. At the start of the twentieth century, London's roads were filled with an uncontrolled jumble of horse-drawn carts, carriages, buses and taxis, early cars, trams and bicycles. Traffic jams on poorly made, narrow streets were common and made for extended journey times; long-distance journeys from the capital to the provinces were particularly problematic. The building of the inner ring of Victorian suburbia had added 1.6 million people to London's population in a period of twenty years.[12] These newcomers were housed in a densely packed set of regular streets formed alongside the main exits to the capital. Once traffic had negotiated this newly built suburbia, its next hazard was the narrow streets of the small towns on London's periphery. These towns, soon to form contiguous suburbs in Greater London, had traffic jams of their own. At Kingston, Croydon, Brentford, Bromley and Barnet, traffic was frequently at a standstill.[13]

The car's arrival was the initial catalyst that drove much discussion on the building of new roads. In the early 1900s, traffic patterns altered dramatically as motorized vehicles competed for space with traditional horse-drawn transport. Political disputes and the First World War delayed affairs and it was not until 1922 that the national arterial road scheme started, providing employment for almost 10,000 labourers.[14] Some 266 miles of arterial road were constructed in Greater London before the beginning of the Second World War.[15]

Road building programmes in Italy, Germany and the United States matched and in some cases exceeded these developments. Italy and Germany concentrated on motorway projects to reinforce the image of dynamic national development fostered by their fascist governments. The United States, in contrast, emphasized arterial parkway systems that excluded common carrier traffic and promoted leisure and commuter driving.[16]

Some of the better-known London roadhouses are shown in Table 4.2 and Map 4.1, all of which were located on new arterial roads. These roads were

Table 4.2 Major London roadhouses

Map Key	Roadhouse	Location
A	Ace of Spades	Kingston Bypass
B	Gay Adventure	Lammas Lane (Esher)
C	Ace of Spades	Great West Road
D	Berkeley Arms	Great West Road
E	Myllet Arms	Western Avenue
F	Spider's Web	Watford Bypass
G	Thatched Barn	Barnet Bypass
H	Comet	Great North Road
I	Spinning Wheel	Great Cambridge Road
J	Kingfisher's Pool	North Circular Road
K	Galleon	Sutton Bypass

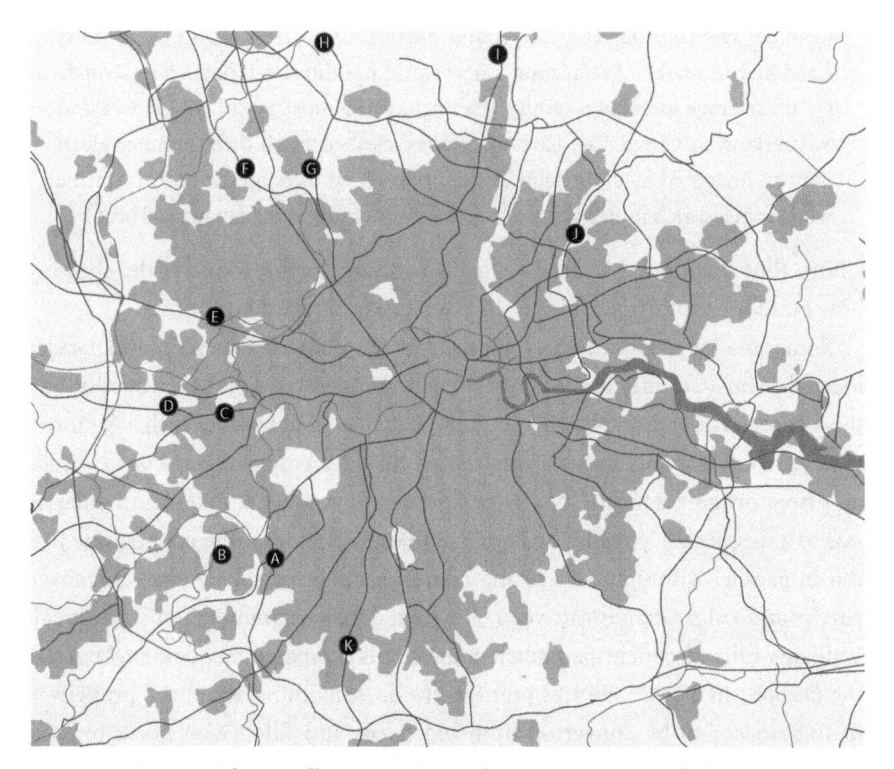

Map 4.1 Major London roadhouses. (Map author – ChrisO, modified from colour to black and white and amended to include roadhouse locations. Licensed under the Creative Commons Attribution-Share Alike 3.0 Unported license.)

quite a contrast from their pre-war antecedents, allowing in their early years for modern high-speed motoring. Each mile of road cost the government £60,000.[17] Unlike the old trunk roads that followed ancient routes and field boundaries with consequent tight and dangerous bends, the new roads were planned by engineers and mostly ran in straight lines with carefully designed gentle bends. The new highways, formed in either concrete or asphalt, gave a consistent, predictable drive, a welcome contrast to the wooden blocks, setts or cobbles of their predecessors.[18] They were originally thirty feet in width, but as traffic increased, were expanded into dual carriageways, sometimes accompanied by cycle paths and service roads. In these cases, the overall width of an arterial road could be as much as 100 feet. These roads were planned so as to bypass town centres and employed roundabouts and full width bridges, which allowed for a more consistent and safer drive.

Travel writer Harold Clunn gushed that

> the great new arterial roads leading out of London constructed since the Great War, are amongst the finest in the world ... [they] have made the Home Counties seem like one vast playground laid out almost at our doors. To the busy Londoner in search of relaxation a new world has thus been opened up, which, for the average individual of fifty years ago, was almost as difficult of access as Switzerland or China. The Home Counties, clothed in all their summer glory, may be imagined as a portfolio of the finest views of domestic scenery in the world, not less rich in architectural and historical interest than in natural beauty.[19]

Clunn thus positioned arterial roads as conduits to the countryside, showing how London's motorists could exploit them to facilitate their journey.

Some smaller roadhouses developed from tearooms, blacksmiths and garages located on busy country roads. Their rural location was part of their attraction and this tied into the early exploratory culture of driving that became such a feature of the 1920s. Country roadhouses emphasized this idea employing excessive bucolic and twee ornamentation. They were at the centre of what elite commentators saw as a despicable 'ye olde England' commercialization of the countryside that ran in parallel with ugly advertising hoardings, tatty petrol stations, charabanc parties and vulgar *arriviste* drivers. One such derisive commentator was Clough Williams-Ellis who identified much of this in his campaigning book *England and the Octopus* in 1928.[20] He was prepared to do something about the propensity of roadhouses to be converted from old barns and filled with horse brasses, 'Tudor' furniture and electric lights designed to look like candles. His modernist roadhouse, Laughing Water, at Cobham in Kent was the antithesis of most rural establishments and met the exacting standards of *Country Life*.[21]

Identified by their scale and by the range of facilities, super roadhouses were distinguished by their location; they were most often found on the suburban stretches of arterial roads. There are numerous reasons for this. The first and most obvious was the need to attract sufficient numbers of customers. Super roadhouses required a very high initial investment, reflecting the construction costs of large swimming pools and American bars. For the Thatched Barn, this reached around £80,000.[22] Clearly, to make an economic return on this level of investment meant attracting vast numbers of possible customers. Arterial roads offered a direct route for drivers from the city centre to the super roadhouse. Roadhouse marketing emphasized how quick and easy the run was from town, specifying approximate journey times from London.[23]

The second factor was super roadhouses' scale of operations which demanded a large physical area with the possibility for future expansion. Archery, swimming and the like all used much ground. Building plots next to new arterial roads afforded the space for a successful roadhouse. In London much of this land, previously used for farming or market gardens, was flat and easy to develop. Thirdly, this land was also cheap. Land prices were depressed in the late 1920s due to economic difficulties and the need for aristocratic landowners to pay higher estate duties. At least 10 per cent of arable land was lost during the 1920s.[24] Much of the arable land became new suburban housing estates, but some was bought by roadhouse owners.

Finally, building super roadhouses on arterial roads generated a strong sense of modernity. This can be reconstructed in viewing the stark white roads cutting through the virgin countryside. Williams-Ellis, a modernist early in his career, praised the modern road:

> There is surely something rather noble about the broad white concrete ribbons laid in sweeping curves and easy gradients across the country – something satisfying in their clean-planed cuttings and embankments.[25]

Another writer remembered the modernity of arterial roads from his childhood:

> There was a certain excitement and even prestige about our proximity to this tumultuous new highway. You felt *au courant*, up to date, as along its modern dual carriageway bowled the compact little motors adventuring to the coast for the day.[26]

Car usage in Britain was transformed between the wars. The 190,000 cars in use in 1920 grew tenfold in the next two decades, radically transforming the motoring landscape.[27] From the 1920s, car usage expanded steadily as middle-class families realized the practical advantages and status of owning their own car. Before the First World War, only the rich or adventurous owned a car. Hand-built in small numbers in workshops rather than factories, cars were expensive. Car manufacturing was under the control of the former coachbuilders who had been quick to adapt to the new technologies of internal combustion engines. Such companies continued with the craft skills that had worked for them in the previous century, adding beautifully handmade wooden cabins onto bought-in chassis. Because of laborious construction and time-consuming painting, each car cost £300–400 apiece, priced well beyond anyone save the privileged wealthy.[28]

Poorly maintained roads explain why cars of this period were very unreliable. In order to complete a journey, a motorist would need to confront the probability of punctured tyres and mechanical breakdowns, both of which required much physical strength to repair. Thus, men overwhelmingly drove cars, either as chauffeurs or hearty middle-class outdoorsmen, who welcomed adventurous motoring for its speed or lengthy challenging journeys. The latter found in the car the possibility for adventurous motoring, either to drive fast or for a long period. Accounts of daring-do by Britain's wealthy and intrepid motorists pervaded the *Autocar*, journal of record for the elite driver. Though this type of motoring continued after the First World War, something fundamentally had altered. Experiences of loss and grief, together with a sense of Britain's imperial power slipping away to the United States combined to convert a masculine and outward sensibility into something more reflective, quieter and nostalgic. For motorists, this became a fashion or even a need to use the car to understand and become reacquainted with the deep emotional attachment of the countryside. This trope was riven with internal contradictions as it saw one of the most visible icons of modernity as a means of encountering and bonding with antiquity.

Historian Alex Potts, describes this as

> Discovering the beauties of the English countryside became a commitment and an obsession among a not-so-privileged middle class who on many counts felt marginal and who wished to possess a true inner identity more valuable than its external social persona.[29]

John Urry sums this up as 'the interwar transformation of the car, from alien threat to a "natural" part of the rural scene'.[30] This idea was at a peak in 1925 as car sales began rising and ownership widened. As one writer put it, with a definite sense of agency, 'how little we knew of England before cars came to show it to us'.[31] These themes were also seen in the popularity of motoring guides to Britain by such authors as H. V. Morton.[32]

This shift in focus for the drive, from the speed or endurance trial to a family outing to explore the countryside, pointed to the increased feminization and domestication of interwar life. According to Alison Light, this idea can be placed alongside the contemporaneous suburbanization of England and middle class withdrawal from the public sphere to the private and domesticated world of the suburban country garden.[33]

By the mid-1920s, when car prices had started falling and ownership figures continued to rise, couples and families began using cars as ways of exploring the countryside. Cars soon became familiar sights at Home Counties beauty spots, such as Box Hill and Newlands Corner. Not all motorists were reverent in their approach, and complaints rose against car-borne visitors who left their litter, or danced noisily to a portable gramophone.[34] Motoring families were also eager to visit the seaside on summer weekends, and bank holiday traffic jams were commonplace on the roads leading to those holiday resorts popular with the middle classes. John Prioleau, writing in *Motoring for Women* (1925), recalled one such occasion:

> It was my extraordinary luck to drive up from Brighton to London in the evening between 6 o'clock and 9 o'clock and as a result of those three appalling hours, I decided that nothing but life and death shall drag me either in my own or someone else's car to Brighton during the summer. From the Brighton aquarium to St James Street, I was not for one moment out of what I can only describe as a queue of private cars.[35]

The title of Prioleau's book might suggest that motoring had reached across the gender barrier, but few women held licenses and men accompanying them usually drove.[36]

With the general predilection for country roads and the seaside as driving destinations on the one hand, and the disproportionally high level of car ownership in the south-east of England on the other, enterprising business owners started to cater to motorists. Increasing numbers of motorists wanting to add a pleasure stop to their day out were happy to break their journey for a cup of tea, a slice of cake and to go to the toilet. The outcome was a plethora of roadside tearooms and small roadhouses on the roads leading to beauty spots and the seaside. Some of them evolved into roadhouses.

Early in the 1930s, a new form of the car, mass production and suburbanization transformed motoring culture. By replacing craft skills, where one man built most of a car, with job specialization, introducing assembly lines and finally a moving line, where the car travelled to meet the worker, Henry Ford through mass-production techniques radically improved his model T car.[37] This increased production efficiency enormously, greatly facilitating car adoption in the United States. Morris and Austin Motors employed these techniques in Britain and produced cheaper, smaller cars. Between 1923 and 1937, the real cost of car ownership fell by 40 per cent.[38]

Mass production realized its full impact only on the introduction of two new technologies: pressed steel panels and spot welding. With these two new processes, the Dodge Brothers Motor Company radically improved the form of the motor car. Pressed steel panels had two important benefits. Cars could now be rapidly assembled from prefabricated body parts into a whole body shell, which allowed for new integrated roofs. Because the body was now all metal, painting times took days rather than weeks, releasing large amounts of a manufacturer's working capital, and reducing warehousing space as well as finance costs and delivery times.[39] Thus, the new technologies of the closed pressed-steel car replaced the open-topped, hand-crafted car of the 1920s. By 1929, as much as 90 per cent of new car sales consisted of the closed bodied type.[40] Price reductions associated with the introduction of pressed steel cars combined with the development of new suburbia generated a much wider group of motorists who wanted to go to roadhouses.

In 1930, a typical early roadhouse motorist was male, sporty, fairly wealthy and the driver of an open-topped car, perhaps a two-seater sports car, a Bentley for the very rich or an MG or a Swallow for those with more limited finances. In order to reach one of the famous arterial road roadhouses, a driver, typically based in central London, would motor cautiously through the inner ring of Victorian suburbia and then, on reaching the new road, let rip. In this way, he could re-live the early, unconstrained years of 'scorching' motoring before the Great War.[41] Patrick Hamilton, who liked to write about roadhouses, recorded this sensation in 1932,

> [they] were ripping up the wide, smooth, deserted spaces of the Great West Road… Gee! it was like a racing track–no wonder he put on speed. It was like being in an aeroplane! 'Go on. Let her rip!' cried Rex.[42]

Drinking alcohol was a central component of roadhouse life. Although restricted licensing hours implemented during the First World War had accelerated falling levels of drinking, the average middle-class roadhouse customer probably consumed more alcohol than his pre-war cousin, as a consequence of a loosening of middle-class *mores* that permitted respectable people to drink in public (see Figure 4.1). This was coupled with a fascination with

Figure 4.1 Opening night of the Ace of Spades, Kingston Bypass, 1931. Sasha/Getty Images.

America, which led to a long-lived interest in drinking cocktails. These changes were particularly apparent for women, for whom it first became permissible, then fashionable, then widely acceptable for them to drink in public.[43]

As has been shown, restricted licensing hours of pubs and hotels were a key factor in roadhouses' success. Roadhouses used the ruse of club membership and continuous serving of light meals to obviate restrictions on sale of alcohol. To satisfy thirsty customers, roadhouse proprietors were only too happy to encourage – even openly and brazenly advertise – that patrons might bring their own drink in their car's boot, effectively transforming this part of the vehicle into a portable cocktail bar. As a result, it was a common observation that roadhouse drivers drank more than was good for them.[44]

Fast driving prompted rapid changes of location and, behind the closed roof of a modern saloon, more anonymity. By using cars to transport prostitutes between nightclubs in the 1930s, criminals grasped this fact.[45] There is no 'smoking gun' evidence connecting roadhouses with motorized prostitution, but it seems plausible that because of roadhouses' connection with fast roads that this occurred there too. What we do know is that coaches and charabancs transported homosexuals to parties at the Ace of Spades for an unconventional night out, its anonymity enabling them to enjoy the blurred sexual boundaries unavailable elsewhere.[46]

British interwar roadhouses depended completely for their customer base on widening car ownership. Roadhouses were initially popular with the metropolitan and wealthy, the first group to have access to cars in any number. As car ownership widened, so did the type of roadhouse customer. Development of the interwar arterial road programme made driving more attractive, with London's arterial roads soon home to most of Britain's super roadhouses. This was inevitable, since only new arterial roads had access to large numbers of passing cars and the cheap, open, former farming land needed to develop a large roadhouse and car park.

Much of the attraction of roadhouses was in their provision of alcoholic drinks around the clock, subverting the licensing laws that applied to those without a car. The car allowed roadhouse patrons to very easily be in the wrong place. In the centre of major cities, the rules for who might go to a night club and where it might be awkward for a lower-middle class person to go were known and understood; because the major roadhouses were new and on the fringes of town, the rules were less easily understood and much more flexible. From about 1935 onwards, as greater numbers of suburbanites owned cars, it became possible, then likely, for someone from the 'wrong' gradation of the interwar middle classes to drive to roadhouses, which resulted in them becoming far less attractive to the metropolitan elite as a destination.

5

Negotiating Class

One fascinating dimension of roadhouses concerned the changing nature of their clientele. Initially, the group was self-selected, based on those owning automobiles, possessing the requisite time and enjoying well-understood forms of leisure. Money and status of course became a prerequisite for entrance. As roadhouses grew in numbers, acquired new amenities and became located further outside London's main orbit, public perceptions began altering. With the select set no longer monopolizing automobiles, those one step socially below turned to roadhouses as a new source of relaxation. For roadhouse proprietors, their clientele loomed large as a marketing problem in which differing expectations had to confront the realities of class interaction. Negotiating class at roadhouses thus became a delicate, continuing and fluid issue with far-reaching consequences.

As a new, stylish icon of the 1930s, roadhouses have aroused remarkably little historical scrutiny.[1] Misconceptions naturally abound. Of the many contemporary commentators about roadhouses, Osbert Lancaster in a satirical book was most responsible for inaugurating what became a stereotypic image with enduring influence. For him, the roadhouse, then at the apex of its popularity, was the product of a three-stage evolutionary process best witnessed in the south-east's coastal development. His *Progress at Pelvis Bay* (1936) depicted roadhouses as starting as tea houses, becoming brewers' improved public houses built in a Tudorbethan style and finally culminating in roadhouses. He dubbed his archetypal roadhouse the 'Hearts are Trumps'.[2]

The fictional stereotype shown in *Pelvis Bay* had some basis in reality.[3] Lancaster was certainly correct in portraying roadhouses as the product sometimes of an evolutionary process based on catering to tea drinkers in the southeast. In the same year as *Pelvis Bay* appeared, Elsa Dundas, formerly a secretary, for instance, invested an inheritance of £700 in a modest Kentish roadhouse, and, though ignorant of catering, experienced steady success so that profits from her popular tearoom funded building of a swimming pool.[4]

Tea also proved a draw for Miss M. J. Fisher-Brown, a recognized authority on Angora rabbits. She first opened a Surrey farm of some 7,000 Angora rabbits that created demand for a tearoom as a fitting conclusion to the tourist experience. With capital from eighty friends and customers, she formed a private club, which soon swelled to some 1,000, enabling members alone to enjoy the restaurant, cocktail bar and horse-back riding. As the enterprise flourished, Fisher-Brown rejected the predictable swimming pool and opted instead to incorporate tennis courts and a miniature golf course, transforming her farm into the White Rabbit Roadhouse.[5]

Likewise, tea was originally the making of Commander Tomlinson. He retired from the Navy, beckoned by the bucolic sedentary life of his Hildenborough farm. Tourists nevertheless marvelled at his old barn, pleading for 'a real old-fashioned farmer's tea'. Curiously, the ancient past meeting the modern present proved decisive: a film company wanting to photograph some scenes visited Tomlinson and convinced him an opportunity awaited the ambitious entrepreneur. Accordingly, visitors flocked to the Old Barn. Others enjoyed the modern swimming pool, observed exotic animals in his garden, or watched airplanes land on his private landing field. Nearby, the Tudor House, planned by aircraft designer Eustace Short as a Kentish roadhouse, came on the market and Tomlinson promptly acquired it. Building a superb ballroom with a maple sprung floor, Tomlinson created 'a ballroom second to none in the country'. Dancing and tennis afforded guests ample exercise; superb food fed the inner man and woman.[6]

Tomlinson's entry into the roadhouse business was scarcely unique. 'Road houses and country inns have created in the public a definite demand for out-of-door refreshment facilities', pronounced a newspaper in 1935. Travellers undertook long journeys simply to sup tea beside 'a rhododendron bush' or underneath a tree. Based on these observations, a shrewd reporter concluded: 'There is money in tea-gardens.'[7] This was the same year Lancaster published his book. Tomlinson typified one type of investor/proprietor who became roadhouse proprietors.[8]

Tourism rather than tea became a catalyst for transforming other phenomenally popular tourist sites into roadhouses. When it opened in 1927, Wookey Hole Cave, a natural geographic site, catered to 16,000 visitors, but numbers soon quadrupled. By 1936, visitors reached a staggering 150,000, and then one year later skyrocketed to 250,000. This astonishing demand reflected in part additions of a swimming pool, restaurant and liquor licence. To accommodate these ever-expanding crowds, Captain Hodgkinson, its owner, rebuilt the premises nearby, again with a swimming pool, but this time included a huge restaurant with

300–400 seats. As the Cave assumed the guise of a characteristic roadhouse, it also boasted a lounge, mock Elizabethan fireplace and a dancing room. Completing this metamorphosis, the Wookey Hole Cave Restaurant became a roadhouse, the Swimming Pool Restaurant.[9]

Notwithstanding Lancaster's stereotype of brewers' money fuelling roadhouse growth, class diversity remained the hallmark of roadhouse promoters' backgrounds throughout the 1930s, with a willingness to risk money the chief prerequisite for opening one. During the first stage, guest house proprietors, building contractors, service station operators, cinema chain owners and peers primarily became investors. Just two had roots in the retailing of alcohol. London brewers Barclay, Perkins & Co. rebuilt the Five Bells (St. Mary Cray, Kent) in 1933, spending lavishly to transform a run-of-the-mill pub into the Bridge House Hotel, which boasted a swimming pool and dance hall.[10] Another brewer, A. C. Reavenall, invested in Rural Restaurants Ltd, which ran the Spider's Web.[11]

Aristocrats, motor car agents, engineers, swimming pool builders, nightclub proprietors, an aircraft designer, a dairy owner, retired military officers and enlisted men, a solicitor's typist and members of a Canadian syndicate – all these joined the ranks of roadhouse promoters in stage two, which began in 1934. Now, too, people with liquor interests outnumbered petrol station owners. Overall, however, the eleven roadhouses promoted by those with drink ties still represented no more than one out of ten of the total, by any yardstick a relatively modest number.

Aristocrats such as Lord Weymouth, owner of the Caveman Restaurant in Somerset, had a hand in designing this roadhouse, a logical commercial extension of the nearby caves which some 250,000 people visited annually.[12] Monica Ewer thus added authenticity to her novel, *Roadhouse*, in having the financial backing for the Harbour Bar come from an old and quite rich Scottish gentry family.[13]

Careers of some promoters underlined not just their unorthodox entry into the roadhouse business, but often limited prior experience. For Humphrey L. Richardson, running the Silver Slipper (Herne) followed stints as a club proprietor and tea shop owner, enterprises which incurred losses. Wiped out by a devastating fire at the Silver Slipper, he proved no more successful in working as a waste paper and metal dealer. Unable to pay off creditors owed £1,663, he declared bankruptcy. Coming further downmarket, he worked as a cinema manager, with £7 weekly wages.[14] The proprietor of Asker's Roadhouse in Dorset received glowing reviews in the inaugural 1935 issue of *Signpost*, but not even this could ensure survival. More astute was his successor, a sailor who on leaving the service dedicated himself to learning the basics of hotel keeping before buying the roadhouse. *Signpost* thought highly enough of the new owner to continue listing Askers in this select guide.[15]

Not all such entrepreneurs bereft of catering experience failed. Undoubtedly the Hersey brothers, the most famous exception, had no prior contact with roadhouses. In fact, they had visited just one before opening the Ace of Spades. Nor did their training and background as engineers offer any insights to running what became a quite complex business with a huge staff and two geographically separated sites. These brothers sensed intuitively as much as any entrepreneur what the market demanded for success. So did another novice owner. Employed in various capacities with twelve different shops as a semi-skilled labourer who worked his way up to manager over a quarter of a century, W. R. Clarke promptly retired in 1932 to achieve his life-long goal, the building of an 'ultra-modern' roadhouse. Some 1,000 customers celebrated the opening week of his Popular Road & Guest House at Easter, drawn by not only tastefully presented food, but also a bowling green, a tennis court, a riding school, even a sports' field. Clarke clearly appreciated the value of being on the cutting edge of technological change: his roadhouse boasted of being the first one in England entirely electrically wired.[16]

Ready capital, not prior experience, constituted the decisive factor in establishing a roadhouse. Some imaginative entrepreneurs generated money from unrelated business. Observing growing weekend tourist trade in western Scotland, Charles Ross, owner of Ross's Dairies, financed the Rob Roy Roadhouse near Aberfoyle. On five acres of land, he offered patrons a golf course, a dance hall and a spacious restaurant accommodating 200.[17] Dame Clara Butt's sister ran the Crib, with teas, dining and dancing aimed at the 'brighter people of Bristol'.[18] In one instance, a landowner sought an investor with £2,500 to erect a 'first-class roadhouse'.[19]

Capital for financing speculative ventures came most often from private funds or speculators. Long-established acquaintances, however, proved equally supportive. Miss Fisher-Brown solicited funds from close friends and customers who formed the private White Rabbit Club (Newchapel) as a prelude to her applying for a club liquor licence. Once the coveted licence (and respectability) had been achieved, she turned the club into a hybrid club/roadhouse. This was a classic example of exploiting ties with intimate contacts, whose money buttressed a strategy for justifying her application for a liquor licence.[20]

Money went hand-in-hand with sound business sense as the basis for success. Shrewd promoters selected roadhouse sites following considerable forethought.

Though motorists making unplanned discoveries became customers, the mainstay of the business derived from planned outings of those living in nearby urban areas who used published motorist guides which began appearing from 1934. Ringing London, visible from trunk roads and strategically placed often on arterial roads, roadhouses were overwhelmingly concentrated within 35 miles of suburbia, so that the journey took at most slightly over an hour.[21] Closest to London's Hyde Park Corner, for example, were the Ace of Spades (Great West Road, 9 miles), followed by its namesake (Kingston Bypass, 12 miles) and the Thatched Barn (Barnet Bypass, 12 miles). Proximity to large urban areas drew custom, but so did attractive rural settings.

When motorists could see the roadhouse from the road, an ideal site had been found. As a building type, roadhouses were physically imposing, surrounded by much land needed for recreational activities. Gigantic features extended to car parks, which sometimes accommodated hundreds of vehicles. The Orchard Hotel, three miles from Uxbridge, had room for 400; the Thatched Barn dwarfed this with 1,000; but pre-eminent was the Spider's Web with an astonishing capacity of 2,000.[22] Restaurants could seat several hundreds, and dance floors had no trouble with similar numbers.

Writing in 1940, one knowledgeable architectural historian praised them as a recognizable type, quite distinct from the public house, whether new or old, because of their trait of 'strangeness': they were, he said, 'decidedly queer'.[23] Their appearance projected a visual image that the alert motorist easily associated with recreation. S. Marella, advisor of many roadhouse builders, grasped this point in recommending to potential investors that 'entrance to the interior must be interesting and elegant without being elaborately designed'. Looming large as an architectural feature was the forecourt, with a carefully designed driveway leading to a huge parking area. Night-time floodlit exteriors and swimming pools served as an effective advertisement.[24] Expensive and sprawling, with distinctive names and architecture, roadhouses were not easily confused with bucolic inns.[25]

Initially, the roadhouse emerged from the need for motorists to service their automobiles and be entertained or fed while waiting. In this form, the service station established dominance over other activities. Monica Ewer's novel *Roadhouse* expresses this relationship in depicting the Harbour Bar, located on a bypass near London, with 'rows of petrol pumps and the garage for repairs and the great car park'.[26] But during the early stages the roadhouse premises continued to reflect their plebeian origins. One unimpressed reporter noted that 'the visitor has to pick his way through oil-drums, derelict cars, repair jobs in full swing, parked caravans, and an all-pervading smell of petrol'.[27] Yet, inside the chief purpose of the petrol station was temporarily forgotten. 'While your car is being valeted by experts', assured W. G. McMinnies, 'you can dance to a radiogram any evening or take dinner'.[28]

Three of the earliest and most famous roadhouses – the Clock (Welwyn Bypass) and the twin Ace of Spades (Great West Road and at the Kingston Bypass) – began as inconspicuous petrol and service stations late in the 1920s.[29] Brothers Walter and Frederick Waters ran the Clock House Service Station exclusively as a petrol and repair shop. The next step involved taking on new partners, the Kennedys, who helped bankroll the building of an adjoining café, serving superb but inexpensive meals and specializing in teas and cakes, which one well-travelled motorist thought 'cannot be beaten anywhere'. Further expansion came soon with a ballroom, filtered swimming pool and finally Wendover Lodge, a group of 'small, chic bungalows' placed well back from the bypass, in a rustic setting rented unfurnished to motorists annually between £75 and £200.[30] Of the twin Ace of the Spades, the second one completed in 1927 was more innovative and influential, aggressively exploiting the potential of the Kingston Bypass which opened that same year. The two brothers purchased land initially to store their equipment, and introduced petrol pumps with a garage to defray costs of the site. Unplanned, the enterprise developed and thrived; lock-up garages, washing facilities, a tearoom and a liquor licence soon followed. Eventually the Ace of Spades stayed open twenty-four hours, with a staff of some 200. The brothers then built a huge ballroom for 350, a cavernous restaurant (capable of seating 700–800), a swimming pool and, for the exotic, a polo ground. Its landing ground, remarked proprietor George Hersey, 'has been used by many customers who fly their own planes'.[31] The Ace of Spades never truly escaped its origins as a workshop. Hersey stressed that three pillars – catering, entertainment and a flourishing motor business – sustained the business. 'We have', he related in an interview, 'never allowed our catering and entertainment side – extensive though it has become – to be top heavy'.[32]

For some leading roadhouses, the link with automobiles persisted in part as a deliberate marketing strategy. The Spider's Web, Clock and Ace of Spades (Great West Road) served as the start or finish of chief motor sporting events, a key factor in establishing their 'reputations'. Outside London's orbit, both the Rob Roy and the Mile Three held driving tests and car trials.[33] Bereft of swimming pools and so ranking in the second tier, northern roadhouses attracted custom as centres for test driving or general car trials.[34]

Other roadhouses pioneered the use of exotic amenities to attract patrons. Beyond facilities for the predictable tennis, squash and bowling, some went to great lengths to separate themselves from rivals. Riding schools came first to the Ace of Spades and then several competitors emulated it, but just a few introduced shooting galleries, baseball grounds, gymnasium equipment, lawn croquet, badminton, skittles, deck tennis, miniature golf and an underwater restaurant. To surpass the competition, the Spider's Web had a genuine nine-hole golf course and golf pro in residence.[35]

The cost of sporting equipment again excluded the working and many of the middle classes from roadhouse sports. Golf, tennis, squash, shooting and riding all required a capital outlay generally beyond the means of those without a substantial budget. Even swimming, its suit requiring the latest fashion and materials, placed those with limited incomes at a distinct disadvantage.[36]

Sporting attractions provide some clue of who used such establishments, but roadhouse customers nevertheless defy easy classification. W. G. McMinnies, whose best-selling annual motorist guides for recreation dominated the market for decades, portrayed customers at the Ace of Spades as 'the young and beautiful of London and its suburbs come to enjoy themselves', while the 'brighter people' visited Bristol's Crib.[37] But types of patrons were much broader socially with ages quite older but no less exclusive than McMinnies described. Porte, a well-known public house architect, divided drinkers into three categories; with the top class – 'the best people' – frequenting lounge or quality smoke rooms in roadhouses and pubs. Having acquired the Thatched Barn, close to the West End and one of the most costly roadhouses, brewers Barclay, Perkins & Co. categorized patrons as those 'to whom the amenities of the place mean more than any consideration of its cost'. From its opening, the Thatched Barn expected some patrons to undertake an outing without definite travel plans. Laundered swimming costumes, flannels, stiff collars and full dress evening clothes – all these could be rented at a special valeting room. Thomas Warrington, proprietor of Chez Laurie in Kent, aimed to attract 'the really high-class trade' desiring outstanding food and 'those facilities, comforts and luxuries that one got in the modern high-class restaurant'.[38] Here one could be assured of meeting people of similar social standing. The Hertford Motor Company, manufacturers of such expensive automobiles as Rover and Chrysler, advertised in a county directory in which a drawing portrayed a man and woman leaving their vehicle with a roadhouse in the background. Prices alone for dinner and dancing excluded all but the inquisitive of the middle classes with automobiles: at the Maybury Roadhouse, west of Edinburgh, customers paid 8s. 6d. for dinner and dancing. To drive the point home, proprietors insisted on evening dress not just for dancing, but sometimes even for dining. The social elite also embraced roadhouses for special social occasions – wedding receptions, hunt and regimental balls and private parties. Perceptive roadhouse managers, such as Mrs Bester at the Spider's Web, held charity and other balls knowing 'the best people of the neighbourhood' would attend, especially in the slower winter months. Soon after opening, the Bell House, located strategically on the London-Uxbridge-Oxford Road, had booked six twenty-first birthday parties.[39] Still more successful was the newly opened Popular Road and Guest House (Leigh on Sea, Essex), where scarcely a week went by without a wedding reception.[40] For afternoon tea, Pantiles (Bagshot) became 'one of the accepted social rendezvous of the district'.[41]

Such a clientele would have rebuffed social interlopers, and no roadhouse promoter, certainly not from a sumptuous super roadhouse, seriously contemplated challenging the prevailing status quo. Commander Tomlinson, who established one prosperous roadhouse, the Old Barn (Hildenborough), and then purchased another, the Tudor House (Bearstead), with great success, encountered one pronounced variation of this class prejudice on being interviewed by an ambitious entrepreneur. An aghast Tomlinson learned of this man's plans to create an establishment with multiple parking areas, restaurants, even swimming pools, all segregated by class, quite reminiscent of the first railway carriages in the first half of the nineteenth century.[42]

Generally, social exclusion was achieved in subtler ways, with expensive meals, fees for swimming and dancing, mandatory evening dress on weekends for dinner and dancing, and sometimes even an annual subscription charge for joining the private club. Patrons of the Bell House could enjoy 'dinner dances with a London band and cabaret at 7/6 a head, evening dress essential', McMinnies noted in his guide.[43] Those motorists interested in egalitarian leisure needed only one encounter to be disabused of the roadhouse as a democratic establishment. 'Prices charged for everything, from a cloak-room ticket to a champagne supper, were out of proportion to the service given', complained one disgruntled motorist who resented an ambience catering to socially select patrons.[44]

Beverages, too, assumed social importance as class indicators. Associated with plebeian taste, public houses and low-profit margins, draft beer – served in pint and half-pint mugs – seldom was available. Bottled beer, more expensive than draft and served in small eight ounce glasses, had acquired a more refined reputation as suitable for the domestic consumption of the upper classes. Residual hostility to bottled beer still prevailed at the most selective restaurants well in the 1930s.[45] One patron recalled that customers of the Ace of Spaces (Kingston Bypass) consumed far more champagne than beer. The Thatched Barn tried to straddle rigid class distinctions, promising 'no fancy prices for anything'. Here, patrons could order wine, spirits and beer at prices charged at public houses.[46]

That chauffeurs were thought to determine the ultimate destination of an outing elevated them into a group worth cultivating. Some roadhouses aimed specifically at this custom, creating a separate room equipped with darts and charging 9d. for a good tea. According to one reporter, 'many chauffeurs have been instrumental in introducing new custom to the place'.[47]

Mrs Bester, proprietor of Spider's Web, was scarcely alone in deliberately cultivating the image of 'a West-End restaurant set in the country', with the head waiter committed to guaranteeing 'West-End service'. Because bucolic roadhouses escaped London's high rentals, their prices were markedly lower.[48]

Newspaper commentaries with a mass audience left readers in no doubt about who frequented exclusive roadhouses. 'When the [West-End] theatres close', wrote the *Daily Mail*, 'the arterial roads are ablaze with the headlights of cars containing merry parties of fashionably dressed women and their escorts, eager to listen [at roadhouses] to music and to dance in the open air.'[49] Sometimes the well-heeled paid for a taxi ride from the West End, arriving in full evening dress after 11 pm, joining countless others eager to escape the summer's heat.[50] Others, fashionably dressed, arrived at roadhouses in automobiles – new and old as well as big and little ones – filling the car park.[51] Serendipity also played a role in the social elite arriving at other times. Following a picnic in the countryside, socialite Lady Pamela Smith and her party 'stopped to dance at an inviting roadhouse on the homeward journey'.[52]

The type of clientele that roadhouses wanted was equally inferred from what social class they recruited as managers and staff. According to Arthur E. Bennetts,

> Roadhouses were often 'managed' ... by the 'old school tie' type of individual who displayed only a very languid interest, amounting often to outright rudeness to any customer who did not belong to what he believed to be his own social sphere.[53]

Even when roadhouses engaged staff, some managers specified former public schoolboys.[54] Promoters carefully designated room names as a strategy for targeting the type of clientele they sought. Like improved pubs, roadhouses invariably included a (saloon) lounge, where customers could sit while consuming refreshments. But in sharp contrast to improved pubs, roadhouses referred not to toilets, lavatories or water closets, but to cloakrooms, a term reserved for the most refined establishments.[55]

Figure 5.1 Spider's Web, 1935. Fox Photos/Hulton Archive/Getty Images.

Unlike hotels or country clubs, roadhouses seldom expected letting rooms to form a major portion of the profits. Letting rooms some did, but roadhouses catered to those wanting leisure for the day or evening, with the manageable return journey making this possible. They existed, in one contemporary's apt phrase, 'for *recreation*, rather than *necessity*'.[56] Nowhere else could patrons enjoy themselves into the early morning hours – dancing, eating and sometimes drinking alcohol – without police supervision or a subscription fee as required by country clubs.

Many roadhouse builders sought to project a theme, sometimes no more adventurous than the ever-popular Tudor style, with oak beams and thatched roofs (see Figure 5.1). More imaginative was the Houseboat where everything reminded customers of sailing, from the houseboat shape of the premises to the deck rails, lifeboats and games – deck tennis, quoits and shuffleboard. Such attention to detail certainly impressed the *Herts Advertiser* reporter. 'As one enters', he observed, 'there is a comfortable lounge with cunningly devised lighting to resemble the portholes of a ship'. Impressed, he reflected that 'one might well imagine that this was the lounge of one of our modern luxury liners'. Yet, being located in Radlett, 20 miles northeast of London, the Houseboat was a long way indeed from the sea. Its popularity owed much to the social class that the owners endeavoured to attract. 'The pleasures of a cruise cannot be enjoyed by all', admitted the reporter, 'but some of its delights have been embodied in the "Houseboat"'. At the same time, it had a modern ambience, with the most fashionable kitchen and tubular furniture. Family Rest Ltd paid £10,000 for all these features, suggesting how much might be incorporated in such second rank establishments.[57]

All these facets of roadhouses underlined one defining trait: they cost a packet to build. The economically minded could get by with as little as £1,000 in construction costs, but the image of roadhouses, so consciously projected by promoters, required something more exalted, befitting the clientele such establishments pursued. Prices escalated sharply during the decade, reflecting competitive pressures to build the biggest, most modern pool. Glorious summers beginning in 1932 encouraged roadhouse entrepreneurs to take the plunge, and invest £1,500–2,000 in building a pool 75' × 30', with a maximum depth of 6' or even 7'. The Thatched Barn established primacy with a heated, floodlit pool measuring 150' × 50'. In the race for the biggest and best, the Havering Court Club and Swimming Pool soon displaced it with a pool measuring 150' × 75'. Advertisements stressed the Club having 'the most beautiful swimming pool around London'. Not slow to capitalize on this reputation, the Club approved of its new nickname, the Havering Court Wonder Swimming Pool, and from its opening in 1936 promised patrons pool hours until midnight. Huge outlays for construction could be recovered in large part at popular establishments with standard admission charges of 1s. 6d. on weekends and a shilling on weekdays.[58]

Two distinct phases characterized the roadhouse's evolution. Between 1927 and 1933, thirty-nine roadhouses appeared, located overwhelmingly in the southeast and promoted by those outside the liquor business. Premises were more often purpose built than conversions of farms or barns. Of the latter, the most famous was Pantiles, based in a 300-year-old barn near Bagshot, Surrey, opened in 1930. Another such example was Aldermaston Mill (Berkshire), which exploited the pond for boating, bathing, fishing and swimming. Elsewhere the southwest accounted for three roadhouses – the Wookey Hole Cave Restaurant (Wells, Somerset), the Crib Roadhouse (Westbury-on-Trym, Severn Beach, Gloucestershire) and the Fenn Green (Bridgnorth-Kidderminster Road, Worcestershire). No roadhouses in the North or Midlands existed at all during these years.[59]

In the second stage of the roadhouse's development, from 1934 to the outbreak of the Second World War, the southeast remained the most popular area, with three of every five new establishments being set up here. Compared to the Southeast's thirty-seven, twenty-six appeared in other parts of the country, including four in Scotland.[60] More roadhouses in the second phase were purpose built, and their cost soared, partly because the scale and the amenities increased enormously.[61] Likewise, by the mid-1930s, a dance hall with a maximum capacity for 200 couples was deemed small in the *Caterer and Hotel-Keeper*'s view.[62] Ballrooms now reached staggering sizes, with Kent's Tudor House built in 1934 capable of accommodating 500 couples in a class by itself.[63] Opened the following year, Askers Roadhouse on the Bridport/Dorchester Road in Dorset had room for 400 couples, the second biggest roadhouse dance hall in the country.[64]

Undoubtedly one of the grandest roadhouses was the Thatched Barn (Barnet Bypass).[65] With its ten-acre site, parking facilities for 1,000 cars, five hard tennis courts, immense swimming pool, sprawling dance room and a thatched roof spanning a 500-seat restaurant resembling an old barn, the aptly named Thatched Barn was erected on a gigantic scale, rightly earning the title 'super road-house'. A roadhouse of unmatched splendour, the Thatched Barn afforded in McMinnies' words 'deluxe social and sporting facilities on the grand scale'. Where else could the adventurous turn to a gymnasium, shooting gallery, sports field, squash courts or games rooms for unorthodox entertainment within 12 miles of London?[66] By way of comparison, the Havering Court Club, a sprawling 32-acre Essex estate, was converted from a mansion into a roadhouse for £60,000. Here was the unmatched swimming pool, tennis courts, golf course and a putting green. Inside, dancers enjoyed the 'Couriers', the live orchestra.[67]

Few breweries had the money, much less the desire, to compete at this exacting level. By far the most exalted was the Myllet Arms, which Benskin's built on the Western Avenue, near Perivale (Middlesex), offering 'food, wine, service and surroundings that you'd expect, and pay through the nose for, in a smart West End restaurant'.[68] Two London breweries each built impressive but less costly establishments, also in Middlesex. Several years earlier, for just under half the price of the Myllet Arms, Whitbread erected the Hendon Way at Hendon. With a large restaurant for 130 people, late-night dancing, a cocktail lounge and a colour scheme designed for each room, the Hendon Way earned the praise of one expert as a 'palatial roadhouse'.[69] At Hillingdon, Fuller, Smith & Turner built the Golden Lion for £20,000. Food and dancing again enticed customers, but the brewery also hired a West End chef to guarantee quality. Though superpubs, with food, dancing and cocktails as major draws, constituted the most expensive of brewers' interwar improved public houses, none of them had swimming pools, eccentric attractions or environments redolent of the past.[70] Only one brewery in fact included this amenity, Barclay, Perkins & Co., which spent £11,000 rebuilding the Five Bells before renaming it the Bridge House Hotel.[71]

Converting existing premises into roadhouses also often entailed huge financial outlays. Winwood Roadhouses Ltd specialized in this end of the market in the Midlands. In transforming a recognized Staffordshire landmark, the Stewponey Hotel (Stourton), into a modern lido, Winwood spent lavishly, reaching some £60,000. It offered the standard amenities found elsewhere – swimming pool, dance hall, restaurant and cocktail bars – but on a grander scale than early roadhouses.[72] Nearby in Worcestershire and being converted at the same time was the Crown Inn in Wychbold, near Droitwich, where Winwood advertised more exotic entertainment. Guests could not only dine, dance and swim, but also visit kennels (naturally filled with pedigree dogs), a monkey house and a bowling green. Just how much Winwood invested on all these attractions was not disclosed to the press, but the sum must have been comparable to what it spent on the Stewponey.[73] Rudimentary premises on a popular junction convertible to a roadhouse, with little save the freehold, filling station, café and car park, carried a hefty price tag – £15,000.[74]

A step below these staggering amounts were establishments in the £10,000–20,000 range, the second tier of roadhouses. One of the most stylish was the Maybury Roadhouse, strategically located on the Glasgow-Edinburgh road, which cost its promoter, an Edinburgh restaurateur and wine merchant, £12,000. The *Times* considered it 'the finest and best-known roadhouse in Scotland'.[75] Projecting a modern image with a long narrow structure covered in reinforced concrete, the building had a flat roof and steel windows. Inside, the same modish theme prevailed with tubular steel furniture, plastic painted walls, indirect lighting and cavernous rooms devoted to drinking – the 'Court lounge', 'lounge bar', 'balcony bar', 'stag bar' and 'cocktail bar'. The Maybury also featured huge dance and dining rooms as well as a tea garden, though no swimming pool.[76] Slightly more expensive was the Chez Laurie, which cost Thomas Warrington £13,500 to build in 1937. On about an acre and a half of land, he proposed to offer customers tennis courts outside, and a dining room, lounge and dance hall inside.[77] In opening the Houseboat in Hertfordshire, Family Restaurants spent £10,000 building a boating lake, a car park accommodating 300 cars and the premises.[78]

Second tier roadhouses reassured investors of profits almost as impressive, between 12 and 15 per cent per annum.[79] With easy access from London, the White Rabbit earned average annual profits of 8.5 per cent during its first three years.[80] Roadhouses in the third tier cost thousands less, averaging around £5,000–9,000, provided they offered suitable attractions.[81]

Investors who bought into the business at the lowest entry level – rock-bottom prices – risked considerably less money. Typically, £2,000–3,000, depending on the location and amenities, would secure what one advertiser hyperbolically called the 'ideal roadhouse'. A medieval property in Suffolk, its six bedrooms, tennis courts, lake pool and dance floor being the chief attractions, was advertised in the *Times* for £2,500 (including freehold) in the mid-1930s. Basic premises, devoid of amenities and offering just the leasehold, could be had for a mere £700, including in some cases a club licence.[82]

There was great variety in the more economical premises. While the Willow Barn (near Worthing, West Sussex) advertised food and dining as standard enticements, patrons had a stunning view of the channel amid the charm of a restored Elizabethan barn. The outlay for such premises was a modest £5,600, £2,000 less than the average improved pub in these same years.[83]

Women sometimes owned roadhouses, too. Mrs Lucy-Hulbert, for instance, owned and managed the Gay Adventure in Surrey. Further north, McMinnies characterized MG's as 'the Midland's best roadhouse', with the dancing area in 'an old world setting'. Giving her initials to the establishment, the proprietress too shunned a swimming pool and provided customers with live music on Saturday night dances, trout fishing, accommodation in two Tudor cottages and 'food at any hour'.[84]

Further up the social spectrum, upper-class women showed no hesitation in running roadhouses, another indication of the type of clientele to which such establishments catered. Lady Hatherton built the Pottal Pool, near Cannock Chase, exploiting the nearby water in advertising bathing, boating and dancing. Those eager to enjoy foreign lands vicariously found the layout of the Pottal Pool based on tropical rest-houses irresistible.[85]

That roadhouses felt no inhibitions about employing women, even from the gentry, as managers underlined new norms of gender drinking. Two married women ran the upmarket Spider's Web near the Watford Bypass, and another served as manager of a Harlow roadhouse (Essex).[86] In reconfiguring drinking habits, roadhouses represented a striking departure from existing practices prevailing in leisure. Newsreels and photographs disclose almost equal numbers of men and women as customers. This gender balance was highly unusual and would not have been true in superpubs or pubs (save in the gender-neutral lounge, the most refined room). It may have been true of the Embassy and some other clubs, but they might have had more wealthy men as well as some prostitutes. Thus, the roadhouse ought to be understood as a very modern place with gender equality prevailing long before the 1960s supposedly changed everything. This same phenomenon of roadhouses desegregating leisure had also occurred earlier across the Atlantic.

What generated a rapidly expanding clientele for roadhouses catering to the social elite? First, there was the matter of convenience. 'No longer is it necessary to make a five-day plan in order to secure a sufficiency of dancing, bathing, motoring and mischief in the evenings of a summer week', applauded one habitué. As part of its appeal, the Spider's Web boasted of its 'day long attractions' – swimming, golf, deck tennis, dancing and rife shooting. Second was the ubiquitous swimming pool, which met for those who wished it the English concern for modesty. Third, nocturnal creatures keen to escape into the countryside had few palatable alternatives. Pubs closed promptly at 10.30 pm outside London and country hotels repelled with 'bad coffee and reluctant service'. But roadhouses like the Tudor Rose (Cheshire) assured courting and married couples that on Wednesdays 'there's a supper dance … from 7:30 p.m. to midnight'.[87] Fourth, roadhouses specialized in exquisite cuisine; thereby justifying the time spent travelling. One of the closest to London, the Spider's Web, McMinnies noted approvingly, 'still aims at providing the kind of food and wine and the same sort of surroundings that one would expect in a first class restaurant in London, but … the prices are considerably less'. Likewise, the Tudor House in Kent served meals from 8 am onwards.[88] Fifth, the roadhouse created the unexpected in which patrons were transported into the countryside to an unusual locale, yet entered premises remarkably familiar. Sixth, roadhouses appealed to younger men more conscious of gender differences. 'The "Red Lion" cannot compete with the "Blue Lagoon" for the favour of a generation which thinks less of the inner man than of the outer woman', observed Barbara Worsley-Gough in the *Spectator*.[89]

One way of further underlining the distinction between roadhouses and pubs was to form a social club with an annual subscription as a separate social group, granted special privileges (notably the consumption of alcohol), within the roadhouse. The membership fee of £52 charged at the Hilden Manor Roadhouse (Kent), for example, effectively excluded all but the wealthy, who doubtless saw such social clubs as gentlemen's clubs in another guise. To achieve social exclusion had obvious appeal to the enormously rich, and explains why social clubs enrolled vast numbers of members – the one at the Thatched Barn counted over 2,000.[90] Like gentlemen's clubs, social clubs served members alcohol and enjoyed greater freedom of action than pubs, though all possessed liquor licenses.

Roadhouses had little in common with the public house, whatever commentaries such as Osbert Lancaster and subsequent scholars argued. Most entrepreneurs entered the business with just one establishment, and declined to expand it into a chain with a common theme. Roadhouse promoters came from diverse backgrounds, and relied on their own personal financial resources, sometimes with assistance from friends. At the entry level, such premises could be built for £2,000–3,000, but the most popular and exclusive cost far more, starting at £20,000 and climbing sharply to a pinnacle of £80,000. Amenities distinguished them as much as cost – swimming (in heated pools), tennis, dancing to well-known bands, entertainment and sumptuous dining. Overwhelmingly, the clientele came from the smart set, people who read the *Times*, attended public schools and Oxbridge, frequented theatres as well as West End or Soho nightclubs, drank cocktails or champagne, danced and dined on weekends in evening dress and played golf, tennis, badminton, squash and lawn croquet. Patrons might rub shoulders with the Prince of Wales and other members of the social elite, at least at the most select places. In the boom years, whatever your background, roadhouses were seen as a way of making a small fortune: 'These words occur in many books on road-houses' .... 'And the fact that I know of at least one proprietor who runs a Rolls Royce shows that there is money to be made in road-houses.'[91]

Distancing themselves from pubs, however expensive or well equipped with unusual amenities, roadhouses became positioned as an alluring attraction along Britain's new arterial roads. Their architecture, layout and siting not only catered to those seeking recreation and leisure, but also provided essential services for motorists – petrol, tune-ups, tyre changes, food and something entertaining to occupy attention – while awaiting their car's servicing. In combining the two dissimilar spheres, roadhouses adroitly filled a niche between pubs and inns, on one hand, and hotels and country clubs, on the other. That roadhouses had few brewers as financial backers reassured patrons they were visiting premises not artfully disguised as pubs gone upmarket. Image, closely associated with films, expensive and exclusive West End clubs, public schools and class captivated the interests of the 'smart set' drawn to roadhouses' select clientele.

6

Americanization and Modernity

British roadhouses were not transatlantic in origin, but in the public imagination they were often associated with America through the services they provided and in how these services were offered. Simultaneously, people thought roadhouses to be very modern destinations, reflecting not only their innovations but also a conflation of the ideas of modernity and Americanization in interwar critical discourse.

British society's identification of Americanization as a problem was not an invention of the 1930s but had a much longer history dating back to the mid-nineteenth century. This was when cheap American products such as shoes, clocks and sewing machines arrived in Britain, starting a destabilization of the economic hegemony that Britain had previously enjoyed.[1] By the first few decades of the twentieth century, America's cultural offerings joined its physical products and found a ready audience in Britain willing to enjoy a change from Victorian constraint. American literature, sheet and recorded music from ragtime to jazz, and movie stars from Clara Bow to Clark Gable influenced how many British people thought and acted.[2]

J. B. Priestley led the way in identifying the impact that Americanization was having on interwar British life. Famously he coined the phrase 'Third England' to describe the suburban Home Counties that were now increasingly consumerist, secular, mobile, classless and Americanized. This 'Third England' was located in the same topographical area as most of the well-known British roadhouses. It was certainly to be found in the same cultural area, as roadhouses provided services that Priestley considered as typical of this style of living such as cocktail bars and swimming pools.[3]

Other writers of the period saw roadhouses as a direct derivation of American society and culture. As has been noted, cultural commentator Thomas Burke remarked that

The Londoner did not know [what he was missing] until New York impregnated him with the modern need for all-night swimming pools, dance bands and badminton courts ... some place to go.[4]

Rawdon Hoare, an Imperialist and Quaker, observed the new roadhouse phenomenon; stopping at the Ace of Spades on the Great West Road, Hoare noticed a 'rather Americanized looking lad'.[5] He found the Ace of Spades of particular interest:

> I had seen – since my return – other magnificent petrol stations; I had seen places that were not unlike American roadhouses. But here on the Great West Road was a combination of the two – super petrol filling and a café that will eventually (I have no doubt) become a roadhouse. But why the youth with a rather feeble attempt at an American accent? I asked him where he came from, 'the East End of London' he said.[6]

The components that made the roadhouse modern and Americanized were varied and sometimes contradictory. This chapter considers how roadhouses managed the pressing calls of British nostalgia and American modernity in their practices, architecture and design and in how they presented their cocktail bars, swimming pools, music and cabaret.

The roadhouses of the 1930s varied from conversions of ancient barns through to purpose built modern structures, but most attempted an awkward mixture of modern and traditional ideas. This rather obscure negotiation with the future and the past can also be seen in their choice of names. Typically, roadhouses either used their name to advertise a rural situation and origin or used something self-consciously American and modern. Either way, they asserted their individuality and differentiated themselves from public houses. To an age accustomed to encountering the King's Arms or the Queen's Head in the countryside, these were strange names indeed.[7] Rural names were an attempt to capitalize on a key aspect of 1930s life, which was an attempt to re-connect with an imagined 'deep' England that referenced life before industrialization and before that ultimate product of modernity the First World War.[8] Examples of this sylvan version of the roadhouse were Moat Farm, Old Roman, Hilden Manor, Old Well, Pantiles and Willow Barn. In marked contrast other roadhouses chose names to reflect modern life. In this category can be found the Ace of Spades, the Spider's Web, the Clock, Chez Laurie, the Showboat and the Cave Man Restaurant. Some went further in the process of self-delineation, and made roadhouse part of their name: Monkey Puzzle, Rob Roy, Askers, Mile 3, Maybury, Houseboat and Majestic were just a few which wanted patrons to know unmistakably how they differed from nearby licensed premises. To capitalize on their swimming pools, some establishments used the adjectives 'blue', 'plunge' or 'lido' in their names. Water mills transformed into roadhouses likewise had an inherent advantage in projecting one of their activities.[9]

One complication of this bifurcation of ancient and modern was the use of mock-Tudor architecture in newly built roadhouses. This practice was far more complex than an attempt to mimic the visual appearance of those roadhouses that had been converted from ancient barns, as mock-Tudor was at the height of popular taste in the 1930s. Easily derided by modernists, this nostalgic architectural style was most usually found in the new suburban housing estates that had sprung up around Britain's major cities between the wars.[10] Part of the attraction was in referencing deep England, partly it reflected the wider fashion for Tudor brought about by the success of the film *The Private Life of Henry VIII* (1933), starring Charles Laughton.[11] Most of all, it was a tribute to and imitation of elite and expensive suburban houses executed in Arts and Crafts style just before the First World War.[12]

This fashion for all things Tudor explains why London's most prestigious roadhouses wanted to be both modern and old-fashioned. The Ace of Spades on the Kingston Bypass, the Thatched Barn, the Spider's Web and the Clock all adopted Tudor, with the enormous Thatched Barn being the most comprehensive in its use. There were some exceptions to this general trend. As we have noted, the Showboat in Maidenhead adopted the *moderne* style, and was in the form of a massive white ocean liner. The Maybury roadhouse in Edinburgh and Chez Laurie in Herne Bay also adopted this style.

Proprietors were keen to demonstrate their modernity by being on the cutting edge of technology. At the Mile 3 Roadhouse (near Bristol), McMinnies approvingly chronicled that 'a special feature is made of a table-to-car sandwich service, in fact everything about the place is extremely modern and efficient. You can fill up your car from electric pumps and take your supply of oil from a spotless cabinet with a strong resemblance to a cocktail bar'.[13]

Part of the roadhouse's allure was its symbolism as a sophisticated venue of 'ultra-modern' design, embodying 'what the modern motorist looks for on the road in the way of cooking and accommodation', McMinnies remarked.[14] At the Popular Road and Guest House, opened early in 1934, customers enjoyed the first roadhouse with all amenities electrically wired. In practical terms this meant a radiant, cosy environment with food served around the clock.[15] Whitbread's installed air conditioning at its new Hendon Way, where all the letting rooms had built-in radios.[16]

Modern design was important in projecting the right image. Despite Tudor dominating the external design on most roadhouses, this was not always carried through in their interiors, where modern design in metals and glass might sit uneasily alongside Windsor chairs and wood-panelled rooms. On entering an 'elegant' interior, patrons would see the lounge hall, leading to the ladies' and gentlemen's cloakrooms. Close to the hall would be a cocktail bar and tea lounge. These terms – lounge hall, cocktail bar, cloakrooms and tea lounge – bespoke refinement, never seen in a public house. Tubular steel and chromium furniture presented the modernity that promoters most wanted.

In advertising in the *Bartender*, a periodical offering advice on diverse topics including cocktail mixing, roadhouses again indicated their preferred clientele. The Hilden Manor Roadhouse's advertisement featured a photograph of the cocktail bar and identified the cocktail mixer. Amenities at the Hilden Manor – first-class restaurant, squash courts and one of the country's leading swimming pools – were stressed. One experienced bartender suggested customers sit 'on a brightly coloured stool', its stems preferably stainless or chromium-plated steel and seat coloured leather. No public house in Britain would have decorated premises in this way, save at the upper end of the market that emulated roadhouses.[17]

The Ace of Spades (Kingston Bypass) exemplified a roadhouse that used mock-Tudor for its exterior, but was intensely modern in its interior décor. In 1932, the owners of the Ace of Spades commissioned Ernest B. Musman, a well-known public-house architect, to design its new clubroom. Earlier photos of the Ace of Spades show a rather ramshackle collection of buildings, so this new building was constructed to update and improve the roadhouse's appearance and facilities. The clubroom was a roadhouse's inner sanctum where only members (in theory) were permitted to enter and where licensing restrictions limiting the times that alcohol was sold did not apply. Musman, architect of the restrained modernist Comet Hotel in Hatfield and Nag's Head Pub in Bishop's Stortford, went for an all out 'fancy dress' art deco for this clubroom.[18] *Architectural Review* featured Ace of Spades' new clubroom in a double spread when interest in new leisure architecture was at its height:

> [Its] lighting is arranged for dimming and the colours can be changed at will. The lower ceiling and walls are finished in black cellulose on laminated wood ... The dance floor surround is covered in black rubber and the dance floor is laid 'with the grain' in maple. The ace of spades [motif] is introduced as a central panel to the floor. The bar is finished in black cellulose with aluminium strips and peach mirror to the cabinet ... Half of the door is covered with grey and half with silvered mirror. The shape of the ace is cut out of the silvering. The furniture throughout is sealing wax red and upholstered in beige.[19]

This glamorous and unrestrained use of colour and deco style was outrageous, even for the early 1930s, a time when many leisure buildings employed this design fashion. The clubroom's design was far more vulgar and *outré* than other well-known comparators, such as the silvered lobby of the Strand Palace Hotel from 1931.[20]

Novelist, Monica Ewer suggested in her writing that roadhouses were flimsy, artificial and two-dimensional.[21] This idea was reflected in real life; roadhouses differed from other competing leisure establishments in their projection of a filmic fantasy world. 'Flood-lights made it all look rather attractively unnatural, like a scene in a film', thought one motorist who stopped, looking to replenish his oil. One critic equated the Chez Laurie with 'a Metro-Goldwyn palace', but such a characterization merely confirmed the thousands of customers of their superior taste.[22] There was no more fitting person than Marion Lorne, a well-known film and stage actress, to open the Gay Adventure roadhouse. A recurring image in McMinnies' pithy commentaries was the association of roadhouse restaurants and cocktail bars with films. He thought the cocktail bar at the luxurious Myllet Arms redolent of what appeared in films.[23] As he updated his entries in a new edition almost annually, McMinnies offered guides for the motoring classes – based on their popularity for over two decades – serving as a reliable index to the thinking of his customers. Ironically, film producers fostered this view. In his very first edition of *Signpost to the Road Houses*, published in 1935, McMinnies recorded that the Thatched Barn's 'steeply sloping Norfolk reed thatched roof and timbered walls dominated by its water tower lend it a unique appearance which the film studios at Elstree have not been slow to appreciate'.[24] He typified the reaction of many interwar Britons.

No roadhouse entrepreneurs went further than those at the Thatched Barn in linking their establishments with popular entertainment. Its location, two miles from Elstree film studios, certainly facilitated the Barn's exotic reputation. On its reopening, Florence Desmond, famed for her film and radio appearances, presided. Later, after dinner, when guests prepared to dance, Josephine Bradley and Frank Ford, 'England's premier ball-room dancers', performed.[25]

Roadhouses likewise served cocktails as way of portraying a modern, chic and fashionable image (see Figure 6.1). Prior to the rise of cocktails, patrons at upmarket establishments, such as the Sports Club in London's Fleet Street, ordered various gin mixtures or peach bitters right up to the end of the First World War.[26] The Americanization of drinking habits developed when US bartenders moved to Britain because of prohibition; the best qualified worked in London's West End, some of whom later migrated to leading roadhouses.[27] Literally, Americans taught the British about cocktails. 'The Americans still know more about cocktails than anybody else', observed a connoisseur at the

Figure 6.1 Ace of Spades, Kingston Bypass, cocktail bar, 1933. Architectural Press Archive/RIBA Collections.

Savoy, unofficial headquarters of serious drinkers. Estimates suggested that Americans had consumed staggering amounts – over 100,000 cocktails alone during the summer of 1925 at this single hotel. Five years later, the Garrick Club, embarrassed with the deficient quality of mixed spirits, dispatched a servant to the Savoy where he would be 'shown how to make cocktails'. Predictably, the Americanization of drinking habits went one step further with coining of the term 'American bar', designating an international bar serving diverse drinks far wider than available at pubs. Roadhouses introduced them as quickly as possible.[28]

The Americanization of drinking can be discerned in other ways. Google's 'ngram' viewer shows major increases in usage of the word cocktail in Britain from about 1920 with a peak at about 1933, suggesting that a strong transatlantic exchange was in place, with the rich and famous in constant travel between Southampton and New York.[29] Another dimension of this was the unofficial first edition of *The United Kingdom Bartenders' Guild Guide to Drinks*, published during US prohibition in the 1920s, describing how to mix exotic potions such as 'Twelve Miles Out', 'Between-the-Sheets' and 'Bosom Crasser'.[30]

The cocktail, roadhouse and female short hair – the 'bob', modelled after the page-boy haircut – arrived almost together. Hostess Madame Alfredo de Peña inaugurated the cocktail party into London in 1922, characterized by late-night revelry and attendance chiefly of the young. American songwriter Cole Porter had popularized cocktail culture with a series of songs: 'Cocktail Time' (1922) and later with 'Say It with Gin' (1930), among others. The Ace of Spades (Great West Road) opened in 1926, the year after Frederick Lonsdale's *Spring Cleaning* (1925) first featured cocktails as part of a play. Florence, in Noel Coward's play *The Vortex* (1926), declares 'It's never too early for a cocktail', the same year in which the low-cut cocktail dress became fashionable. The cocktail craze 'swept the country', wine merchant Harry Caplan recollected, and the cocktail bar 'became the resort of the *elite*'. For ladies, cocktails quickly displaced champagne.[31] So popular was the cocktail that homes without a cocktail cabinet as part of the standard furnishings were regarded as old-fashioned. According to McMinnies, the cocktail bar at Woodside Hotel and Country Club on the main London-Eastbourne Road 'might have been transferred lock, stock and barrel from one of the smarter resorts in London'. He regarded the cocktail bar at Kingfishers' Pool as in no way inferior to London standards.[32] Thomas Warrington decorated the walls of his Kentish roadhouse with pictures of cocktails.[33] Cocktail culture played a critical role in fostering Americanization: 'Mayfair and Manhattan were the twin centres of the universe, and the activities of the "fast set" were eagerly reported by the Press.'[34]

The cocktail added immensely to the attractions of roadhouses. By the mid-1930s, without either a cocktail bar or lounge a roadhouse's claim to sophistication seemed questionable. Projecting the appropriate image, the Monkey Puzzle advertised its dancing and dining facilities, with pictures of well-dressed, elite patrons drinking cocktails. Cocktail mixing acquired its own mystique, worthy of special recognition. When the Hilden Manor Roadhouse advertised in the *Bartender* in 1938, for instance, the cocktail mixer, J. Baverstock, received as much attention as the restaurant ('first class'), squash courts (unusual as an amenity) and swimming pool ('one of the finest … in England').[35] At the Nautical William, patrons could request cocktails from a list featuring names of over eighty different mixtures, while at the Spider's Web a house cocktail gave it cachet. Roadhouse bartenders and old-style publicans, in fact, had little in common. No publican would go so far as to name a cocktail (or beer as an equivalent in the different context) after a favoured customer, or send a patron on holiday a letter wishing him an enjoyable time. Yet, this is precisely what one experienced bartender recommended as part of a barman's 'sociability'.[36] Though knowing virtually nothing about serving beer, bartenders had vast expertise in mixing cocktails. To draw eager explorers of suburban nightlife, the Myllet Arms advertised an unbeatable cocktail bar, offering 'every known drink under the sun'.[37]

In making swimming pools a standard feature at roadhouses, promoters assumed a leading role in pioneering the desegregation of leisure for the motoring classes. Formerly, when swimming, as in almost all other recreational sports, the sexes could not mix. Change came from the United States in the 1920s, with new attitudes to sun tanning and greater emphasis on physical fitness. Within a decade, beaches became desegregated, Hollywood films began glamorizing swimming as a new cultural activity, and swimming suits (more form fitting than costumes), manufactured with a new elastic thread, Lastex, enabled the rich to emulate the attire of film stars. For British middle- and upper-class women, mixing with men when swimming, dancing and on the automobile journey itself all gave roadhouses a special allure, which no other set of activities could rival, as venues for interacting with eligible young men in what now became part of new dating rituals.[38]

The 1930s saw a nationwide craze for swimming, encouraged by three factors. First, swimming was part of a more general interwar preoccupation with fitness and the outdoors. As leisure time increased, forcibly for the unemployed and as working conditions improved for the waged, much of it was spent outdoors. This saw a rapid rise in rambling, cycling and swimming and was part of a rediscovery of the countryside by town dwellers whose lives had been dominated by work and church.[39] Second, sweltering summers in 1933–35 with temperatures soaring into the upper 80s encouraged swimming in outdoor pools. Third, authorities across Britain constructed many new pools and outdoor lidos. By 1935, 1,000 council baths existed, with 300 more being added each year. The municipal push for outdoor swimming was part of local government policies aimed at improving public health, which was also seen in the construction of health centres and improved council housing. The amounts spent on such bathing facilities reached staggering proportions, estimates reaching some £10 million in 1935. Britons joined 1,900 swimming clubs, causing booming sales of bathing costumes that topped one million.[40]

For the public, the pinnacle, Empire Pool (Wembley), required an outlay of £150,000, and rivalled Olympia's main hall in size. Other public bathing pools established an enviable reputation: Clacton (1932, £50,000) and Prestwich (1931, £34,000). Skegness had demonstrated the profitability of luring swimmers and spectators, who spent some £25,000 annually. Whatever the location, they generated 'a packet of money for the locality'.[41] Lidos and seaside resort pools often adopted a glamorous *moderne* style, reflecting Hollywood taste and its projected modernity. Saltdean Lido in Brighton is a good example of this trend.

The typical roadhouse customer was not attracted to swimming pools for the general public. The middle-class, motorized swimmer would have found the atmosphere of a municipal pool impossible, with the danger of meeting the family's greengrocer on equal terms and in bathing costumes.[42] Within a few years of their introduction, George Orwell viewed municipal lidos as the centre of a new naked, democratic Britain, which was just the reason that roadhouse customers wished to avoid them.[43]

Before the roadhouses' advent, motorists eager for a swim had to drive to some secluded spot, strip down to the bathing suit and then steel themselves for entering 'the inhospitable Thames, unwarmed, unfiltered and unlit'.[44] By the late 1920s, roadhouse proprietors recognized the opportunity to provide exclusive swimming. Pantiles, opened in 1930, was reputedly one of the first roadhouses with a swimming pool in the country, and certainly its 50,000 patrons in the first season established it as pre-eminent in the field.[45] Swimming pools offered patrons irresistible amenities: privacy, convenience, hygiene, comfort and, most important, protection from social interlopers. Fitting rooms – the Pantiles boasted over 100 – guaranteed much-craved seclusion. A daily entrance fee to the pool, excluding the unwelcome masses, afforded social privacy.[46] Hot summer weather well into the evening demanded innovative thinking. Proprietors at the Pantiles floodlit the swimming pool at night, much to the gratification of some 50,000 bathers in 1934.[47] The pool at the Ace of Spades on the Great West Road premises promised poolside catering, ample bathing and sunbathing facilities to four or five hundred people, with floodlighting at night as an added attraction.[48] Other roadhouses stayed in front of the competition with submarine lighting in pools (see Figure 6.2).

Patrons dived into heated, filtered water, assured of its cleanliness. At the Firbeck Hall Roadhouse (Great North Road, Rotherham), the newly built swimming pool established hitherto unreached standards with water 'sterilised by the ozonair process'.[49] Uncovered swimming pools comprised the quintessential attraction of roadhouses, which together with ideal temperatures fuelled a boom in 1933–34 generating enviable profits.

Typical was the Bell House. In his motorist guide to suitable bucolic oases, McMinnies lauded its 'curtained cubicles', and the pool, its water 'remarkably clean' with 'the very latest filtering and sterilising plant'. As owners of a popular recreational venue on the London to Oxford Road, 23 miles from the capital, the Bell House's proprietors saw the importance of staying in front of

Figure 6.2 Thatched Barn swimming pool, from a postcard, late 1930s. Author's collection.

the competition – the Ace of Spades on the Kingston Bypass was promising 'luxurious dressing accommodation', poolside catering and water heated to 75 degrees perfectly sterilized by the new 'Katadyn' process.[50] Within several years, the Bell House even upgraded its water purification system. McMinnies recorded with approval the newly certified chemist who sampled the pool water daily to 'ensure its purity', an increasingly popular tactic at many roadhouses designed to capitalize on public fears about impure, cloudy water.[51] Other improvements included not only installation of loud speakers in the pool area and throughout the premises, but also the hiring of a qualified swimming instructor.[52]

Driving swimming pool improvements at roadhouses was the compulsion to retain their pre-eminence as fashion leaders in an increasingly competitive market. Fashionable Jantzen and Forma bathing suits, their new styles each season marketed exclusively for wealthy patrons, were displayed in a separate area with a fitting room at the back at the Bell House. Those eager to appear fashionable could rent the latest swimming suits for a mere six pence.[53]

Amid the sweltering summer of 1935, the hottest in sixty-five years, observers thought swimmers numbered over 100,000 on weekends in London. One roadhouse alone counted 2,000 and more weekend swimmers. By 9 pm roadhouses in June, filled to capacity and responsible for one of London's largest traffic jams, turned thousands of revellers away. 'During the summer months crowds fill open-air pools during week-ends and evenings, so that actually the swimming pool becomes a recreation centre', remarked *Hotel*.[54] Such was the nature of the swimming craze that the newly opened Nautical William in the midlands drew over 2,000 patrons daily on weekends and even in the spring holidays of 1937 had to turn customers away.[55]

Temperatures soaring into the 80s in the summer of 1938 sent perspiring Britons to roadhouses in the southeast in droves, the bathers seeking relief during the day replaced with still more in the evening. August proved no less oppressive, and bathers, enjoying the floodlit pools, frolicked into the early morning hours. Geography proved no barrier to the boom. Outside Manchester, ambitious swimmers started from East Lancashire to participate in the craze.[56]

Bathing was not always the chief recreation, especially at a minority of roadhouses using lakes instead of purpose-built pools. Clough Williams-Ellis designed Laughing Water at Cobham, Kent, for Lord Darnley. Recognizing the vagaries of English weather, owner and designer agreed on using swimming in the lake as 'an agreeable excuse for waterside amenities and gaiety of all sorts'. Customers exploited leisure activities – socializing at the Lido restaurant, boating, rambling, dancing or listening to music – as 'alternative diversions to mere immersion in cold water'. To supplement meagre numbers of virile masculine swimmers, roadhouses like Laughing Water offered 'what the cinemas call strongly supporting programmes as a standby'. One of these, Cobham Woods, enticed with birds, wild flowers and rhododendrons.[57]

Aimed at a refined clientele, roadhouse promoters fully grasped the marketing rationale, expressed by one architect in the *Hotel Review* early in 1935.

> The equipment of new Atlantic passenger liners, fiercely competitive ... in their eagerness to capture traffic, is usually indicative of what is being demanded ... by the wealthier travelling public, and one could scarcely imagine a modern ship of any size or pretension without something pretty generous in the way of a swimming pool.[58]

Roadhouses used their swimming pools to project an Americanized modernity, and deployed newsreel films to advertise this service by suggesting that life at their establishment was quite similar to the Los Angeles Country Club where Johnny Weissmuller might pop in for a swim. Almost all of the roadhouse newsreels still available for viewing today show swimmers and swimming pools in action. The most common images are of poolside fashion parades of young women in their new swimming costumes, synchronized swimming, made popular by glamorous American films, and a general splashing around of revellers.[59]

Musical entertainment most differentiated exclusive super roadhouses from those below them. 'If you are offering the very best in food and drink you must also provide first-class – which means expensive – entertainment', one roadhouse design expert stressed. Orchestras were virtually mandatory for such a setting, so famous band leaders, especially if the show was broadcast live, performed as an added attraction. Putting such a feature on an entertainment programme excluded all but the super roadhouses. They often booked well-known bands from West End restaurants that could cost £12,000–13,000 per year. Cabaret turns, much in demand at this end of the market, offered no financial relief – the going rate for the best approached £1,000 weekly.[60]

Star names generated roadhouse custom. Top band leaders, often poached from London's West End such as Ben Oakley and the famed Barnstormers, received wages commensurate with the clientele they were hired to attract; Oakley earned the fabulous sum of £55 weekly for performing and broadcasting at the Thatched Barn. The Spider's Web recruited bandleaders Fred Bretherton from the Gargoyle Club, and Bill Airey-Smith, one of the most sought after musicians for 'the smartest of all the London road houses'.[61] Music likewise contributed to the success of the Ace of Spades (Kingston Bypass) and to widening the clientele's scope. Proprietor George Hersey advertised music, dancing and dining nightly until 3 am as a deliberate marketing tactic to attract people who worked well into the night, especially theatrical employees, and in this he was not disappointed. It was, McMinnies thought, 'one of the most successful enterprises of its kind'.[62] Lampooning the Ace's cultural pretensions, Osbert Lancaster depicted the 'Hearts are Trumps' roadhouse, where 'Edward Sugarprong and his Twenty-Seven White-Hot Tubthumpers provided the hottest jazz to be heard between Hammersmith Broadway and Pelvis Bay'.[63]

Dancing in fact ranked as third only to swimming and dining as popular attractions. 'Decide your entertainment policy with the pockets of your customers in mind', advised an authority on roadhouse building. 'Entertainment', he added, 'can be the secret of a roadhouse's success'.[64] At the most exclusive establishments nothing but a live orchestra, often based in London, would do. On Saturday nights at the Barn (Bayfordbury, Hertfordshire), a famed dwarf singer led a band. The Crib imported West End dancers and variety artists. On their opening night as a full-fledged nightclub, the Ace of Spades (Kingston Bypass) advertised that then famous dance instructor Santos Cansani was to appear.[65] In Monica Ewer's novel, *Roadhouse*, the proprietor hired the well-known bandleader, 'The Terry', whose band members wore white naval mess jackets echoing the roadhouse's blue and white resplendent colour motif.[66] Below this exalted level, owners could economize with a gramophone – the newest types intended specially for use in large spaces – or radio.[67] Whatever the format, casual dress was permissible for an informal lunchtime dance, but many roadhouses considered evening dress mandatory for dinner dances.[68] For example, the Spider's Web permitted dancing in everyday clothes, but reserved one room for evening dress.[69]

Exclusive roadhouses drew custom with cabaret shows, 'featuring West End night-club artists' and water carnivals, especially in winter. Newsreel cameras were present to record a few of these cabaret acts, through which we can gain a picture of an evening at a London super roadhouse. It is likely that when the newsreels attended, roadhouse managers would have booked acts already well known to cinema audiences. Based on this source, roadhouse cabarets comprised singers, comedians and speciality dance acts. The two singing acts recorded by the newsreels used American material. This is entirely to be expected. In the 1920s and 1930s, American musical sources dominated British popular culture, consolidating a successful export programme that had been in play since the days of ragtime. Mass methods of music reproduction, such as the radio and the gramophone, had accelerated this process; the arrival of sound and the Hollywood musical in 1929 provided further reinforcement.[70] In both of the songs shown in the newsreel archives, the American material is modified for its English audience. For example, Betty Astell, star of British movie *This Is the Life* (1933), which was filmed at the Bell House, sang there for the newsreels to publicize her film.[71] Her visual appearance was entirely the Hollywood star, singing an American song, 'Heigh Ho'. Her hair was bleached a platinum blond, she wore a slinky evening gown, evincing a domestic version of Jean Harlow; but her vocal styling was entirely English as Astell sang in a received pronunciation throughout.[72] Astell's adaptation of American popular music typified how Britain handled transatlantic cultural imports; British dance bands softened the edges of American music, adding strings to produce a gentler domestic offering. Astell's performance is a synecdoche for much of British roadhouse life, generating a British modernity by adapting American cultural archetypes.

It seems unlikely that British roadhouse proprietors visited the United States to get the information necessary to imitate American country clubs, which, in the services they provided and the clientele they attracted, were far closer to the British roadhouse offering than American roadhouses. The process was, in reality, far more heuristic and haphazard. As soon as rising middle-class incomes met reducing prices for motor cars, a signal change in British society occurred with the arrival of large numbers of wealthy, newly mobile middle-class motorists who wanted to add fashionable leisure to the modern excitement of motoring.[73] Once this modernity started to play out, smart business owners responded by building roadhouses, made exclusive by both pricing and accessibility to automobiles.

In order to attract these new customers, roadhouses offered swimming, cocktails, dancing and cabaret. Introduction of swimming pools in the early 1930s was not a roadhouse innovation, but a response to an already well-established craze discernible in municipal and seaside lidos. What roadhouses offered was swimming in exclusive company and surroundings, the opposite of the democratic lido. Cocktails were, of course, American in origin, but had been standard in sophisticated West End clubs long before roadhouses' ascent. Roadhouse cocktails shifted this habit from central London to rural locations. The interior décor and exterior appearance of roadhouses reflected two competing and contradictory modern fashion trends, art deco/*moderne* and mock-Tudor. Art deco cocktail bars can trace their origins to Los Angeles, New York and continental Europe, but were, perhaps, most influenced by the impact of Hollywood movies on British culture. Although Beverly Hills' mansions occasionally employed mock-Tudor, it was a British fad, and its use made roadhouse art deco interiors even more shocking. This odd combination of styles was an adaptation of an American culture found in most of the super roadhouses near London. In a roadhouse evening, the food offered was French, or past midnight, British bacon and eggs, but the newsreel archive shows that the music and dancing and some of the cabarets were usually adaptations of American archetypes.

Roadhouses were self-consciously modern establishments established to furnish entertainment for the mobile, wealthy middle classes. Their interior and exterior appearance and the services they provided were mostly adaptations of American cultural sources, often mixed jarringly with British styles.

7

The Roadhouse in the Public Imagination

One intriguing aspect of the roadhouse is that it is almost forgotten; it has disappeared from popular memory and, even for most interwar historians, is an obscure relic of the period. This obscurity is in marked contrast with the acclaim and notoriety that roadhouses achieved in Britain in the 1930s, still evident today from their contribution to popular culture in that period. Roadhouses were the locus of the action in popular fiction, in at least one successful play, in movies and in musicals.

In fiction, roadhouses appear in three main guises. First, they were a setting for Americanized romance, imitating the themes shown in local cinemas with their regular diet of Hollywood movies. Second, writers identified roadhouses as a centre for crime and gangsters, themes that also displayed a good deal of Americanization. Finally, authors used roadhouses as a metaphor for change, setting mobile modernity against the themes of continuity and traditional Englishness. Roadhouses were an appropriate place to reflect these themes in films, plays and fiction of the 1930s, because they were not widely experienced or understood by audiences. In effect, roadhouses formed a *tabula rasa*, a clean slate on which writers imposed their ideas.

This chapter explores the relationship between important roadhouse texts and popular culture in the interwar years, picking out novels from Edgar Wallace, Graham Greene and short stories in the Sexton Blake series but concentrating most of its attention on Monica Ewer's novel, *Roadhouse*, written in about 1933. Research for this book has identified three further books and two short stories that have the roadhouse as their main setting and a further fourteen where roadhouses play an important role.[1]

Roadhouses often employed American namesakes and adopted American practices, and were, therefore, well positioned to demonstrate the impact of Americanization in fiction. Edgar Wallace's roadhouse novel *The Coat of Arms*

(1931) is a good example. Edgar Wallace, Britain's most successful author between the wars, wrote successive inexpensive, best-selling thrillers. Graham Greene described him as 'the giant of the cheap edition... the human book-factory'.[2] He remained popular for years after his early death, but his work has not stood the test of time and his writing is now something of a curiosity.[3] Working- and lower-middle class readers enjoyed Wallace's novels, which epitomized interwar popular fiction.[4]

By the late 1920s, Wallace, always keen to adapt his writing to the latest trends, had replaced his imperial fiction with Americanized content.[5] For example, in *The Hand of Power* (1927), the hero is 'a young American reporter-cum-advertising copywriter called Bill Holbrook who is in London working for Pawter's Intensive Publicity Service'.[6] It concludes with the hero and his girl leaving Britain for Manhattan to get married. At this stage in his career, Wallace had to use Hollywood movies and his imagination to inform his writing because he had not yet visited the United States.

To clear his substantial debts, Wallace took a job at RKO studios in Hollywood, arriving in the United States in November 1931. He lived there until his death the following February. Despite living in Los Angeles for only a few weeks, Wallace wrote a diary for publication, full of detailed gossip of his life there describing his excitement at the modernity of Beverley Hills and the movie studios.[7] Wallace was alone in California and prone to making expensive transatlantic phone calls, bridging the two worlds.

In the year preceding his emigration, Wallace's novel, *The Coat of Arms*, was published, which was more subtle and interesting in its treatment of Americanization than in his earlier writing.[8] In this book, 'The Coat of Arms' is a small hotel near Guildford in Surrey recently converted into a roadhouse, a location that Wallace uses to describe an aspirational form of Americanization where snobbery is central. He introduces us to its residents most of whom had recently arrived from North America. Wallace was clear, unlike other commentators, on the origins of this new English phenomenon. As one character explains: 'it's the English equivalent of a road-house isn't it?'.[9] The very English proprietor

> planned to cater for the better-class week-end custom, to make a road-house of this rambling Tudor inn, and to that end had furnished expensively and with considerable taste, had rescued and ... had used so much paint that [the village] smelt of it.[10] At week-ends it was rather overcrowded and the big paved yard a little too full of cars.[11]

The Coat of Arms presents an idealized locus of new mobilities in Britain powered by the car. This thought is extended to its customers, who travel frequently and seemingly without barriers across the Atlantic. It is so modern in its assumptions about movement and its sharing of British and American cultures. The rural proprietor concludes that 'I like him, I like most Americans.'[12] One of the book's characters is an American captain of police, and as expected in an Edgar Wallace novel, others turn out to be criminals, producing an early example of the use of roadhouses in crime and thriller fiction.[13]

Later in the decade, Graham Greene, a far more sophisticated but, at the time, a much less well-known author than Wallace, also deployed roadhouses as pivotal locations in his novels *The Confidential Agent* (1939) and *Brighton Rock*. In *The Confidential Agent*, Greene's Tudor Club roadhouse was the location for the agent's first encounter with the British criminals who pursue him throughout the novel. Writing in a filmic style, Greene positioned this roadhouse on the foggy and deserted Dover road,

> This sort of thing was new since the days when he came to England as a youth… an old Tudor house – he could tell it was genuine Tudor – it was full of armchairs and sofas and a cocktail bar where you expected a library… The lavatory was certainly not Tudor, it was all glass and black marble.[14]

Greene presents his roadhouse's clientele as potentially decadent, vulgar, snobbish and violent. The proprietor explains his recent move to Kent,

> You've heard of *The Spanish Galleon*? No I don't think so, it was my first roadhouse near Maidenhead, but I had to sell out in the end. The west you know it's losing caste a bit. Kent's better, even Essex. On the west you get a rather – popular – element on the way to the Cotswolds.[15]

This reflected the idea that the first roadhouses based in western London such as the Ace of Spades and the Gay Adventure had become dominated by suburban customers and had lost their metropolitan *cachet* of the early 1930s. Despite the Tudor Club's pretensions to glamour and exclusivity, the confidential agent is threatened with a beating from a violent chauffeur in the roadhouse's deco toilets.

Earlier in the decade, a Sexton Blake story paper, *The Roadhouse Murder* (1933), written in a cruder style for a younger and more masculine audience, also dealt with these themes.[16] Such stories aimed at boys and young men searching for the excitement and thrills that matched Hollywood movies, but located themselves in the more familiar world of everyday Britain. *The Roadhouse*

Murder uses America as the source for much of its content, juxtaposed with an English location and an English hero, Sexton Blake.

Sexton Blake stories, first published in the last decade of the nineteenth century, were still going strong into the 1930s. He was

> a consulting detective, but also a bit of an action hero. As his exploits unfolded during the twentieth century, he also tackled a range of problems from private disappearances to international conflicts.[17]

The Roadhouse Murder's author, Anthony Skene, was a journeyman writer who contributed to the long-running series, the Sexton Blake Library.[18] In *The Roadhouse Murder*, Sexton Blake tracks down a gang of Americanized criminals who had set up their base at the High Card roadhouse at Caterham in Surrey. Blake 'knew the place, it had lately been the resort of "high kickers" expensive if not exclusive'.[19] This is an accurate summary of British roadhouse clientele in the early 1930s, backed by René Cutforth's reminiscence 'it was considerably unbuttoned for the period: almost anybody could get in there so long as he had his hair appropriately slicked back'.[20] Caterham would seem to be the one of the last places to look for violent gangsters, but Skene chose a correct location, beyond the Metropolitan Police reach but quite near London.

After some unlikely encounters with machine-gun toting criminals on London's streets – 'Bang! A streak of flame came from the shadows' – Blake followed the gang to their roadhouse lair. Unusually, he needed help and this came from recently arrived American detective Lawrence Hackby of the Interstate Agency, New York and they worked together to infiltrate the High Card.[21] This establishment had all the features that would define a large interwar suburban roadhouse, boasting a grand swimming pool (in which the gangsters tried to drown Blake), a restaurant, bars and back offices where the gangsters met.[22]

Skene took his dialogue for Hackby straight from the 'B' Movie talkies. Hackby summed up the situation: 'I guess we're after the same dame. Well now I want to make the pinch. You may have the publicity, but I gotta have the pinch!'.[23] Hackby was a transplant from the world of American movies, used to lend glamour and veracity to such a suburban and English location. Like Wallace's Police Captain, this character linked Hollywood to England's suburban Home Counties. Skene provided a good description of a British roadhouse, transformed into the headquarters of a Chicago gang, with gang members who were a pastiche of those seen in Hollywood movies. 'I am the hostess here. Miss Latimer is the name. They call me The Doll.'[24]

Even in the late nineteen-fifties, the roadhouse still provided sufficient fascination to be the fictional location for another Sexton Blake roadhouse story, *Roadhouse Girl* (1957). Many of the themes of *The Roadhouse Murder* are repeated:

> Of course I knew it! Do you think I didn't know why he was putting money into the club that had my name on it – the Roundabout? He was using that place as he used the other one he controls, the Marengo on the Great West Road.[25] He was using both places to get men and women into trouble; to get them into deep water with drink or dope, or worse so that he could blackmail them.[26]

The years leading up to 1934 were the highpoint of public interest in British roadhouses and in that year Monica Ewer's romantic novel, *Roadhouse*, was released in weekly instalments in a magazine and shortly after was published in book form.[27] This novel is an unexpected repository of pertinent information about super roadhouses and is analysed in some detail in the paragraphs that follow.

The plotting and characters in *Roadhouse* suggest a romantic period-piece, with stereotypical heroines, good-time girls, heroes and villains. Even so, a study of this novel and Ewer's descriptive writing affords a number of possibilities for analysis.

Figure 7.1 Monica Ewer in 1930, aged 41. Photo by Planet News Archive/SSPL/Getty Images.

First, *Roadhouse* tells us much about roadhouses' contribution to the developing modernity of the 1930s. It provides clues to the significance of a newly motorized culture and of the new spatialities generated by new forms of leisure. Second, at another level, *Roadhouse* offers us, in its detailed descriptions of the Harbour Bar roadhouse, an unusual and unique access to the organization of large roadhouses and the people who went to them, all filtered through Ewer's distanced view.

Monica Ewer was the daughter of William Thompson, a Protestant Irishman, who had edited *Reynold's Newspaper* (see Figure 7.1).[28] Raised in a family with radical leanings, she naturally associated herself with the socialist politics emerging in Edwardian Britain.[29] Most of the colleges in the old universities excluded clever young women because of their gender, so Monica, with her modern tendencies, was educated instead at London's Bedford College.[30] In 1912, she married journalist Norman Ewer, who, like Monica, was a committed socialist. Ewer's radicalism not just persisted, but moved further left in her thirties; she was a Fabian, an associate of Sydney and Beatrice Webb and a member of the Communist Party.[31] One close colleague described her as 'charming and Irish', remembering her as 'possessed of an Irish Puritanism which would have recoiled a mile from any irregularity'.[32]

Ewer wrote for the *Daily Herald* in the 1920s as a film and stage critic. She was also a playwright, her first play, *The Best of Both Worlds* (1925), examined poverty through the eyes of a privileged female observer. From 1925 to 1928, she edited a theatrical series, *Plays for the People*, aimed at working-class audiences.[33] Heedful of the advice of those who urged her to write about what she knew, Ewer wrote her first novel, *Insecurity* (1930), in which she documented the difficulties of being a female journalist on Fleet Street.[34] Ewer followed up this effort with some forty romantic novels aimed at female readers, often making a young woman the leading character. Ewer was an author in a well-populated field of women writing for women between the wars competing with big names, such as Ethel M. Dell and Ruby M. Ayres among many others. The *Times*' obituary, written in a kind if condescending manner, described her work as a 'genre which was very much her own'.[35] She also wrote dialogue for a number of films.

Because of Ewer's background, politics and values, she did not take her fictional writing seriously. Historians must be careful in their response to novels and there is a need for special caution with popular works. Nevertheless, novels, such as *Roadhouse,* can provide reliable historical information. John Tosh stresses that 'all creative literature offers insight into the social and intellectual milieu in which the writer lived and, often, vivid descriptions of the physical setting as well'.[36] Mindful of this idea, this book uses *Roadhouse* not only as a unique source for investigating the topography and culture of the British roadhouse of the early 1930s, but also as a vehicle for positioning roadhouses as locations of modernity.

Roadhouse typifies many interwar romantic novels. Ewer's heroine, independent, young and attractive but not that pretty, falls in love with a very masculine, proud and taciturn father figure. As Rachael Anderson has proposed, 'the heroine of the thirties was still uncertain whether she wished to be liberated from man or dominated by him'.[37]

Ewer's interest in theatre and film provided a connection to the world of romance. Historian Alison Light notes that

> Film, and especially Hollywood cinema, together with the spate of film magazines, which became a craze in the late 1920s and '30s made romance even more visible as the major form for a more heterogeneous class of audience.[38]

Roadhouse aimed at its female audience through two forms of popular literature. It first saw the light of day in *Home Notes*, a competitor to the better-known *Woman's Weekly*, comprised of recipes, dressmaking hints and romantic fiction. Literary historian Ros Ballaster describes it as a 'cheap, popular magazine', cultivating a domestic audience.[39] *Home Notes*' content suggests a lower-middle-class suburban audience of housewives, looking for romantic and escapist fiction. In its later book form, *Roadhouse* appeared in hardback, an expensive option. As a consequence, most of Ewer's readers would have got their copies through circulating libraries such as W. H. Smith and Boot's and from municipal public libraries, whose numbers grew considerably during the 1930s. The majority of customers for these libraries were the middle class, not intellectual, and conservative in their choice of authors.[40]

Placing *Roadhouse* in the category of undemanding romantic fiction provokes further concerns that it might be an unreliable source for analysis, owing to Ewer possibly exaggerating the roadhouse's glamour for literary effect. Ewer's background as much as her sensibilities counteract this risk. Ewer, ever the socialist and 'puritan', intellectually and temperamentally distanced herself from her subject matter, and this can be seen in the descriptive passages that make this book so interesting. In reviewing *Roadhouse*, the *Evening News* thought the novel's 'crisp reality of its background and detail' primarily differentiated it 'from most frankly sentimental tales' of the genre.[41] To minimize the difficulties of this source, the ensuing analysis concentrates its attention on roadhouse architecture, features, culture and customers and ignores the romantic narrative of the novel.

Roadhouse is a useful source for details on the minutiae of roadhouse life unrecorded in other documentary sources. Naming her roadhouse 'the Harbour

Bar', Ewer provided us with a good deal of information about the features and organization of that imagined building.[42] She located her roadhouse in the outer reaches of Greater London alongside a new arterial road. A journey to the nearest small town needed a bus or car. The name, the Harbour Bar, presents two avenues for investigation; the first being the punning name itself and the second being in the frequent direct and metaphorical nautical references found in the book.

Ewer introduces us to her roadhouse: '"the Harbour Bar" it said in letters a foot high'.[43] Emphasizing the size of the lettering was her way of showing the scale and modernity of the roadhouse. This sits well compared to a slightly later, real roadhouse pub, the Prospect Inn, which had 18-inch red neon lettering to advertise its name.[44] The Harbour Bar is quite a good pun; its first meaning suggesting that you are entering the calm waters of the harbour, away from the fraught dangers of the open sea or the open road. Second, it suggests a cocktail bar. By using the term 'bar' rather than hotel or pub, Ewer is conjuring up a sense of modern and Americanized drinking. In that same year, the pioneering roadhouse, the Ace of Spades on the Kingston Bypass, had installed a new art deco cocktail bar in its clubroom. By using a pun, Ewer mimicked the fashion for jokey names popular in both roadhouses and suburban homes in the late 1920s and early 1930s.[45]

Ewer described the Harbour Bar as 'The great white roadhouse whose most distinctive feature was a flagstaff'.[46] It was a shrewd choice; many roadhouses adopted this nod to modernism in their appearance. The most likely candidates for inspiring the Harbour Bar are the Ace of Spades and the Spider's Web, both well-known roadhouses set adjacent to an arterial road on London's outskirts. The Spider's Web had white elevations and a mock-Tudor red tiled roof.

Roadhouse's detailed description of its garage and filling station seems again to be using the Ace of Spades as its example,

> If you leant a little to one side, you could see the rows of petrol pumps and the garage for repairs and the great car park. You could see the perpetual coming and going. Every movement became familiar. The men in their blue overalls bending to open the bonnets of the cars, carrying the petrol pipes, filling the oil cans, the noise of a spanner thrown on a running board, the impatient hooting, the shouting of orders – all these sights and sounds fitted into the daily pattern of life. They were all part of the business of the by-pass.[47]

Newsreels and photographs of the Ace of Spades showed the extensive filling and garage facilities available there. This establishment epitomized a roadhouse with petrol station origins. Aerial shots revealed a large structure with 'GARAGE' painted in enormous white letters on the roof.[48]

Ewer also set out the entertainments available to her roadhouse customers, centred on a large, floodlit, swimming pool with a moustachioed swimming instructor. There was a tennis court, with a trainer selected for his good looks, and the possibility of a game of clock golf. This was quite a restrained list compared to actual roadhouses where patrons might try horse riding, archery and flying lessons. The Harbour Bar resembled actual roadhouses in providing alcoholic drinks into the small hours. It was a 24-hour business: 'Someone always had to be on duty in the roadhouse that never closed.' Both cocktails and beer were on offer. Mike, the bartender, was on hand to suggest new ideas for novelty cocktails, including one called 'love-all' as a tie-in to a special tennis promotion. The roadhouse's restaurant served a formal lunch with white tablecloths, switched to a 'gay check' for tea, and then, perhaps, back to formal dressing for evening meals.[49] Francois, the head waiter and a key figure in supervising these transitions, embodied the continental experience associated in the public mind with the highest quality of the best West End establishments. Large brewers also employed the approach of hiring continental waiters and chefs to add class and cachet to their large arterial roadhouse pubs.[50] The Harbour Bar's resident dance band, 'Terry, Chita and the Boys' provided the evening's entertainment, central to this roadhouse's success. Much roadhouse popularity derived from the following generated by its well-known bands, as live music was so necessary for couples to enjoy the full pleasures of dancing.

Ewer's use of a nautical name reflected the real-life Prospect Inn, which its architect provisionally named H.M.S. Prospect. Its owners, perhaps thinking a naval reference a little odd for a pub some miles from the sea, rejected this suggestion.[51] Ewer took the nautical naming of her roadhouse further as a way of creating a more general maritime theme for the book. By so doing, she connected her *Roadhouse,* on one hand, to a dislocation and placelessness associated with the sea, and, on the other, to the transatlantic ocean liner, an epitome of 1930s modernity.[52] In carrying out this literary exercise, Ewer simultaneously made her novel more interesting and *au courant,* but elevated the writing well above the more workaday romantic novel of that period, a critical fact unappreciated later in her *Times* obituary.

In dressing up the Harbour Bar in a nautical style and providing the bellboys with midshipmens' uniforms, she establishes a theme for her descriptive writing.[53] For example, in her introduction to the isolated location of the roadhouse on a new bypass, Ewer wrote: 'Like a fleet of great ships the lorries moved majestically down the bypass.'[54] Later in the book, our heroine, Alison Reed, considers the night-time prospect from her new place of employment:

> Far away along the by-pass a red light blinked at a crossroad. They were all at sea. In his nautical decoration, Mark Gaynor [the Harbour Bar's manager] had had the right instinct. The roadhouse was like some great luxury liner, the one incongruous amid the Atlantic breakers, the other incongruous amid the silent fields. Both incongruous and unsafe. Alison shivered and turned back to the warmth and light and companionship.[55]

Ewer cleverly intimates that the red traffic light mimics a light on a ship in the dark. This was a theme that, more famously, John Betjeman turned to in his nostalgic poem 'Harrow-on-the-Hill'.[56] Ewer makes a direct connection to the transatlantic liner and suggests a sense of dislocation, another consistent theme in the book. The idea of the transatlantic liner contained elements of new technology, time-space compression, Americanization, speed and glamour, facets which all became associated with roadhouses. In the 1930s, the New York to London journey became the route for a competition between France, Germany, Great Britain and Italy to produce the fastest transatlantic crossing. Ships such as *Normandie*, *Bremen* and *Queen Mary* attempted to win the Blue Riband crossing record for their respective country.[57] These ships, not stripped down for maximum speed, were the last words in luxury travel. Their interiors were decorated in a glamorous Hollywood style that was also seen in roadhouse designs.

The Showboat exemplified this, built in a long, low style that combined art deco with modernist architecture in an uneasy mix featuring decks with railings in its design. Sunbathing on the Showboat's terraces overlooking its swimming pool was as close as one could get to being on the *Queen Mary* without leaving port.

In embracing the possibilities of new mobilities, breaching of class boundaries, unfettered consumption and being both modern and American, roadhouses were well positioned to act as a focal point for the concerns and opportunities of Britain in the 1930s. At the simplest level, in the more undemanding sort of story, roadhouses represented modern Britain in a way that readers thought both possible and unusual. For example, in a terrible book, *Rally Round Rosalind*, its heroine rescues her fortunes by turning an old house into a new roadhouse:

> What about a garage for a start? And a band, and, of course, a dancing-floor… and a brace of tennis courts… and a swimming pool, we must simply have a pool, no roadhouse is complete without one.[58]

An old house being converted for a new purpose is also seen in less optimistic circumstances in the final chapter of *They Come They Go* (1937), a history of a fictional rectory whose conversion into a roadhouse is the final secular indignity imposed on a centuries-old world of tradition and Christian service: 'Ye Olde Rectory Road House! What a shame!'[59] Rex Warner explored a similar idea in a much more sophisticated manner. His novel *The Aerodrome* (1941) describes how militarism and fascism overtake the rural traditions of an English village. Much of the action centres on the village squire's ancient manor house, transformed into something with a strong resemblance to a roadhouse or country club for the aerodrome's officers, wives and girlfriends.[60]

Ewer addressed the theme of modernity throughout *Roadhouse* and proposed that the Harbour Bar provided a life that differed greatly from traditional urban and rural settings. Her roadhouse made a connection to the older world through new transport technologies. This is evident from the very first page:

> Hooting and jostling, the private cars vied with one another in passing and re-passing. The bare road, broad non-skid utilitarian, had a strength of purpose. It ran straight as a Roman road. It was a pioneer road with a difference. It opened up not a new country but a new route through an old country.[61]

This addresses numerous themes of modernity and modernism. The 'hooting and jostling' suggested an unease and restlessness, of ever-increasing speed in modern life, only available to those who had access to a fast car; a modernist architect might have written her description of the road as clean and efficient. Ewer's suggestion of pioneer exploration hinted at American origins. Later in the book, she made more explicit claims for modernity:

> [She] led the way into the big restaurant. Through the great windows at one end you could see the cars tearing up and down the by-pass. They gave a sense of perpetual movement to the room. It was as if a newsreel unrolled forever before your eyes.[62]

Much is modern about this paragraph. By deploying an observer who is distanced from the subject and views anonymously through the screen of the roadhouse's great windows, Ewer is proposing a cinematic experience that positions the reader as if he or she were watching a movie. She reinforces the point by describing the view as a newsreel. In proposing a sense of perpetual movement, Ewer gets to the heart of the roadhouse experience because it revolves around mobility and speed.[63] As Ewer puts it, unconsciously supporting the argument that sees time–space compression as being central to modernity: 'The pace of life was unduly accelerated'.[64]

By positioning her roadhouse 'at sea', Ewer generates a strong sense of dislocation in her writing. This wording shows the roadhouse isolated from the norms of interwar society, not part of the town, the suburb or the countryside. This makes the roadhouse a place only accessible to motorists, an elite group at the beginning of the 1930s, whereas by the end of the decade one that had become much wider in terms of class.[65] It also enables the Harbour Bar to be isolated for dramatic purposes, an island disconnected from the normalities of Ewer's readers' suburban homes.

Ewer referenced alienation directly in her text:

> The night air was sharp and clear and still, and after the heated restaurant it smelt fresh and clean. The stream of cars had slackened. Beyond in the darkness stretched the empty fields. Once more Alison was struck with a strange sense of isolation.[66]

Here, Ewer is making another claim for modernity. Had the Harbour Bar been a real-life roadhouse, our typology would have categorized it easily as a super roadhouse, one of those many establishments suddenly appearing in London's outer reaches alongside new arterial roads. With their clean lines of white concrete passing through open fields, these roads exemplified modernist construction projects, producing a rather unworldly and modern aesthetic effect. The placing of a roadhouse onto this new landscape heightened the sense of dislocation or isolation. Here was an establishment expected, through its clientele and its cultural production, to be metropolitan but was located in the empty countryside, accompanied by the noise of a constant flow of cars and lorries. Ewer drives the point home:

> They [the customers] were crowded together for reassurance, and around them lay the threatening empty spaces and the fields of which they knew nothing.[67]

As the years progressed, London's rapidly expanding suburbia encroached on lonely roadhouse sites. As early as 1934, Ewer noted roadhouses' movement from isolation to becoming surrounded by suburban homes and customers. Consider the Ace of Spades, a real-life roadhouse that also experienced this effect. Early photos show the Ace of Spades in the open country adjacent to the new Kingston Bypass. Within a decade of its establishment, the Ace was literally engulfed by suburban sprawl, losing its reputation as an exclusive venue and image as geographically separated from nearby communities. Similarly, Ewer portrays her fictional roadhouse in irreversible decline: 'There are lots of homes for sale round here. A real home, half a mile from the roadhouse.'[68]

Ewer's thought that a home near the roadhouse could be 'real' emphasized the artificial nature of roadhouse life. This is an interesting idea and presages much later debates on the nature of place in man-made locations such as the roadhouse. In short, writers such as Marc Augé argue that airports and motorway service stations are placeless because the people using them are transient.[69] Ewer went further to suggest the Harbour Bar was an artifice, a sham, with 'fake décor'.[70] A little earlier in the book, Ewer portrayed her roadhouse as if it were a film set,

> Through the other window you could see the trim impersonal gardens, supplied by a multiple firm, gardens in which no amateur had ever planted a hopeful seed or set a crooked inadequate stake. Beyond lay the swimming pool, that smelt faintly of chlorate of lime, but that looked gay with its blue paint and its red matting.[71]

Ewer was suggesting that the faint smell of chlorine hid some deeper concerns, despite superficial appearances of the modern.

Ewer correctly identified many roadhouses as fakes. In their employment of mock-Tudor, both the Thatched Barn and the Ace of Spades were phoney, particularly when (as in the case of the latter) patrons moved straight from an Elizabethan facade to a replica of an American bar borrowed from a film set. Tearooms on country roads were, perhaps, less false than the super roadhouses, but their projection of a country day out, with tea in an old barn, coupled with jokey signs and objects of interest, was, in its way, artificial.

Ewer conjured up the Harbour Bar as a transplanted version of a Hollywood film set. This is not surprising, given her background as a writer of film dialogue, as the author of a book on stage production and her occupation as a film critic. She borrowed her plot and production values from Hollywood, while at the same time acknowledging them as phoney-baloney. This was perhaps one of the few elements in the book where Ewer revealed her anti-establishment leanings. Graham Greene also wrote novels in a filmic manner, a technique he employed to great literary praise. In *The Confidential Agent*, he attempted to produce a hybrid between a novel and a film script. Greene, like Ewer, was, significantly, both a novelist and a film critic.[72]

Ewer used the conventions of a Hollywood movie in her cast of characters. Her heroine, Alison, is a feisty girl from an ordinary background who fights to keep the man she loves, Mark Gaynor, the manager, tall and square-shouldered, and universally known as 'The Chief'. Alison is introduced to the roadhouse by a flinty-eyed good-time girl, saving up to move to the United States. Alison's other love interest is Terry, a drunken, dissolute but handsome bandleader who makes love to her, but does not care for her. In effect, Ewer deployed Hollywood clichés for all her main characters.

Calling Gaynor 'The Chief' was a particular nod to American culture. Ewer was reflecting the influences of American films, but also reproducing the culture of the British roadhouse, in so many ways Americanized. The *moderne* architecture of the Showboat and the deco styling of roadhouse cocktail bars exemplified this, but music produced the greatest impact of Americanization on the British roadhouse, 'the band sighing for the Carolinas, the popping of balloons, the band's hot rhythm from Harlem'.[73] Newsreels of British roadhouses illustrated the direct imitation and adaptation of American musical forms.[74]

The plot of *Roadhouse* pivots on the problem of competing roadhouses. The building of a new roadhouse called the Good Pull-up on the same arterial road, but nearer to London, threatened the Harbour Bar: 'Ted pointed to a big house in course of construction. See that is going to be a rival. Folks have tumbled to the idea that there's a lot of money to be made this way.'[75] Gaynor's boss, who turns out to be the secret owner of this establishment, tricks Gaynor into buying the Harbour Bar when it seemed likely to fail. Ewer proposed that whether a roadhouse attracted the fashionable, sophisticated and free spending determined its initial success. For Ewer, the Harbour Bar's elite customers enjoying the best of what such establishments could offer embodied 'the great caravanserai, crowded with city folk, rich, idle, sophisticated, their clothes from Paris, their music from Africa, their slang from America, and their morals from Bloomsbury'.[76] Here was Ewer's 'puritan' side, voicing a common position among interwar intellectuals that Americanization, deracination and immorality had degraded British society.[77]

Both of Ewer's roadhouses attempted to attract celebrities and members of the West End set to increase their level of fashionability as a way of gaining clientele who also considered themselves up-to-the-minute. The Ace of Spades emphasized the quality of its cabaret and, at least whenever the newsreels visited, attracted stage and screen stars.

Unlike the sophistication of the evening clientele, in the daytime, Ewer proposed that her roadhouse had a very wide selection of customers:

> The restaurant was packed with a great diversity of people. Over in one corner a couple of lorry drivers were contentedly drinking beer. Another group of drivers, taking the chassis of half a dozen cars to the London finishing works, occupied the next table.[78]

This is a surprising idea. The use of roadhouses by working-class customers has little support from documentary sources. Admittedly, a game of darts could be played in the public bar of the Berkeley Arms, which, perhaps, betrays that establishment's brewery origins. Roadhouses did not have public bars, and Ewer placed her road transport drivers in the restaurant. It seems unlikely, but Ewer may not have been exaggerating. Ewer noted how roadhouse clientele changed as afternoon turned to evening:

> There was a bustle of new arrivals, sports cars disgorging laughing young people, some in berets and jumpers, some in full evening dress. There were still a sprinkling of drivers on business and one or two family parties.[79]

Family parties using roadhouses during the day accords with documentary evidence. Roadhouse swimming pools were a big attraction for families on hot summer days. A newsreel of sunbathers at the Showboat roadhouse shows family parties, including small children and their pet dog all enjoying the sun terraces.[80] Ewer's description of youthful bohemian customers driving sports cars and wearing berets seems surprising, but was corroborated by Rawdon Hoare's commentary *This Our Country* (1935) published in the same year. He found the behaviour of roadhouse customers infuriating, reckless and juvenile.[81]

Ewer was very perceptive about the contingency of roadhouse fashion and consequent financial success. She proposed that 'A luxury business built on a craze never lasts.'[82] This was prescient; within a few years roadhouses struggled against changing fashions and losing their wealthiest customers (see Chapter 8). In *Roadhouse*, the Harbour Bar had to adapt to changing fashion, by embracing more local, suburban customers and 'regulars' such as commercial travellers. Ewer's apparently incongruous portrayal of *déclassé* roadhouse customers becomes quite plausible when placed in the chronological context of the roadhouses' second phase (1934–39). Past their peak of popularity, no longer fashionable, and steadily losing wealthy patrons, roadhouses now struggled, forced to explore creative ways to ensure financial survival.

This chapter is in effect an exercise in literary palaeontology. As scientists can deduce which creatures swam in our seas millions of years ago from their fossilized remains, so we can today recreate the popularity and manners of roadhouses, which like the sea creature have also disappeared, using their literature. Like fossils on certain beaches, this forgotten aspect of the 1930s to the 1950s turns up all over the place; sometimes, as with Graham Greene's novels, it can be seen in writing that is still known and well regarded. More often, roadhouses appear in obscure works. The various recent projects to digitize old books have provided word searching that has revealed references to roadhouses in British fiction that earlier methods would not have uncovered.

These novels are vital but difficult sources to interpret correctly, requiring their substantiation with more traditional documentary evidence. They are, however, a unique, previously unexploited source revealing not just a reality about roadhouses, but how the public conceptualized them. From them, we visualize that for a few years roadhouses epitomized modern, exciting and Americanized fun enjoyed by an elite clientele, then known as the smart set.

8

Death of the Roadhouse?

Given the sheer luxury offered at roadhouses, contemporaries predictably presented the roadhouse as an extremely lucrative business. In 1933, the Automobile Association (AA) helped substantiate this view when it noted that a roadhouse near London with quite modest pretentions had experienced such a huge turnover that its proprietor declined a generous offer for the premises. The following year, Thomas Burke went still further in his appraisal, regarding roadhouses as profitable whatever the season. 'In the summer they do well with their all-night swimming-pools, and in the winter they do equally well with their dance-bands and badminton courts'.[1] Business seemingly boomed in the second half of the decade. 'Up to the outbreak of war' he remarked, 'those places, almost any night of any season, had full houses'.[2] No sooner had the Monkey Puzzle Roadhouse opened in 1933 than its popularity led to expanded accommodation.[3] Likewise, on opening the Popular Road and Guest House in the following year, proprietors were inundated with customers, 1,000 of them being served in the first four days.[4] Monica Ewer was thus apparently on solid ground in portraying the fictional Harbour Bar as doing a booming trade, with the chief backer earning a 25 per cent return on his investment.[5]

Diverse sources reinforced this image of flourishing roadhouses. For £12,000, a syndicate offered freehold premises and 150 acres to an investor wanting 'a chance to make big money with ample security'.[6] Elsa Dundas' account of her 'carefree' life in running a Kentish roadhouse projected the rags to riches experience of a working-class woman – with some inherited money in-between – that readers of the *Daily Mirror* must have envied. So successful was she that, had Dundas decided to sell, she thought that her modest but prosperous roadhouse 'would keep me in comfort for the rest of my life'.[7] An *Evening News* story recorded that one roadhouse restaurant's takings for a single night surpassed £200. Swimmers, numbering 500 or more on hot days, generated money, but so did 'another big crowd who got their fun just by watching the merry antics of others'.[8] Advertisements specifying capital of no more than £4,500 to earn astonishing annual profits (45–83 per cent) must have struck potential but well-informed investors as fanciful.[9]

Had business at roadhouses boomed as much as such advertisements and commentators suggested, there would have been no need for a publicity pamphlet to contain vouchers offering discounts of either 25 per cent on the total costs or 50 per cent on entrance fees to swimming pools as initial introductory offers for five establishments in 1934. This was still more surprising, given the inclusion of two of the most prominent super roadhouses, notably the Clock and the Bell House.[10] Another super roadhouse, the Barn (Bayfordbury), drew special praise for its 'magnificent seventeenth-century tithe-barn'. McMinnies thought highly enough of the Barn to put it in his inaugural guide, stressing its catering to exclusive functions, such as hunt balls and outstanding teas as well as farm produce. Opened in 1934, a mere twenty-five minutes trip from London and featuring an impressive list of attractions (notably a restaurant, dancing, deck tennis, a bathing pool and pedigree puppies), the Barn was nevertheless put on the market for a quite modest £2,250, including freehold, the following year. As a prognosticator, the publicity pamphlet, appearing in the same year as the Barn's opening, had promised parties of no more than four persons a 25 per cent discount on all cash bills during their initial visit.[11]

By 1935, roadhouses had just passed their high point of newsreel-driven publicity. The days of visits to the Ace of Spades by the Prince of Wales were over, and roadhouses were no longer quite so attractive to London's Bright Young Things.[12] In consequence, roadhouses looked a little nearer down the arterial road at the newly motorized suburban customer. Earlier, when they were very fashionable, from 1930 to 1933, most roadhouse customers came by car from central London. As early as 1933, encroached on by new suburban housing, the Ace of Spades had begun to advertise itself to local residents in the *Surrey Comet*.[13]

The change in fashion that made super roadhouses less attractive to the St. James' *beau monde* was met, or most likely generated, by the growing access to cars in suburban London. As has been seen, René Cutforth thought that anyone could get in as long as they looked the part.[14] This referred to a preoccupation dating back to clerks dressing up as gentlemen in the late Victorian era, and was in effect a fear of impersonation.[15] Sharing a roadhouse with a respectable but despicable suburban car owner would have been enough for the smart set to move back to the West End. As the decade progressed, car access widened, prompting the *Daily Mirror* to worry about the sexual safety of its young working-class women readers. In 1936, it featured an article, 'If I had been a cad', which explained how easy it was to pick a girl up and take her to a roadhouse:

> Why go on with my experiences? ... except to mention the girl who said she was a film extra, then when I mentioned some people in the business, confessed she was a shop-girl out for the night. Oh yes, if I had a car she would love to come to a roadhouse, she'd been once – that was in the summer.[16]

This idea is suggestive, even after discounting the sensationalist journalism. It assumed that the topic would sufficiently resonate with the paper's audience to understand how roadhouses operated and where they were located. It is plausible that in driving young working-class women to roadhouses, their boyfriends had begun to gain access to cars for the first time. It is also consonant with J. B Priestley's observations on the 'Third England' consisting of 'cocktail bars, Woolworths, motor-coaches, wireless, hiking, factory girls looking like actresses, greyhound racing and dirt tracks, swimming pools'.[17]

Jack Isow's ill-fated entry into the world of roadhouses underlined their economic fragility. Associated with a series of sleazy Soho nightclubs, he now expanded into London's suburbia, leasing the Thatched Barn and paying a hefty £3,000 annual rent. Within fifteen months, he had incurred debts of almost £8,000. It was the Thatched Barn and several other establishments that gave credence to some roadhouses' unsavoury reputation. Liquor sales after permitted hours and unlicensed gambling (with Chicago style slot machines), dancing and singing prompted a police raid on the club, and, following his arrest and conviction, Isow was imprisoned for three months. Released in 1938, he appeared in court again the following year, this time for bankruptcy.[18]

The Thatched Barn's subsequent fate reflected how roadhouses were losing their distinctive identity. With a new owner and a professional catering company installed as manager, the Thatched Barn recovered from this debacle, acquiring a liquor licence and becoming a respected venue for motorists. The formula was aimed at dancing, with well-known bands hired – 'the best that can be obtained from London'. To draw patrons on Sunday, the new owner, London brewery Barclay, Perkins & Co., hired a twelve-piece orchestra, which performed in the afternoon and evening. Further respectability came when the brewery rebuilt the Thatched Barn in 1937 for an undisclosed sum of money.[19]

One factor that limited the appeal of roadhouses in an intensely competitive market was the absence of a swimming pool. So quickly did the fad spread for swimming that by the mid-1930s a roadhouse without one seemed an anomaly.[20] Having converted a former Essex rectory into a roadhouse on the Southend

Arterial Road, promoters thought dancing, billiards and a buffet counter virtually guaranteed success at the Crossways Roadhouse. Soon, however, proprietors capitulated, forced to advertise in the *Times* in 1937 that with nearly 17 acres, more than sufficient space existed for building a swimming pool.[21] This last point might have proved decisive in its survival, for the swimming pool would have catapulted the Crossways into becoming a super roadhouse.[22] As Albert Campion, Margery Allingham's amateur sleuth, reflected 'These things usually flop because the promoters will rely on one or two good features to carry the others.'[23]

The Houseboat's short history was another inauspicious sign of how economic reality began impinging on the fantasy world of the roadhouse as early as 1935. Resembling an elegant houseboat that cost Family Restaurant Ltd £10,000 to create, a luxurious tier-two establishment, the Houseboat opened in Radlett, Hertfordshire, on 25 July 1935. Less than four months later, however, the premises depicted by the *Caterer and Hotel-Keeper* as 'one of the ... most attractive roadhouses in the Home Counties' had been sold rather humiliatingly at public auction.[24]

A similar fate befell the Showboat, one of the super roadhouses, its amenities including a ballroom, restaurant, cocktail bar, sizable swimming pool with the latest technology and sprawling car park, all laid out on some 41,000 square feet. Yet, within five years of opening the proprietors declared bankruptcy, its equipment, fittings and fixtures auctioned off.[25] That same year, the High Tower Roadhouse (Jersey) also closed, evidently pre-empting a similar fate.[26] Monica Ewer points to precarious financial backing as the chief explanation. In *Roadhouse*, which appeared in 1935, Mrs Eve Merrick, whose husband bankrolls the Harbour Bar, sees no threat from promoters of the newest rival, the Good Pull-Up. 'If they don't get a quick return they'll go under', she predicts.[27] The short-lived existence of the Showboat, Houseboat, High Tower Roadhouse and doubtless others lent credence to this conclusion.

Undoubtedly the most startling news came in 1938 when three more super roadhouses closed, all of them auctioned, but not sold. Of the Spider's Web, one of the country's pre-eminent establishments, McMinnies as late as the previous year had written glowingly of it as 'one of the most popular places of its kind near London and on a sunny week-end, it is not unusual to find its great car park full of smart cars'. Its seven acres, swimming pool, miniature golf links, tennis court and a car park perpetually crowded with 400 cars nevertheless failed to ensure success.[28] Even a well-established roadhouse such as the Bell House, which never lost McMinnies' confidence, was forced to close. Finally, to the far north in Durham, Finchdale Abbey, its £30,000 cost having few rivals anywhere in the country, lasted just nineteen months before succumbing to a public auction; still worse, not one bidder came forward.[29]

Not all indebted roadhouse investors closed their doors to pay off creditors. Larkfield House, for example, opened in 1933, its menu, amenities and ambience directly aimed at the motoring public, with club facilities (including liquor sales for members), specially prepared hampers for picnic lunches, an all-night restaurant, and twelve electric petrol pumps, together with service facilities. Proprietor John Collins had grandiose plans for a swimming pool and tennis courts. By 1938, he, like Jack Isow, had sold out to brewers Barclay, Perkins & Co., which rebuilt the premises for almost £10,000 and transferred the liquor licence and name from the nearby Bull Hotel. Still called a roadhouse, the Bull now became *déclassé*, consciously cultivating the customers arriving at the local bus stop who inquired solely about tea, not outstanding cuisine, dancing or a panoramic view. Nothing more was heard about a swimming pool or tennis court.[30] Even before the Second World War, the roadhouse business was therefore in serious difficulties, perhaps involved in a protracted death.

Heightening competition in the leisure sector complicated the business of roadhouse proprietors. Shrewd brewers constructed big, imposing improved public houses that offered couples a lounge for comfort and refinement, together with pleasant dining facilities. Sensing a commercial opening, brewers had begun to misapply the name 'roadhouse' to their new premises. On the well-travelled Western Avenue near Ealing, Barclay spent almost £16,000 erecting the Park Royal Hotel in 1936. Without a swimming pool or dance hall, the Park Royal was just an expensive pub; the brewery nevertheless described it as 'our new roadhouse'.[31] Though Barclay, Perkins & Co. expended nearly £39,000 on the Abbey Hotel on the North Circular Road in West Willesden the following year, it was no more a roadhouse than the Park Royal Hotel.[32] Similarly, Benskin's Watford Brewery ran a competition for an architectural design that consciously cultivated the image of a London West End hotel relocated to the countryside for motorists' convenience. The anonymous winner was E. B. Musman, one of the outstanding interwar pub architects who produced an unconventional design that combined a French château with a Scottish baronial castle, paying tribute to Dutch and classic influences.[33] First of a triumvirate of Benskin's expensive superpubs, each costing £25,000 or more, Musman's Berkeley Arms was located within a half hour's trip from London. Here as well as at the Myllet Arms and the Comet were installed foreign chéfs.[34] To reinforce the image of refinement, Benskin's lured managerial staff from West End hotels. With a cocktail lounge, sprawling restaurant, chauffeur's room, lock-up garages and letting accommodation, these superpubs (save at the Myllet Arms) aped roadhouses without incorporating two of their quintessential features – dance halls and swimming pools.[35]

Competition also came from other directions. Rivals appropriated standard amenities – swimming pools, dance halls and upmarket food – at roadhouses, blurring the distinction between them and offering motorists a broader range of choice. Ambitious proprietors of upmarket rural hotels and country clubs, for instance, quickly appreciated the draw of swimming pools, especially after the hot summer of 1932, and introduced such facilities. About 25 per cent of the entries in McMinnies' first edition of *Signpost*, published in 1935, already advertised them.[36] This development forced him to rethink his categories. By 1938 not only had the special section on roadhouses disappeared, but the aggregate number of such establishments integrated with other entries had diminished enormously. Of the forty roadhouses listed separately in the first edition, just five remained three years later.[37]

Wartime conditions disrupted the business of many roadhouses (see Figure 8.1). In 1945, the *Scotsman* forecast that just 37 of the AA's list of 250 roadhouses in 1939 would probably reopen once the government ended the rationing of petrol.[38] Some of them the government had requisitioned or converted into hospitals. For example, the Showboat in Maidenhead was commandeered to become an 'All Services Club' and was then converted into a factory to make wings for Spitfire fighter planes.[39] The Thatched Barn certainly provides the most interesting example. During the war, this enormous, well-known roadhouse was requisitioned to be Station XV, the home of the Special Operations Executive (SOE), a secret organization responsible for devising ways of sabotaging enemy forces with ingenious and devious means. Frederic Boyce, historian of the SOE, reported that 'with private motor transport drastically reduced in wartime, it provided a useful site, with public rooms being converted into workshops and bedrooms into accommodation for the staff'.[40] The SOE reported through the Ministry of Works and after the war ended, the Ministry continued to use it well into the 1950s as home to the Building Research Centre to test the use of steel in concrete.[41] In 1949, the Ministry actively considered derequisitioning the Thatched Barn so that its new owner, Billy Butlin (of the eponymous holiday organization), might convert it into a 'vacation village' which could be used by middle-income American tourists and thus attract much needed dollars for the British economy. The Ministry had already invested £40,000 in expanding the Thatched Barn, so was perhaps reluctant to let it return to the private sector.[42]

Contributing significantly to financial problems of roadhouses was their targeting of an overly narrow segment of the motoring public as customers, the offspring of the super-rich, the Bright Young Things. Roadhouse managers and promoters acquired a well deserved but commercially disastrous reputation as notoriously haughty, an image largely responsible for driving custom away. With public school 'old boys' as managers, these establishments catered exclusively to the same social elite from which their proprietors sprang, snubbing customers of less refined social standing.[43] In Graham Greene's novel, *The Confidential Agent*, the monocled manager of a Kentish roadhouse describes his customers – pointedly denying his own snobbishness – as 'only the best people', one of them the twenty-year-old daughter of a peer.[44]

Cultivating an upmarket clientele involved hefty overhead costs. Modest roadhouses could offer inexpensive music from a radio or phonograph, whereas more exclusive establishments had no choice but to hire orchestras to provide live music. 'If you are offering the very best in food and drink you must also provide first-class – which means expensive – entertainment', warned S. Marella.[45]

Too many roadhouse promoters, especially in the more prosperous southeast, thought themselves as catering solely to Society, a term characterizing a small group of individuals, probably numbering no more than 40,000, fond of social display and radiating glamour, fashion and affluence. According to historian Ross McKibbin, 'membership required an acceptable mix of breeding, education, wealth, and cultural assumptions, and anyone without that mix was not a member of Society'.[46] The sophistication, luxury, style, commitment to modernity and elegance that roadhouse proprietors' consciously projected and Society upheld mirrored the fantasy world created by Hollywood. Anglo-American hostesses gave Society unity and helped Americanize it.[47] Within this elite, the Bright Young Things received widespread publicity, especially their escapades at night clubs and roadhouses.[48]

Certainly roadhouses had lost the allure possessed before 1939, in part because Society became fragmented. The economic base of the roadhouse, on one hand, had changed in a way that reduced its glamour: before 1939 it had been easy to see the roadhouse as a creation for the 'idle rich', with Bertie Wooster, Anthony Blanche, Lord Peter Wimsey and all the other people who might whip down to a roadhouse for a spot of dinner (that phrasing is more Wooster than Wimsey). Post-war taxation, on the other, meant that living the life of the pre-war idle rich was hardly possible.[49]

Prosperity, however, had not vanished from the face of the earth. Active businessmen made money after the war, and income tax arrangements made it

Figure 8.1 Rawlin's garage and roadhouse, 1945. Copyright The Francis Frith Collection.

relatively easy for them to spend it on roadhouses. Exchange controls went on for thirty years after the war, and had their effect on foreign travel. Package or charter tours, tailored to fit within the exchange control limits, were developed, but they were not going to be much fun for the rich, because they could take only a tiny fraction of their money overseas (or else evade the controls, which could be complicated or illegal or both). So they had money that could much more easily be spent in England than abroad.[50]

Some roadhouses thus proved to be quite resilient, at least initially, despite the disruptive war. Government price controls, limiting the cost of meals to five shillings, left proprietors with three viable options – going down market, charging more for liquor or offering overnight accommodation.

Billed in McMinnies' first edition as 'easily the most modern and comfortable road house in the west of England', basing its reputation on repairing automobiles while customers dined or danced, the Mile 3 Roadhouse in 1947 went in search of customers without transportation. Its advertisement proclaimed 'Your Transport Problem Solved!' and offered to ferry patrons to and from dances on Wednesday and Saturday evenings. A broader clientele could have also been attracted if the roadhouse became a family venue. To a miniature nine-hole pitch and putting course, a Leicestershire roadhouse with four acres added a children's playground.[51] Just how many roadhouses emulated these tactics is unclear, but establishments outside London's orbit might have lacked an alternative.

The two remaining strategies, raising liquor prices or letting rooms, offered greater scope for increasing profits. Though both were adopted, the huge demand for rooms prompted many roadhouses to transform themselves into motels.[52] Owners of nearly half of the roadhouses advertised for sale in the *Times* in the 1940s, 1950s and early 1960s understood this, and so specified the number of letting rooms in their establishments as a sales feature. In 1948 one Midland roadhouse, its huge flood-lit swimming pool and licensed bar attractive facilities, had secured approval for adding twenty bedrooms to the twelve it already possessed.[53] Roadhouses also began using receipt of planning permission to develop a motel as a key selling point in advertisements.[54]

Impetus for the metamorphosis of roadhouses into motels or hotels stemmed from a property boom, beginning early in the war and lasting well into the 1960s. Intimations of a boom appeared unexpectedly in 1941 from a distant place generally unassociated with roadhouses. Equipped with a lounge, restaurant, ballroom and central heating, the Maybury went on the market for £45,000, nearly four times its original cost in 1935.[55] Though the owner displayed considerable ingenuity in providing patrons with deck tennis, parvo tennis, skittles, chucker and darts as recreational diversions on its huge flat roof, he put forward this astonishing figure for premises without a swimming pool.[56]

In the ensuing quarter of a century, about £1 million of freehold property changed hands with the sale of forty-two roadhouses, reported in the *Times*. While the boom's pace remained constant, prices escalated sharply in what constituted spirited bidding wars. Three-quarters of the total value of sales involved property worth over £20,000. The four most expensive establishments – £45,000, £60,000, £66,000 and £85,000 – came at the boom's end in the 1960s. London was the epicentre, with these four all in the Home Counties. To entice buyers, many advertisements of the more modest priced premises disclosed astonishing levels of turnover: nine such establishments had cumulative annual revenues of £161,000.[57]

Ration-free patrol, announced in 1950, further stimulated the boom, especially in suburban London. At one roadhouse on the Watford Bypass, the impact was immediate, with diners quadrupling in numbers almost overnight; another southern roadhouse 'had the biggest evening trade since 1939'.[58] In the *Daily Mail*, Tom Pocock's lead line was striking: 'The roadhouse is back to stay'. He based this conclusion on the half-dozen roadhouses near London that had reopened to gigantic crowds and rave reviews. Of this handful, he focused on the Spider's Web, its three restaurants, two dance floors, 2,000 yards of plush carpeting and panelling rescued from a medieval English castle, making it the quintessential post-war establishment. Everything was on an unimaginable scale, at least for a roadhouse, with eight French chefs, six gardeners and a total staff of 150. Outfitting the premises ran to £25,000, excluding the buildings themselves and the swimming pool. Weekdays some seventy customers motored there for a tea-bathe, while another 150 for a dinner-dance-bathe. Altogether the weekend was different. Then, some 5,000 motorists and companions jammed the car park, their automobiles backing up the Watford Bypass as far as the eye could see. Since government controls limited cover charges for meals to five shillings, hefty alcohol prices generated the revenue necessary for overhead charges of £1,000 weekly.[59]

Flocking to this new oasis of pleasure, 750 well-heeled Americans arrived every week, having read of its delights in the *Queen* magazine. To secure their cultural moorings, the roadhouse had outfitted 'a flossy Hollywood boudoir'. For an international flavour of sophistication, manager Leonard Colosanti planned to import palm trees from the Riviera the following year, integrating them with the 40,000 flowers festooning the ambience. Pocock's lingering image of his visit suggested how the divergent Anglo-American crowds intermixed, despite their dissimilar cultural backgrounds:

> Americans, indistinguishable from the wealthy merchants of Golders Green, sip their mint juleps and help set a scene that somehow looks as unreal as would the Pyramids on Clapham Common.[60]

Pocock, in referencing Golders Green, was making it obvious to conventional readers of the *Daily Mail* that these vulgar customers were Jewish, showing that roadhouse attendance in north London was popular with that community both before and after the war. The Spider's Web led the way in post-war roadhouses, and was identified by a *Men Only* cartoonist as a site of prostitution in 1952. This roadhouse lasted until 1970 when it was destroyed by fire and was replaced by a hotel of the same name.[61]

Other leisure resorts available to well-heeled post-war British motorists exploded in numbers, amenities, diversity of cuisine and overall comfort. Swimming pools, the quintessential feature of pre-war roadhouses and country clubs, had lost their glamour, with other facilities now paramount, especially – and not surprisingly in an era of rationing – appetizing cuisine. Country clubs, too, shrank in numbers, with two-thirds fewer listed in the 1951 edition of McMinnies' guide compared with 1935.[62] Both roadhouses and country clubs had received special treatment in separate sections in 1935 and 1936. Unlike his 1930s guides with their south-eastern concentration, McMinnies' post-war editions were more broadly based, reflecting the greater reliability of automobiles, appearance of vast numbers of new resorts and a widening array of establishments having to compete in an expanding, more sophisticated market. Leisure for the smart set thus underwent a vast change, hitherto unexplored by scholars.

Post-war roadhouses, even as an elite form of leisure, could not immunize themselves against broader societal changes emphasizing domesticity, with women now urged to withdraw into the home and assume their rightful roles as wives and mothers. Anxiety over prostitution caused a moral panic in the 1950s, depriving women of public spaces for leisure, unless some male acted as escort. Pubs regained their predominantly masculine subculture, reversing women's influx into drinking spaces during the Second World War. Women's patronage of pubs in the post-war era stood at 17.5 per cent from the late 1950s into the early 1970s, remarkably lower than in the war itself.[63]

Standardization became a pronounced feature of the 1950s, with clothing, food, design and even beer following this trend.[64] The roadhouse had attracted patrons in large part because of its unique appearance, amenities and reputation as the most fashionable leisure resorts for the social elite. That market steadily contracted as other new venues appeared as formidable competitors.

Changes in youth leisure habits transformed the potential market for roadhouse patrons. Of these, none was more important than the espresso bar, first established in Soho early in the 1950s, a development which John Burnett characterized as marking the 'modern renaissance of coffee-drinking'. Certainly, the modernistic image of such bars – Formica, indoor plants and fashionable décor – projected a general ambience of brightness, cleanliness and exotic décor. Seen by the younger generation as a 'trendy social centre', espresso bars expanded in response to various factors: increased disposable income of the young; the dramatic expansion of foreign holidays; and leisure's democratization. Two other factors – invention of the espresso machine and mass advertising of 'instant' coffee – stimulated the espresso bars' popularity.[65]

With airlines instituting 'tourist' fares and pioneering 'cheap mass air travel', foreign holidays burgeoned. Almost twice as many Britons ventured abroad as in the pre-war era. Espresso bars became linked with the young and foreign sophistication, fostering the emergence of an 'international culture' in which the introduction of continental lagers played a significant role. By 1960, Greater London accounted for one-fourth of Britain's 2,000 espresso bars, foreshadowing the concentration of wine bars in the 1960s and 1970s.[66]

Romance enacted at espresso bars replaced roadhouses as a rendezvous for courtship and intrigue. A diverse cultural mix of milk and snack bars, cafés and coffee bars produced 'a vibrant subterranean world of jazz clubs and cafés in

Central London, populated by young people from the suburbs'. Italian coffee intermixed with American music played on jukeboxes, enabling youth to establish 'hetero-social public space' where 'friendships, intimate relationships and rivalries' flourished, argues Kate Bradley.[67]

By the 1950s, roadhouses struggled for survival, their exclusivity long gone. The Ace of Spades was thought of locally as a rather déclassé hotel with a swimming pool open to the general public. One local resident recalled spending time at the former roadhouse:

> There was a small hotel on the Hook roundabout called the Ace of Spades where I used to try and learn to swim. One summer day in the early 1950s I met Diana Dors as she was trying to teach Dennis Hamilton how to swim. That was the kind of place it was. People would sunbathe on the lawn to the east side. I cannot be sure but around 1955–56 the hotel went into decline followed by a fire that caused it to cease operation.[68]

Real-life roadhouses thus could not generate enough profits and so often failed, whereas the fictional Harbour Bar in Monica Ewer's novel endures precisely because it deliberately avoids catering solely to affluent, young motorists. Mark Gaynor, the roadhouse's managing director, insists on the importance of a diverse clientele:

> We've got to keep the plain people coming here – here and nowhere else. We've got to preserve our character by supplying all classes. Once we become just fashionable we're dead.[69]

His character had far more prescience than Ewer herself realized when penning these words in 1935. Arthur E. Bennetts concurred with Gaynor's perspective. Charging exorbitant prices, he observed in 1935, 'effectively barred the "family" man who, with his car, represents the vast majority of the present-day week-end motoring public'.[70]

9

Conclusion

The American roadhouse owed its rise not to prohibition but to desegregated leisure, begun in many big US cities early in the 1900s. This process was well under way when Congress implemented prohibition in 1920, destroying the traditional masculine saloon and creating new public drinking spaces in which egalitarian leisure became possible on a wide basis for the first time. Into these spaces stepped men and women who fraternized together without escorts at speakeasies, cabarets, nightclubs and, in suburbs and rural areas, roadhouses.

Soaring numbers of women getting college education, together with spreading ownership of automobiles, fostered a new type of woman embodied in what became an icon of the 1920s, the flapper. Her greater freedom physically in driving an automobile and financially in earning wages enabled her obtaining independence from parental supervision. Thus liberated, flappers asserted a new-found control over their lives, drinking, driving and dancing as they ventured into activities hitherto regarded as disreputable.

Sale of illegal booze, on one hand, and growing numbers of people interested in participating in the 'roaring twenties', on the other, generated a new context for leisure activities unimaginable to those championing prohibition of alcohol. Whatever had been the defects of the old regime, nothing compared to escalating amounts of gambling, vice, prostitution, white slavery rings and gangsters, linked with bloodshed and literally thousands of unexplained deaths. Even without these lurid images, critics decried new immoral dances such as the shimmy, jazz (associated with prostitution and sexual intercourse) and moral threats to juveniles and adolescents, the chief clientele of roadhouses.

Newspaper coverage disseminated an image of lawlessness, violence and bloodshed rooted in new drinking behaviour that the British public avidly imbibed in the 1920s and 1930s. These stories insinuated an image of new drinking customs influencing their view of the roadhouse long before the first British one had appeared.

There was another dimension to this process of Americanization. In juxtaposing crime-ridden Chicago with parts of London's West End and Soho, newspaper commentaries offered a jaundiced view in which similarities easily outweighed differences, even to the most sceptical. With shootouts, brawls, shakedowns, gangland rivalry, police raids and rampant illegal liquor drinking, the two localities could be interchanged as vice capitals of either country.

Americanization too lent credibility to these new disturbing images of depraved drinking cultures in Anglo-America. Edgar Wallace, best-selling novelist of the interwar era, fittingly promoted the idea of direct American participation in British roadhouses in his novel, *The Coat of Arms*. At London theatres several years later, audiences were treated to Walter Hackett's play *Road House* in which corrupt aristocrats, crooks and lascivious females enacted on stage what had appeared in press stories. Perhaps a turning point came in Valentine Williams's short story, 'The Dot-and-Carry Case', carrying decadence further with foreigners, dope smugglers, prostitutes and aristocrats framing the narrative about typical roadhouse life. Amid this context, Britons not surprisingly acquired a jaundiced perspective of prevailing morality at the decade's new stylish icon, the roadhouse.

Desegregated leisure was the product not so much of Americanization as of parallel developments at US and then British roadhouses. Prohibition destroyed the saloon and its masculine clientele, enabling the sexes to interact in the new drinking establishments, notably speakeasies and roadhouses. In Britain, the new leisure for the smart set in roadhouses permitted egalitarian drinking between the sexes and so much more – in swimming, dancing and sporting activities. Middle-class women also enjoyed desegregated leisure in brewers' improved public houses in which an entirely separate room, the lounge, recreated etiquette associated with gentlemen's social clubs.

Roadhouses emerged in Britain with few rivals for the affection of the smart set. Originating late in the 1920s in the rather undistinguished settings of plebeian, dirty and disorganized petrol stations, roadhouse pioneers struck the fancy of the motorized elite, and the Clock (Welwyn Bypass), and twin Ace of Spades (Great West Road and Kingston Bypass) earned accolades in the press and soon huge crowds of enthusiasts.

Two stages characterized roadhouse evolution. In stage one (1927–33), roadhouses achieved their pinnacle of fame, becoming an integral part of the elite metropolitan set of the young and highly mobile. Starting in 1932, scorching summers drove Britons outdoors, fostering a craze for open-air swimming and a boom in constructing swimming pools. Cars, swimming and more generally leisure defined offerings at super roadhouses. The following year represented a peak in numbers of roadhouses being constructed (see Figure 9.1).

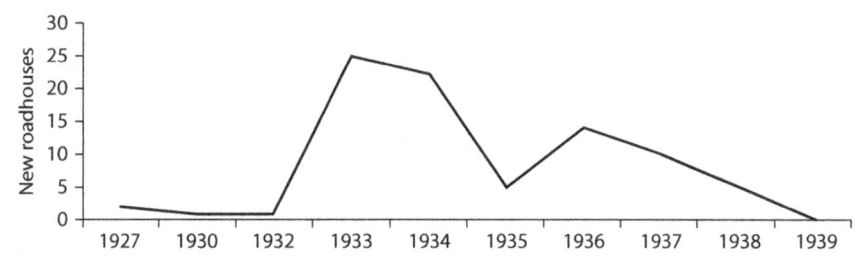

Figure 9.1 Roadhouse openings, 1927–39.

In retrospect, the roadhouse business seemed buoyant, catering to a privileged, well-heeled clientele who relished newsreels publicizing their cavorting, wealth, materialism and tastes. These members of the smart set welcomed admirers from afar, not interlopers who sought to emulate the social elite at play.

Growing numbers of automobiles with their middle-class drivers and passengers dramatically affected roadhouses in stage two (1934–39). Encroaching on elite leisure playgrounds, these uninvited motorists transformed roadhouses into places far less exclusive, depriving the smart set of their previous private club ambiance, and ensuring they rubbed elbows with those further down the social ladder.

The roadhouse's startling commercial success faded quickly. Appearing in 1934, the first motorists' guide to roadhouses enthusiastically acclaimed the new icon as a resort for the select set. Yet, at the very moment of seeming triumph, the illusion of continuing, upward prosperity received a serious check. Inside the pamphlet, motorists were offered two types of discount vouchers.[1] Of the five discounted roadhouses, moreover, three – Clock, Bell House and Barn (Bayfordbury) – were super roadhouses. In that same year, the last roadhouse newsreel was completed, suggesting a loss of their exotic appeal to the general public.

One year later, McMinnies produced his first national motorist guide, in which he dedicated a special section to outstanding roadhouses. One of these, the Barn (Bayfordbury), opened in 1934, and received two pages of coverage, including praise for not only its 'first rate teas, farm produce, home-made cakes and warm hospitality', but also for serving as the unofficial headquarters of social functions for the landed classes. Publicity, steady custom (patrons 'arriving in parties and in pairs, in cars of every shape and size') and diverse attractions (notably a Macaw which oversaw tea parties) – all the hallmarks of super roadhouses – nevertheless failed to avert financial disaster.[2] That same year the Barn went on sale for the modest price of £2,250, including freehold. Still more startlingly, another Hertfordshire roadhouse, the Houseboat, though expensively outfitted for £10,000, lasted less than four months before closing and being sold, not on the open market, but at auction. In pointing to failure to achieve quick returns on investment as an explanation for roadhouse collapses, Monica Ewer displayed more perspicacity than she undoubtedly realized in her novel, *Roadhouse*.

Unmistakable signs of a quite fragile industry in 1936 came from diverse directions. An anonymous south-eastern roadhouse changed hands within months of opening, and, reflecting the turbulent market, the new owner set lower prices. Confusing the public about the refined nature of roadhouses, Osbert Lancaster satirized them, their origins portrayed as nothing more grandiose than tea houses and brewers' pubs. Brewers themselves challenged the elite image of roadhouses, building superpubs aping them, including one that was literally next door to the Ace of Spades, among the country's premier establishments. Benskin's erected the Myllet Arms on Western Avenue, spending the gigantic sum of £60,000 to offer the public a 'combined inn, roadhouse and hotel'. French chefs, exquisite cuisine and wine competed with the Ace, and quite successfully – thrice Benskin's enlarged the dining room in the following five years. Barclay, Perkins & Co. spent considerably less on the Park Royal Hotel, also on Western Avenue, but the brewery still felt its £16,000 outlay qualified the hotel as a roadhouse.[3]

Sleaziness intruded into the roadhouse world when Jack Isow, who as a Jew had been refused service at the Thatched Barn, leased the premises in 1936. Linked with dubious Soho nightclubs and unpopular because of his religion, he quickly outraged vandals, who poured oil and petrol into the Barn's 300,000-gallon swimming pool, leaving behind their signature, a swastika. Replicating many of the traits of gangland Chicago – gambling, illegal drinking, singing and dancing – Isow too followed his discreditable American predecessors in being arrested, convicted and incarcerated.[4] Isow's entry as a roadhouse proprietor signalled the loss of the smart set as a mainstay of the roadhouse's clientele, with those one step below socially replacing them.

Worse news for the industry arrived the next year. That the Crossways (Southend Arterial Road), La Jollon Auberge (Harrogate) and Tudor House Hotel (Tewkesbury) had to be sold may have reflected failure to build swimming pools, the defining feature of super roadhouses. But this explanation seems unconvincing in the light of what happened at the Showboat. All the amenities synonymous with super roadhouses proved insufficient to stave off its bankruptcy, which could not draw a single bid and so was auctioned. Brewers meanwhile intensified competition. On the North Circular Road, Barclay, Perkins & Co. once again competed strongly, its Abbey Hotel, a superpub few other establishments could rival in cost (£38,000), was described as a roadhouse. Another huge brewery, Benskin's, built the last of its triumvirate of superpubs, the Comet, at Hatfield, costing £25,000, which significantly provided a French chef as cook and chauffeurs with a waiting room.[5]

Nothing prepared roadhouse owners, however, for 1938, an unprecedentedly disastrous year. Three super roadhouses – the Spider's Web, the Bell House and Finchdale Abbey Hotel – all underwent auction. Of these, the Finchdale Abbey (Durham) disturbed proprietors most, having cost some £30,000 but lasted just nineteen months. No one bid at the auction. McMinnies too became disenchanted with roadhouses, dropping his special section devoted to them since the inaugural issue. He could only find room for five, compared with the forty listed in 1935. Ironically, he included the Bell House, soon closed and auctioned off. In yet another unsettling development, Barclay, Perkins & Co. purchased Larkfield House, and following rebuilding renamed it the Bull, a rather plebeian pub without any pretence of appealing to its former clientele. What happened to Larkfield House was symbolic. Having spent almost £100 million building, rebuilding and renovating pubs in the interwar era, the financial benefits now became evident: brewers' improved public houses, not just superpubs, vastly outnumbered roadhouses in McMinnies' select guide. By whatever yardstick, brewers' reformed pubs supplanted roadhouses as more desirable sites for respectable leisure.[6] Perhaps fittingly, Graham Greene's *The Confidential Agent* appeared the next year in which he caustically portrayed roadhouse managers as rude and arrogant, targeting an overly narrow elite segment of the market.

In retrospect, the veritable collapse of roadhouses as flourishing commercial enterprises, together with Monica Ewer's acute observations, underline one of our major themes, their 'flash in the pan' business. Expanding quickly late in the 1920s, roadhouses drew many investors eager to make a killing in a booming market, and some certainly did so but all too briefly. Ewer's managing director of the Harbour Bar encapsulates the dismal fate of such entrepreneurs: 'A luxury business built on a craze never lasts'.[7]

It is now sixty years since the last knockings of British roadhouse culture were heard. Although roadhouses are erased from popular memory, they epitomized many fundamental social changes in the 1930s and are, therefore, of lasting interest to interwar British historiography.

Roadhouses' most important claim to historical importance centres on their adoption and adaptation of American cultural transmissions. In reality, roadhouses were quite an ambiguous example of interwar Americanization. In some ways, roadhouses were very British. Early small country roadhouses shared and reinforced the British obsession with the class of their customers; the short period of elite interest in new super roadhouses also spoke to the rigid structures of interwar British society. These same super roadhouses were also likely to project a sense of tradition through their use of mock-Tudor designs. The Ace of Spades, the Spider's Web, the Clock and, in a particularly grotesque manner, the Thatched Barn, adopted this most English of styling. They were acknowledging an architectural trope that was intensely nostalgic but fashionable in its own way. Interiors of famous roadhouses either continued the 'Olde England' theme with Windsor chairs and chintz tablecloths or, as seen at the Ace of Spades, eagerly reproduced Americanized art deco cocktail bars and clubrooms. Juxtaposition of deco and Arts and Crafts seemed not to strike anyone at the time as peculiar. Three roadhouses – the Showboat, Chez Laurie and the Maybury – used a *moderne* style, which reflected both American and continental influences.

Transatlantic influence emerged clearly in the roadhouse's cultural practices. Super roadhouses mimicked American country clubs, but not because of any direct Americanization. Britain's roadhouse owners did not travel to the United States, nor did American entrepreneurs directly own or invest in British roadhouses. Influence of American culture most likely came from the cultural transmissions of Hollywood movies, jazz and swing music, and hard-boiled crime stories. Of course, this reception and subsequent adaptation of American cultural sources was commonplace in British interwar society, but roadhouses were in the vanguard. London's elite adopted the fashion first, and then aspirational and imitative middle-class roadhouse customers followed them.

Roadhouses were without exception located outside of urban centres, the traditional locus of fashion and excitement. Super roadhouses occupied a liminal setting in outer London and other large British cities, in both a physical and cultural sense. Physically, super roadhouse owners chose to locate their businesses on arterial roads just outside the contiguous suburban development beginning to surround Britain's large cities. Although not part of town, neither were they in the countryside. They were typically erected on cheap land formerly used for unproductive farming or market gardening. This scruffy netherworld, later made permanent through green belt legislation, did not conform to contemporary ideals of 'real' countryside.

Rather than sylvan glades and downland slopes, tropes used in 1920s literature to signify deepest England, land bought for roadhouses was flat and nondescript, its margins marked out by rusting barbed wire, home to old bath tubs and abandoned farming equipment. Monica Ewer's depiction of the Harbour Bar as remote and isolated demonstrated a clever and accurate understanding of the cultural positioning of roadhouses. At the height of their elite popularity they formed part of a dislocated metropolis, connected by fast driving to the city in an umbilical link, their success generated by novelty and the transcendental effects of speed. Roadhouse customers might appear to have had little or nothing in common with their nearest neighbours, the suburban citizens living on the city's outer fringes, but both shared a sense of inauthenticity, each in their different way subverting the norms of the town/country binary. As roadhouse clientele changed to embrace local, wealthier car owners, while the smart set slipped away, roadhouses themselves became suburban. New housing estates eventually subsumed them so that their cachet was lost forever.

While roadhouses attracted dissimilar sorts of customers in the interwar years, they consistently failed to draw serious police scrutiny. In Soho, widespread police corruption restricted the authorities' attempts to stamp out a variety of problematic behaviours that included: cocaine, unlicensed drinking, dancing and entertainment, illegal gambling, public displays of homosexuality, and prostitution. Unwillingness to prosecute roadhouse owners sits uneasily with the way that roadhouses were continually depicted in popular culture as epitomizing a new and transgressive 'racy roadhouse' atmosphere.[8] The most plausible explanation is that the consistent literary portrayal of British roadhouses as naughty, dangerous or worse reflected reality rather than some cultural mass delusion, and that authorities' failure to intervene was a consequence of inadequate policing just outside Britain's major cities. This was precisely the case too in the United States, enabling roadhouses to flourish during prohibition. If Robert Graves, a respected commentator, characterized some roadhouses as brothels, then they undoubtedly were. It seems improbable that an all-night drinking club would not provide both cocaine and prostitution. We now know that homosexual men met at the Ace of Spades, though this type of assignation was punished with public disgrace and imprisonment. If it proved possible for the most famous of roadhouses to escape detection, equivalent heterosexual misdemeanours, including illegal activities, almost inevitably happened. In any case, British discourse forever enshrined roadhouses' reputation as anonymous, dangerous, furtive and transgressive. Our evidence, derived from diverse sources, offers compelling evidence of this thesis.

Roadhouses were part of a wide-ranging set of changes to British personal mobility in the interwar period. As early as 1927, they provided a new destination for increasing numbers of middle-class motorists. Before the advent of roadhouses, motorists got the car out of the garage for two reasons: first for quotidian journeys, such as a trip to the shops or driving to work; and second, to speed an outing to the country or seaside. The latter was an important part of the reconnection of the post-war generation with the outdoors, an idea that also found expression in rambling and bicycling.

Driving to roadhouses, just for the point of going there, was an innovative and individualistic practice that allowed car users to enjoy and consume traditional West End entertainments in a new way. This practice contrasted with the rather tedious stasis of much interwar middle-class leisure, which had changed little since before the First World War. Playing golf and bridge, visiting friends and on a special occasion dining out, typified everyday fun for the well off. The highest 'caste' may have enlivened their leisure with events such as the Eton versus Harrow cricket match at Lord's or going to the racing at Ascot.

In contrast, driving out into London's outer reaches at all times of the day and night required an autonomous automobility where car owners almost always drove; some of them would shun their chauffeurs so as to engage directly with the transcendental effects of high-speed driving. Qualities to be found in London's new arterial roads aided and abetted this habit. Most super roadhouses lay adjacent to these fast motor roads, so a journey to the Ace of Spades meant a high-speed drive. That was indeed the whole point. As car usage increased rapidly throughout the 1930s, this became more and more difficult to achieve as road safety interventions such as roundabouts and traffic lights slowed car speeds. As roadhouse use became more normalized, other forms of retail consumption such as cinemas and car showrooms located themselves near to super roadhouses, foreshadowing car-borne out-of-town shopping that became familiar to Britain in the 1970s.

Roadhouses were a development in the late 1920s and early 1930s, but as we have pointed out, they reflected older traditions and practices. Of these, the river club is the most pertinent as it contained many of the elements that roadhouses displayed in their heyday. Both types of establishment offered exclusivity, an out of town location, swimming, dancing, dining, assignation and (most likely) cocaine and other similar pleasures. The first vital difference was the method of getting there, with the car and the arterial road replacing the river steamer and the Thames. A car's particular autonomous properties used technology in an adaptive way, and was, as a result, an important part of the condition of modernity prevalent in the 1930s. The second key difference from river clubs was in roadhouses' diurnal provision of a wide set of entertainments, with family swimming and outdoor games in the daytime and much more adult offerings during the evening and long into the night. This day-round approach is how we consume fun and leisure in the early twenty-first century, but roadhouses foreshadowed all this eighty years ago and then became lost from sight during the decades following the Second World War.

Appendix – Catalogue of Interwar British Roadhouses

This catalogue was collated over a number of years' research from a wide variety of contemporary resources that include directories, guide books, travel books, architectural journals, trade journals, newspapers, advertisements, bankruptcy and sale notices, newsreels and postcards.

As was noted in Chapter 2, the definition of what was or wasn't a roadhouse in the 1920s and 1930s was complicated and varied depending on the writer's perspective. The roadhouses shown below are categorized according to the typology shown in Figure 2.2, and excludes a fair number of small pubs and tea rooms that used the term 'roadhouse' but did not provide anything sufficiently unusual to justify the term. The date of opening and cost of construction of each roadhouse is shown where known.

Super roadhouses

Ace of Spades, Great West Road, Middlesex, 1926.
Ace of Spades, Kingston Bypass, Surrey, 1927.
Bell House, Beaconsfield, Buckinghamshire, 1931.
Clock, Welwyn Bypass, Hertfordshire, 1929.
Galleon Restaurant, Burgh Heath, Surrey, 1929.
Gay Adventure, Esher, Surrey, 1933.
Green Plunge, Royston, Hertfordshire, 1934.
Havering Court, Havering, Essex, 1934 (£60,000).[1]
Hendon Hall, Barnet Bypass, Hertfordshire, 1933.
Hilden Manor, Tonbridge, Kent, 1937.
Nautical William, Kidderminster/Bridgnorth Road, Shropshire, 1937 (£30,000).[2]
Pantiles, Bagshot, Surrey, 1930.
Pity Me, Durham, County Durham, (£50,000).[3]
Showboat, Maidenhead, Berkshire, 1933.

Spider's Web, Watford Bypass, Hertfordshire, 1932.
Spinning Wheel, Hoddesdon, Hertfordshire, 1934.
Sugar Bowl, Burgh Heath, Surrey, 1933.
Thatched Barn, Barnet Bypass, Hertfordshire, 1933 (£80,000).[4]

Hybrid pub roadhouses

Berkley Arms Hotel, Cranford, Berkshire, 1931 (£25,000).
Bridge House, St. Mary Cray, Kent, 1933.
Finchdale Abbey House, Finchdale Priory, Durham, 1936 (£30,000).[5]
Hendon Way, Hendon, Middlesex, 1934 (£25,000).[6]
Houseboat Road House, Radlett, Hertfordshire, 1935 (£10,000).[7]
Larkfield Roadhouse, Larkfield, Kent, 1933 (£10,000).
Maybury Road House, Edinburgh, Scotland, 1935 (£12,000).[8]
Myllet Arms, Perivale, Middlesex, 1936 (£60,000).[9]
Stewponey Hotel, Stourton, Warwickshire, 1936 (£60,000).[10]
Willow Barn Road House, Durrington, Sussex, 1938 (£5,600).[11]

Rural roadhouses

Aldermaston Mill, Aldermaston, Berkshire, 1933.
As You Like It, Fordingbridge, Hampshire, 1935.
Askers Road House, Bridport/Dorchester Rd., Dorset, 1935.
Barn, Bayfordbury, Hertfordshire, 1934.
Laughing Water, Cobham, Kent, 1933.
Manor House, Kingsdown, Kent, 1934.
Moat Farm Road House, Wrotham, Kent, 1934.
Monkey Puzzle, Herstmonceaux, Sussex, 1933.
Old Barn, Hildenborough, Kent, 1935.
Old Mill Pool, Harrow Mill, Essex, 1933.
Old Water Mill, Hellingly, Sussex, 1934.
Tudor House, Bearstead, Kent, 1934.
Watermill, Box Hill, Surrey, 1933.
Wookey Hole Caves, Cheddar, Somerset, 1927.

Pub roadhouses

Chez Laurie, nr. Herne Bay, Kent, 1937 (£13,500).[12]
Prospect Inn, Minster, Kent, 1939.

Hotel roadhouses

Birch Hotel (Haywards Heath).
Chase Hotel, Ingatestone, Essex, 1933.
Comet, Hatfield, Hertfordshire, 1937.
Croft Spa Hotel, nr. Darlington, Durham, 1936.
Great Fosters, Egham, Surrey, 1936.
Oatlands Park (Weybridge).

Unclassified Tier 2 and Tier 3 roadhouses

Adelphi, Slough, Berkshire, 1933.
Bubbling Brook, Cane End, nr. Reading, Berkshire, 1935.
Crib Road House, Westbury-on-Trym, Gloucestershire, 1933.
Crossways, Southend Arterial Road, Essex.
Crown Inn, Wychbold, Worcestershire, 1935.
Fenn Green, Kidderminster, Worcestershire, 1933.
Firleaze Road House, Almondsbury, nr. Bristol, 1933.
Fisher's Pond, Winchester/Portsmouth Road, Hampshire, 1933.
Four Ways, Delamere, Cheshire, 1935.
George & Dragon Hotel, nr. Exeter, Devon, 1936.
Golden Lion, Hillingdon, Middlesex, 1938.
High Tower Road House, St. Ouen's Bay, Jersey, 1937.
Kingfisher's Pool, Oak Hill, Essex, 1935.
La Jollon Auberge, Harrogate, Yorkshire.
MG's, Henley-in-Arden, Warwickshire, 1934.
Mill Stream, Bury Mill, Buckingham, 1931.
Mile 3, Bristol, 1933.
Orchard Hotel, Ruislip, Middlesex, 1933.
Popular Road House, Leigh-on-Sea, Essex, 1934.

Pottal Roadhouse, Cannock Chase.
Rob Roy Road House, Aberfoyle, Wales, 1934.
Silver Arrow Roadhouse, Knaresborough, Yorkshire, 1936.
Silver Slipper, Herne Bay, Kent, 1936.
Spinney Roadhouse, Danbury, Essex, 1937.
Tudor Rose, Two Mills, Cheshire, 1937.
Wagon Shed, Horley, Surrey, 1933.
Water Splash, London Colney, Hertfordshire, 1933.
White Rabbit Club, New Chapel, Surrey, 1937.

Notes

Chapter 1

1. *Racy Roadhouse*, Conrad Leonard and Clarkson Rose (from the British musical *Twinkle*, 1936).
2. *Observer*, 21 March 1971.
3. While acknowledging the difficulties of precise definition (see Chapter 2, 18), the authors have compiled a list of leading roadhouses from many diverse sources (see Appendix).
4. David Slater and Peter J. Taylor (eds), *The American Century: Consensus and Coercion in the Projection of American Power* (Oxford: Blackwell, 1999), 6.
5. Rob Kroes, 'Americanization, What Are We Talking About?' in Rob Kroes, Richard Rydell and Doeko Bosscher (eds), *Cultural Transmissions and Receptions: American Mass Culture in Europe* (Amsterdam: VU University Press, 1993), 302–20.
6. Neil Campbell, Jude Davies and George McKay (eds), *Issues in Americanization and Culture* (Edinburgh: Edinburgh University Press, 2004); Frank Costigliola, *Awkward Dominion: American Political, Economic, and Cultural Relations with Europe, 1919–1933* (Ithaca, NY: Cornell University Press, 1984); Victoria De Grazia, *Irresistible Empire: America's Advance Through Twentieth-Century Europe* (London: Belknap, 2005); George McKay (ed.), *Yankee Go Home (and Take Me with U): Americanization and Popular Culture* (Sheffield: Sheffield Academic Press, 1997); Duncan Webster, *Looka Yonder!: The Imaginary America of Populist Culture* (London: Routledge, 1988); Chris Waters, 'Beyond "Americanization": Rethinking Anglo-American Cultural Exchange Between the Wars', *Cultural and Social History* 4, 4 (2007): 451–59; Andrew Davies, 'The Scottish Chicago?: From "Hooligans" to "Gangsters" in Inter-War Glasgow', *Cultural and Social History* 4, 4 (2007): 511–27.
7. Earl Mayo, 'The Americanization of England', *Forum* 32 (January 1902): 569; Maureen E. Montgomery, *'Gilded Prostitution': Status, Money and Transatlantic Marriages, 1870–1914* (London: Routledge, 1989).
8. *Hotel and Catering Weekly*, 6 October 1933.
9. For interwar transatlantic encounters, see David Gilbert and Claire Hancock, 'New York City and the Transatlantic Imagination: French and English Tourism and the Spectacle of the Modern Metropolis, 1893–1939', *Journal of Urban History*, 33, 1 (2006): 77–107.
10. The term 'super' roadhouse, though not used in the 1930s, distinguishes the group of roadhouses with large premises and the most facilities, notably swimming pools.

11 See, for example, *London's Famous Clubs and Cabarets – The Ace of Spades Club*, [film] Dir. unknown, UK: Pathé, 24 April 1933, reel 1072.14.
12 Viscountess Rhondda, *Leisured Women* (London: Hogarth Press, 1928), 28–30, 54.
13 David W. Gutzke, *Women Drinking Out in Britain Since the Early Twentieth Century* (Manchester: Manchester University Press, 2014).
14 David W. Gutzke, 'Gender, Class, and Public Drinking in Britain During the First World War', *Historie Sociale/Social History* 27 (1994): 368–69.
15 For the CCB's Progressivism, see David W. Gutzke, *Pubs and Progressives: Reinventing the Public House in England, 1896–1960* (DeKalb: Northern University Press, 2006), Chapter 3. Its traits and motivations are discussed in David W. Gutzke, 'Progressivism in Britain and Abroad', in David W. Gutzke (ed.), *Britain and Transnational Progressivism* (New York: Palgrave MacMillan, 2008), 23, 26, 29–32; David W. Gutzke, 'Progressivism and the History of the Public House, 1850–1950', *Cultural and Social History* 4 (2007): 244–45; David W. Gutzke, 'Sydney Nevile: Squire in the Slums or Progressive Brewer?' *Business History* 53 (2011): 965–67.
16 Gutzke, *Women Drinking Out in Britain Since the Early Twentieth Century*, 61; and Gutzke, *Pubs and Progressives*, 210–11.
17 Gutzke, *Pubs and Progressives*, 211–12, 215.
18 Ernest Edwin Williams, *The New Public-House* (London: Chapman and Hall, 1924), 192–93.
19 Gutzke, *Pubs and Progressives*, 158–61.
20 Ibid., 163–73.
21 Steve Humphries, *A Secret World of Sex: Forbidden Fruit: The British Experience 1900–1950* (London: Sidgwick & Jackson, 1988), 113–14.
22 W. G. McMinnies, *Signpost to the Road Houses, Country Clubs and Better and Brighter Inns and Hotels of England* (London: Simpkin Marshall, 1935), 111.
23 Evelyn Waugh, *Vile Bodies* (London: Chapman & Hall, 1930).
24 David J. Taylor, *Bright Young People: The Rise and Fall of a Generation, 1918–1940* (London: Chatto & Windus, 2007).
25 Judith R. Walkowitz, *Nights Out: Life in Cosmopolitan London* (New Haven: Yale University Press, 2012).
26 Sue Bowden, 'The New Consumerism', in Paul Johnson (ed.), *Twentieth-Century Britain, Economic, Cultural and Social Change* (London: Longman, 1994), 242–60.
27 Ross McKibbin, *Classes and Cultures: England, 1918–1951* (Oxford: Oxford University Press, 1998); Frank Gloversmith, *Class, Culture and Social Change: A New View of the 1930s* (Brighton: Harvester, 1980); Alan A. Jackson, *The Middle Classes, 1900–1950* (Nairn: David St. John Thomas, 1991); John Carey, *The Intellectuals and the Masses: Pride and Prejudice Among the Literary Intelligentsia, 1880–1939* (London: Faber, 1992); Roy Lewis and Angus Maude, *The English Middle Classes* (London: Phoenix House, 1949).

28 1931 Census, visionofbritain.org.uk and L. P. Abercrombie, *Greater London Plan 1944* (London: HMSO, 1945).
29 Alan A. Jackson, *Semi-Detached London: Suburban Development, Life and Transport, 1900-39* (London: Allen & Unwin, 1973); Mark Clapson, *Suburban Century: Social Change and Urban Growth in England and the United States* (Oxford: Berg, 2003); John Burnett, *A Social History of Housing, 1815-1985* (London: Methuen, 1986); Paul Oliver, Ian Davis and Ian Bentley, *Dunroamin: The Suburban Semi and Its Enemies* (London: Barrie & Jenkins, 1981).
30 Sean O'Connell, *The Car and British Society: Class, Gender and Motoring 1896-1939* (Manchester: Manchester University Press, 1998); Peter Wollen and Joe Kerr, *Autopia: Cars and Culture* (London: Reaktion, 2002); Peter Thorold, *The Motoring Age: The Automobile and Britain 1896-1939* (London: Profile, 2003).
31 Michael John Law, *The Experience of Suburban Modernity: How Private Transport Changed Interwar London* (Manchester: Manchester University Press, 2014).
32 Brad Beaven, *Leisure, Citizenship and Working-Class Men in Britain, 1850-1945* (Manchester: Manchester University Press, 2005); Alan Delgado, *The Annual Outing and Other Excursions* (London: Allen and Unwin, 1977); Stephen G. Jones, *Workers at Play: A Social and Economic History of Leisure, 1918-1939* (London: Routledge & Kegan Paul, 1986); Jonathan Rose, *The Intellectual Life of the British Working Classes* (New Haven, CT: Yale University Press, 2001).
33 There has been an unpublished doctoral thesis on the topic, D. L. North, 'Middle-Class Suburban Lifestyles and Culture in England, 1919-1939' (University of Oxford, 1989).
34 Lawrence Napper, *British Cinema and Middlebrow Culture in the Interwar Years* (Exeter: University of Exeter Press, 2009); Jeffrey Richards, *The Age of the Dream Palace: Cinema and Society in Britain, 1930-1939* (London: Routledge, 1989); David Atwell, *Cathedrals of the Movies: A History of British Cinemas and Their Audiences* (London: Architectural Press, 1980).
35 Alison Light, *Forever England: Femininity, Literature and Conservatism Between the Wars* (London: Routledge, 1991).
36 Anthony Hern, *The Seaside Holiday. The History of the English Seaside Resort* (London: Cresset Press, 1967); Josephine Kane, *The Architecture of Pleasure: British Amusement Parks 1900-1939* (Farnham: Routledge, 2013).
37 Anthony Powell, *Hearing Secret Harmonies* (London: Arrow, [1997] 2005), 241.

Chapter 2

1 McMinnies, *Signpost* (1935), 136. McMinnies identified country clubs as a separate category of establishment. This was based on their being private clubs and on locations well away from the road.

2. See "roadhouse, n." OED Online (Oxford University Press, September 2011). www.oed.com.catalogue.ulrls.lon.ac.uk/view/Entry/275339 (accessed 12 October 2011).
3. *Indianapolis (Indiana) Star*, 30 December 1924.
4. *Washington Times*, 2 July 1917.
5. University of Houston, Digital History Project, http://www.digitalhistory.uh.edu/database/article_display.cfm?HHID=454 (accessed 2 March 2012).
6. Jack S. Blocker, David M. Fahey and Ian R. Tyrrell (eds), *Alcohol and Temperance in Modern History: An International Encyclopedia* (Santa Barbara: ABC-CLIO, 2003), 520.
7. Warren J. Belasco, *Americans on the Road: From Autocamp to Motel, 1910–45* (Cambridge, MA: MIT Press, 1979), 149.
8. Daniel Russell, 'The Roadhouse: A Study of Commercialized Amusements in the Environs of Chicago', Unpublished Master's dissertation (University of Chicago, 1931).
9. Thomas Burke, *London in My Time* (London: Rich & Cowan, 1934), 199.
10. Ibid., 36.
11. George Long, *English Inns and Road-Houses* (London: Werner Laurie, 1937), 177.
12. There is, though, evidence of British filling station owners visiting the United States to study station design and layout (*The Motor Trader*, 13 December 1933).
13. Long, *English Inns and Road-Houses*, 177.
14. Anon., *Road Houses and Clubs of the Home Counties* (London: Sylvan Publications, 1934), 1. Little is known about the Roadhouse Association, save for this publication. It was perhaps no more than a marketing exercise where space was sold in the guide.
15. S. P. B. Mais, *The English Review*, June 1937, 677–90. The 'lido' in Britain was and is an outdoor swimming pool, often run by the local council.
16. Michael Arlen, *The Green Hat* (London: Collins, 1924); *Outer London Clubs and Cabarets – 'The Hungaria River Club – Maidenhead'*, [film] Dir. Unknown, UK: Pathé, 1933, reel 1088.05.
17. Society of Motor Manufacturers and Traders, *The Motor Industry of Great Britain 1937* (London: SMMT, 1937).
18. See David Matless, *Landscape and Englishness* (London: Reaktion, 1998).
19. Richard Haslam, *Clough Williams-Ellis* (London: Academy Editions, 1996), 51.
20. Clough Williams-Ellis, *England and the Octopus* (London: Geoffrey Bles, 1928); Clough Williams-Ellis and J. M. Keynes, *Britain and the Beast* (London: Dent, 1937).
21. V&A RIBA Drawings collection PA887/1.
22. Clough Williams-Ellis, 'The Roadhouse', *Design for Today*, June 1933, 42.
23. Originating with refined hotels and luxury ocean liners, this term was being incorporated into brewers' improved pubs as a tactic in part to draw a more respectable clientele. Critically, this specially designated room became the most exclusive gender-neutral space for bourgeois patrons (Gutzke, *Pubs and Progressives*, 158–60).
24. Michael John Law, 'Turning Night into Day: Transgression and Americanization at the English Interwar Roadhouse', *Journal of Historical Geography* 35, 3 (2009): 473–94.

25 Williams-Ellis, *England and the Octopus*, endpapers.
26 Commander A. Tomlinson, *Tales from a Roadhouse* (St. Leonards-on-Sea: King Brothers & Potts, [1937] 1954), 7; *Hotel and Catering Management*, April 1937.
27 McMinnies, *Signpost* (1935), 163.
28 Clough Williams-Ellis and John Summerson, *Architecture Here and Now* (London: Thomas Nelson & Sons, 1934), 70; 'A Roadhouse in the Woods: "Laughing Water," Cobham, Kent', *Country Life*, 21 June 1934.
29 RIBA, *Rebuilding Britain* (London: Lund Humphries, 1943).
30 Long, *English Inns and Road-Houses*, 179.
31 McMinnies, *Signpost* (1935), 158.
32 Kenneth Grahame, *The Wind in the Willows* (London: Methuen, 1908) is one literary example.
33 *Outer London Clubs and Cabarets – The Hungaria River Club – Maidenhead*.
34 Arlen, *The Green Hat*, 203.
35 Horace Wyndham, *Nights in London* (London: John Lane, 1926).
36 Ibid., 43.
37 Ernest Dudley quoted in Matthew Sweet, *Shepperton Babylon* (London: Faber and Faber, 2006), 47.
38 Joseph Vecchi, *The Tavern Is My Drum* (London: Odhams Press, 1948).
39 David J. Taylor, *Bright Young People: The Rise and Fall of a Generation, 1918–1940* (London: Chatto & Windus, 2007), 105.
40 *Outer London Clubs and Cabarets – The Hungaria River Club – Maidenhead*.
41 Detail taken from an undated postcard, probably from the 1920s.
42 Other summer river clubs on the Thames were the Hotel de Paris at Bray, a few miles from Maidenhead, and the Palm Beach at Hampton Court.
43 Judith R. Walkowitz, *Nights Out: Life in Cosmopolitan London* (New Haven: Yale University Press, 2012).
44 Michael John Law, 'Stopping to Dream': The Beautification and Vandalism of London's Interwar Arterial Roads', *London Journal* 35, 1 (2010): 58–84.
45 Williams-Ellis, *England and the Octopus*, endpapers.
46 One could have equally chosen the Clock Roadhouse on the Welwyn Bypass or the Spider's Web on the Watford Bypass to represent this type of roadhouse, but much more is known about the Ace of Spades.
47 *London Gazette* (23 December 1930) shows both Ace of Spades roadhouses being registered at the Land Registry.
48 Anon., *Road Houses and Clubs of the Home Counties*, 23.
49 *Autocar*, 17 May 1929.
50 Hulton Picture Archive, gettyimages.co.uk #3312952.
51 *Flight*, 6 July 1933.
52 See 'Pacifism, Nudism and Hiking' in Robert Graves and Alan Hodge, *The Long Week-End: A Social History of Great Britain 1918–1939* (London: Faber and Faber, 1941), 275.

53 Iain Hutchinson, *The Flight of the Starling* (Erskine: Kea, 1992), 23.
54 McMinnies, *Signpost* (1935), 141.
55 Harold P. Clunn, *The Face of the Home Counties: Portrayed in a Series of Eighteen Week-End Drives from London* (London: Simpkin Marshall, 1936), 106.
56 McMinnies, *Signpost* (1935), 140–41.
57 Alan A. Jackson, *Semi-Detached London: Suburban Development, Life and Transport, 1900–39* (London: Allen and Unwin, 1973), 360.
58 Gutzke, *Pubs and Progressives*, 169.
59 Richard Gray and Cinema Theatre Association, *Cinemas in Britain: One Hundred Years of Cinema Architecture* (London: Lund Humphries, 1996).
60 *Maidenhead Advertiser*, 13 April 1933.
61 McMinnies, *Signpost* (1935), endpapers.
62 *Outer London Clubs and Cabarets – The Showboat*, [film] Dir. unknown, UK: Pathé, 18 September 1933, reel 1088.18.
63 Some pubs had recently rebranded themselves as hotels in order to improve their respectability (Gutzke, *Pubs and Progressives*, 172, 185–86).
64 Long, *English Inns and Road-Houses*, 180.
65 http://www.greatfosters.co.uk/hotel/history/(accessed 12 February 2013).
66 *Autocar*, 18 August 1933.
67 See Gutzke, *Pubs and Progressives*, Chapter 8; Basil Oliver, *The Renaissance of the English Public House* (London: Faber and Faber, 1947), Chapters 4–6.
68 Gutzke, *Pubs and Progressives*, 168.
69 Clive Aslet, 'Refuelling the Body, the Soul and the Morris Road Houses of the 1920s and 1930s', in Marcus Binney and Emma Milne (eds), *Time Gentlemen Please!* (London: SAVE Britain's Heritage and CAMRA, 1983), 21; also see Robert Elwall, 'One for the Road', *RIBA Journal* 110 (October 2003): 22. This misconception that roadhouses originated as pubs, improved or otherwise, continues to be made (Thorold, *The Motoring Age*, 138, 140).
70 Michael John Law, 'Charabancs and Social Class in 1930s Britain', *Journal of Transport History* 36, 1 (2015): 41–57.
71 Clunn, *Face of the Home Counties*, 38. Florentine could refer to either the use of marble or rubbed gold décor or perhaps both.
72 McMinnies, *Signpost* (1935), 26.
73 This and other plan details from Oliver, *Renaissance of the English Public House*, 37.
74 McMinnies, *Signpost* (1935), 26.

Chapter 3

1 Raymond Postgate, 'English Drinking Habits', *Holiday* 33 (February 1963): 88.

2   James R. McGovern, 'The American Woman's Pre-World War I Freedom in Manners and Morals', *Journal of American History* 55 (1968): 315–33; Joan M. Jensen and Lois Scharf (eds), 'Introduction', in *Decades of Discontent: The Women's Movement, 1920–40* (Boston: Northeastern University Press, 1987), 34; Mary P. Ryan, 'The Projection of a New Womanhood: The Movie Moderns in the 1920s', in Jean E. Friedman and William G. Shade (eds), *Our American Sisters: Women in American Life and Thought*, 3rd ed. (Toronto: D. C. Heath & Co., 1982), 508–9.

3   Peter Ling, 'Sex and the Automobile in the Jazz Age', *History Today* 39 (November 1989): 18–20; Lewis A. Erenberg, *Steppin' Out: New York Nightlife and the Transformation of American Culture, 1890–1930* (Westport, CT: Greenwood, 1981), 236–37.

4   Erenberg, *Steppin' Out*, 236–37; Madelon Powers, 'Decay from Within: The Inevitable Doom of the American Saloon', in Susanna Barrow and Robin Room (eds), *Drinking: Behavior and Belief in Modern History* (Berkeley: University of California, 1991), 112–31.

5   Perry R. Duis, *The Saloon: Public Drinking in Chicago and Boston, 1880–1920* (Urban: University of Illinois Press, 1983), 105–7; Kathy Peiss, *Cheap Amusements: Working Women and Leisure at the Turn of the Century New York* (Philadelphia: Temple University Press, 1986), 28; Powers, 'Decay from Within: The Inevitable Doom of the American Saloon', 115; Hutchins Hapgood, 'McSorley's Saloon', *Harper's Weekly* 58, 25 October 1913, 15.

6   Daniel Okrent, *Last Call: The Rise and Fall of Prohibition* (paperback ed., New York: Scribner, [2010] 2011), 211–12; Mary Murphy, 'Bootlegging Mothers and Drinking Daughters: Gender and Prohibition in Butte, Montana', *American Quarterly* 46 (1994): 175.

7   Thomas R. Pegram, *Battling Demon Rum: The Struggle for a Dry America, 1800–1933* (Chicago: Ivan R. Dee, 1998), 168.

8   Ling, 'Sex and the Automobile', 18.

9   *Kingsport Times*, 16 April 1929.

10 Ling, 'Sex and the Automobile', 22–23; Gerald E. Critoph, 'The Flapper and Her Critics', in Carol V. R. George (ed.), *'Remember the Ladies': New Perspectives on Women in American History: Essays in Honor of Nelson Manfred Blake* (Syracuse: Syracuse University Press, 1975), 147.

11 'I Know the Price of a Petting Party', *Smart Set: True Stories from Real Life* 76 (1925): 48, 99; also see *Sheboygan Press*, 23 May 1931.

12 *Oshkosh Daily Northwestern*, 1 March 1929; Garry C. Myers, 'Roadhouse Menace to Young Folk', *Hammond Times*, 8 October 1935.

13 *Lowell Sun*, 7 August 1929; *Charleston Gazette*, 9 May 1927.

14 *Oxnard Daily Courier*, 11 May 1923; Paul G. Cressey, *The Taxi-Dance Hall: A Sociological Study in Commercialized Recreation and City Life* (Chicago: University of Chicago Press, 1932), 22; *Charleston Gazette*, 14 June 1926.

15 *Montana Standard*, 7 October 1929; *New York Times*, 7 October 1929.
16 *Lowell Sun*, 7 August 1929; *Charleston Gazette*, 9 May 1927; Jessie F. Binford, 'Cook County (Illinois) Roadhouses', *Journal of Hygiene* 16 (1930): 262.
17 Binford, 'Cook County Roadhouses', 262; *Daily Northwestern*, 16 November 1931.
18 Daniel Russell, 'The Road House: A Study of Commercialized Amusements in the Environs of Chicago', Unpublished MA thesis (University of Chicago, 1931), 53, 80–83.
19 *Gettysburg Times*, 31 December 1931; *Syracuse Herald*, 14 May 1925; *New York Times*, 13 May 1925. Smaller white slave rings, for example, existed in Milwaukee County (*Sheboygan Press*, 8 June 1931).
20 *Atlanta Constitution*, 2 July 1921; *Times*, 31 December 1931; *Atlantic News-Telegraph*, 6 January 1932; *Capital Times*, 6 December 1930; *Albuquerque Journal*, 25 August 1929; *Montana Standard*, 26 August 1929.
21 Binford, 'Cook County Roadhouses', 257, 264; *Salt Lake Tribune*, 18 January 1927.
22 *New Castle News*, 18 September 1925; *Newport Mercury and Weekly News*, 17 October 1930.
23 *Waterloo Daily Courier*, 12 June 1933; *Evening Independent*, 14 August 1931; *Roswell Daily Record*, 8 May 1924; *Sheboygan Press*, 4 December 1925; see also *Edwardsville Intelligencer*, 10 May 1931.
24 *Titusville Herald*, 13 December 1926; *Olean Times*, 3 February 1931; *New Castle News*, 10 June 1927.
25 *Syracuse Herald*, 16 August 1932; *Appleton Post Crescent*, 18 April 1929; *Waterloo Daily Courier*, 12 June 1933; *Evening Independent*, 14 August 1931; *Olean Evening Times*, 28 October 1930.
26 Kevin F. White, 'The Flapper's Boyfriend: The Revolution in Morals and the Emergence of Modern American Male Sexuality, 1910-30' Unpublished PhD thesis (Ohio State University, 1990), vol. 1, 190.
27 *Roswell Daily Record*, 8 May 1924.
28 *Titusville Herald*, 13 December 1926; *Olean Times*, 3 February 1931; *New Castle News*, 10 June 1927.
29 'Dorothy Dix Talks', *Odgen Standard-Examiner*, 9 May 1924.
30 *New Castle News*, 10 June 1927.
31 Rebecca A. Bryant, 'Shaking Things Up: Popularizing the Shimmy in America', *American Music* 20 (2002): 177, 179, 181.
32 Eleanor Early, *Whirlwind* (Chicago: White House Publishers, 1928), 200–3.
33 'Flapper Fanny', *Lima News*, 15 October 1926.
34 Maud Radford Warren, 'The House of Youth', *Burlington Hawk-Eye*, 7 December 1924; Patricia Raub, *Yesterday's Stories: Popular Women's Novels of the Twenties and Thirties* (Westport, CT: Greenwood, 1994), 14; John D'Emilio and Estelle B. Freedman, *Intimate Matters: A History of Sexuality in American*, 2nd ed. (Chicago: University of Chicago Press, 1997), 223–35; Bryan, 'Shaking Things Up', 182.

Notes for Pages 36–41

35 Dashiell Hammett, *Red Harvest* (New York: Alfred A. Knopf, [1929] 2000), 565–66.
36 Marjorie Rosen, *Popcorn Venus: Women, Movies and the American Dream* (New York: Coward, McCann & Geoghegan, 1973), 78; *New York Times*, 6 May 1929.
37 Jessie F. Binford, 'May We Present the Road House?' *Welfare Magazine* 18 (1927): 872–80.
38 *Capital Times*, 7 December 1929.
39 Beatrice Fairfax, 'Advice to the Lovelorn', *Lebanon Daily News*, 27 December 1926.
40 *Scotsman* story reproduced in *Fellowship*, 5 (January 1925): 17.
41 Karl M. Chworowsky to Editor, *Unity*, 20 September 1926, and Dr. Workman to Editor, 9 June 1927, reproduced in *Fellowship*, 7 (1927): 23–24, 162.
42 *Ogden Standard-Examiner*, 18 June 1922.
43 In this case, however, bootleggers were Americans smuggling booze from Britain to their homeland. Meyrick, *Secrets of the 43*, 43–44, 85; Heather Shore, '"Constable Dances with Instructress": The Police and the Queen of Nightclubs in Interwar London', *Social History* 38 (2013): 191, 198; Walkowitz, *Nights Out*, 210, 216–17, 224–26, 228.
44 This and the following paragraph are based on Walkowitz's *Nights Out*, 208–32.
45 Shore, 'Queen of Nightclubs', 189; Pamela Horn, *Women in the 1920s* (Stroud: Alan Sutton, 1995), 36; Humphries, *A Secret World of Sex*, 119.
46 Sir Max Pemberton, 'The Road House – What of It?' *True Temperance Quarterly* 8, November 1934, 5.
47 McMinnies, *Signpost*, 5, 136–37.
48 Tomlinson, *Tales from a Roadhouse* (1936), 3rd ed. (St. Leonards-on-Sea: King Brothers and Potts, [1936]1954), 56–57. Likewise, an anonymous author of a promotional pamphlet about eighteen roadhouses offered his own personal testimony about their 'blameless repute and irreproachable decorum' (*Road Houses and Clubs of the Home Counties*, 3).
49 Tomlinson, *Tales from a Roadhouse*, 92.
50 Monica Ewer, *Roadhouse* (London: Sampson Low, 1935), 5–6, 15.
51 *Caterer and Hotel-Keepers' Gazette*, 20 June 1932.
52 *Herts Advertiser*, 2 August 1935; *Caterer and Hotel-Keepers' Gazette*, 20 June 1932; *Road Houses of the Home Counties*, 41, 45; *Nottingham Evening Post*, 12 January 1934.
53 J. Williams, 'The Roadhouse in Winter', *Hotel and Catering Weekly*, 19 November 1933.
54 Walter Hackett, *Road House: A Play in Three Acts* (London: Samuel French, 1934), 13–14, 16, 41, 43, 47; 'Walter Hackett (1876–1944)', in Anna Rothe (ed.), *Current Bibliography: Who's News and Why, 1944* (New York: H. W. Wilson Co., 1945), 262.
55 Synopsis of 'Roadhouse' and Shooting Script, Special Collections, British Film Institute.
56 T. E. B Clarke, *Jeremy's England* (London: John Long, 1934), 268.

57 Nicholas Blake, *Thou Shell of Death* (New York: Harper & Row, [1936]1977), 69–70, 78, 107, 118, 138, 147; also see Graham Greene, *The Confidential Agent* (London: W. Heinemann, 1939); Thorold, *The Motoring Age*, 139–40.
58 Margery Allingham, *The Case of the Late Pig* (London: Penguin, [1937] 1983), 20–22.
59 Valentine Williams, 'The Dot-and-Carry Case', in *The Curiosity of Mr. Treadgold* (Boston: Houghton Mifflin Co., 1937), 65–81.
60 Graham Greene, *Brighton Rock* (Harmondsworth: Penguin, [1938]1970), 132.
61 McMinnies, *Signpost* (1935), 136–82 and 5th ed. (1939), 53, 87, 263, 277.
62 *Hotel Review*, September 1935; *Caterer and Hotel-Keeper*, 12 June 1936, 23 April 1937, 6 January 1939; McMinnies, *Signpost* (1935), 140; *Aberdeen Journal*, 26 January 1938.
63 *Caterer and Hotel-Keeper*, 5 October 1934.
64 *Manchester Guardian*, 8 August 1935.
65 John R. Greenaway, *Drink and British Politics Since 1830: A Study in Policy Making* (Basingstoke: Palgrave Macmillan, 2003), 166.
66 Arthur E. Bennetts, 'Why Roadhouse?' *Luncheon and Tea Room Journal*, November 1935.
67 'Roadhouse Drinks', *Yorkshire Evening Post*, 31 October 1934.
68 Published in the United States by a wire service, this story has proved impossible to trace in Britain (*Gleaner*, 6 August 1932).
69 Pemberton, 'The Road House – What of It?', 5; Ivor Brown, *The Heart of England* (London: B. T. Batsford, 1935), 61; *Gleaner*, 6 August 1932.
70 *Gleaner*, 6 August 1932.
71 Elsa Dundas, 'I Run a Roadhouse', *Daily Mirror*, 22 May 1935.
72 *Herne Bay Press*, 5 and 15 February 1938, and 4 February 1939.
73 Ibid., 4 February 1939.
74 Ibid., 5 February 1938.
75 Pemberton, 'Road Houses', 5; Horn, *Women in the 1920s*, 32; Martin Pugh, *'We Danced All Night': A Social History of Britain Between the Wars* (London: Bodley Head, 2008), 217.
76 Horn, *Women in the 1920s*, 29, 32; Juliet Gardiner, *The Thirties: An Intimate History* (London: Harper, 2010), 629.
77 Horn, *Women in the 1920s*, 30; Gardiner, *The Thirties*, 628.
78 *Manchester Guardian*, 1 February 1928; *Fellowship*, 5 (March 1925): 49.
79 James Laver, *Between the Wars* (Boston: Houghton Mifflin Co., 1961), 10 1; Horn, *Women in the 1920s*, 27–29; Meyrick, *Secrets of 43*, 53, 271.
80 *Evening News*, 19 August 1932 and 26 July 1933.
81 Long, *English Inns and Road-Houses*, 178–79; Hertfordshire Quarter Sessions, Licensing Committee, Minute Book, Hertfordshire Record Office, QS CE/8, 4 May 1934, 265; Meyrick, *Secrets of the 43*, 53.

82 *Luncheon and Tea Room Journal*, December 1935; Long, *English Inns*, 182.
83 *Caterer and Hotel-Keeper*, 30 October 1936.
84 *Yorkshire Evening Post*, 5 March 1937; Robert Graves and Alan Hodge, *The Long Week-End: A Social History of Great Britain, 1918–39* (London: Faber and Faber, 1941), 380. Bagnios came to be translated as bordellos.
85 Horn, *Women in the 1920s*, 36; Humphries, *Secret World of Sex*, 126.
86 Horn, *Women in the 1920s*, 37; Pringle, *Dance Little Ladies*, 24, 46; Mayo, 'The Americanization of England', 569.
87 Graham Robson, *Motoring in the 30s* (London: Patrick Stephens, 1979), 51.
88 Horn, *Women in the 1920s*, 32; Margaret Pringle, *Dance Little Ladies*, 23, 49.
89 *Gloucestershire Echo*, 25 March 1936.
90 At a Yorkshire roadhouse, where several women had been fined for selling liquor without a licence, police sergeant John Mitchell testified that he 'saw a man with nothing on but his shirt and socks in the front room'. Questionable behaviour went well beyond semi-nudity; he also witnessed 'a man buy drinks for himself' while 'a girl was sitting on his knee' ('Roadhouse Drinks').
91 *Daily Mail*, 30 December 1935.
92 Michael John Law, 'Turning Night into Day', 482.
93 *Men Only* (January 1952), 96; *Times*, 17 April 1953.
94 We are grateful to Trevor Lloyd for this point.
95 *Caterer and Hotel Keeper*, 7 July 1939.
96 Matt Houlbrook, *Queer London: Perils and Pleasures in the Sexual Metropolis, 1918-57* (Bristol: University Presses Marketing, 2006), 71.
97 Ibid., 71.
98 Bennetts, 'Why Roadhouse?'; A. V. Seaton, 'Leisure in Different Worlds', in *Leisure: Modernity, Postmodernity and Lifestyles*, vol. 1 (London: LSA, 1994), 335.
99 McMinnies, *Signpost* (1935), 5.
100 Sean O'Connell, *The Car in British Society: Class, Gender and Motoring* (Manchester: Manchester University Press, 1998), 180.

Chapter 4

1 Greene, *Brighton Rock*, 132.
2 W. G. McMinnies, *Signpost* (1935), 141.
3 *Maidenhead Advertiser*, 13 April 1933; Brown, *The Heart of England*.
4 John Stevenson, *The Slump: Britain in the Great Depression* (London: Routledge, 2013).
5 See, for example, James Marshall, *The History of the Great West Road: Its Social and Economic Influence on the Surrounding Area* (Hounslow: Heritage Publications, 1995).

6   Derived from Society of Motor Manufacturers and Traders, *The Motor Industry of Great Britain 1939*, and www.visionofbritain.org.uk for official census data.
7   Plowden, *The Motor Car and Politics*, Appendix B.
8   Kathryn Morrison, *Carscapes: The Motor Car, Architecture and Landscape in England* (New Haven: Yale University Press, 2012).
9   Pugh, *'We Danced All Night'*, 350; Michael John Law, 'Speed and Blood on the Bypass: The New Automobilities of Interwar London', *Urban History* 39, 3 (2012): 490–509.
10 1931 Census, visionofbritain.org.uk and Abercrombie, *Greater London Plan 1944*, 188. A precise definition of where London's suburbia stops is problematic, but this book uses the calculations of Abercrombie's Greater London Plan (1944) that categorizes Surrey, Middlesex and the inner parts of Essex and Kent as suburbanized. Hertfordshire and Buckinghamshire have been excluded from these numbers as they were less populated and more rural in nature.
11 Michael John Law, '"The Car Indispensable": The Hidden Influence of the Car in Interwar Suburban London', *Journal of Historical Geography* 38, 4 (2012): 424–33.
12 Ben Weinreb and Christopher Hibbert, *The London Encyclopaedia* (London: Macmillan, 1987), 632.
13 This paragraph has been reproduced from Law, 'Stopping to Dream', 58–84, reprinted by permission of the publisher (Taylor & Francis Ltd, www.tandfonline.com).
14 'Note on Working Short-time on Arterial Road Schemes', The National Archives, TNA, LAB 2/729/ED5351/1920, c. January 1922.
15 Rees Jeffreys, *The King's Highway* (London: Batchworth Press, 1949).
16 See Christof Mauch and Thomas Zeller (eds), *The World Beyond the Windshield: Roads and Landscapes in the United States and Europe* (Athens: Ohio University Press, 2008).
17 Raymond Unwin, 'Memorandum No. 2', *Greater London Planning Committee Report* (London: HMSO, 1929), 27.
18 Jeffreys, *The King's Highway*, 115.
19 Clunn, *The Face of the Home Counties*, 2.
20 Williams-Ellis, *England and the Octopus*.
21 Architecture Club, *Recent English Architecture 1920–1940* (London: Country Life, 1947), Plate 28.
22 McMinnies, *Signpost* (1935), 140–41.
23 Anon., *Road Houses and Clubs of the Home Counties*.
24 Paul Bolton et al., House of Commons Library, *Agriculture: Historical Statistics Standard Note: SN/SG/3339* (London: HMSO, 2015).
25 Williams-Ellis, *England and the Octopus*, 162.

26 Paul Vaughan, *Something in Linoleum* (London: Sinclair-Stevenson, 1994), 58.
27 Plowden, *The Motor Car and Politics*, Appendices.
28 Ibid., 39.
29 Alex Potts, 'Constable Country Between the Wars', in Raphael Samuel (ed.), *Patriotism: The Making and Unmaking of British National Identity* (London: Routledge, 1989), 164.
30 John Urry, *Automobility, Car Culture and Weightless Travel: A Discussion Paper* (Lancaster: Lancaster University, 1999).
31 'On the Road', *Autocar*, 3 July 1925.
32 H. V. Morton, *In Search of England* (London: Methuen, 1927).
33 See Rudi Koshar, 'Driving Cultures and the Meaning of Roads' in Mauch and Zeller, *The World Beyond the Windshield*, 25.
34 Williams-Ellis, *England and the Octopus* and C. E. M. Joad, *The Horrors of the Countryside* (London: Hogarth Press, 1931); Matless, *Landscape and Englishness*, 62.
35 John Prioleau, quoted in O'Connell, *The Car and British Society*, 85.
36 John Prioleau, *Motoring for Women* (London: Geoffrey Bles, 1925).
37 Paul Nieuwenhuis and Peter Wells, 'The All-Steel Body as a Cornerstone to the Foundations of the Mass Production Car Industry', *Industrial and Corporate Change* 16, 2 (2007): 183–211.
38 Society of Motor Manufacturers and Traders, *The Motor Industry of Great Britain 1939*.
39 Nieuwenhuis and Wells, 'The All-Steel Body as a Cornerstone to the Foundations of the Mass Production Car Industry'.
40 Michael Sedgwick, *Passenger Cars, 1924–1942* (London: Blandford Press, 1975), 9.
41 Thorold, *The Motoring Age*, 19.
42 Patrick Hamilton, *The Siege of Pleasure* (London: Constable, 1932), 297.
43 Gutzke, *Women Drinking Out in Britain Since the Early Twentieth Century*, 14–42.
44 See Chapter 6.
45 Louise Settle, 'The Kosmo Club Case: Clandestine Prostitution During the Interwar Period', *Twentieth-Century British History* 25, 4 (2014): 562–84.
46 Houlbrook, *Queer London*, 71.

Chapter 5

1 Like so many so other historians, Martin Pugh confuses roadhouses and new improved pubs built in interwar England (Pugh, *'We Danced All Night'*, 227).
2 Osbert Lancaster, *Progress at Pelvis Bay* (London: John Murray, 1936), 63–67.
3 See Chapter 2.

4   Dundas, 'I Run a Roadhouse'; also see *Hotel and Catering Weekly*, 26 April 1935.
5   *Luncheon and Tea Room Journal*, March 1938.
6   McMinnies, *Signpost* (1935), 162–63, 174–75.
7   Adele Lezard, 'There Is Big Money in Tea Gardens', *Hotel and Catering Weekly*, 26 April 1935.
8   *Times*, 16 September 1936.
9   *Hotel and Catering Weekly*, 16 February 1934; *Wells Journal and Somerset and West of England Advertiser*, 6 and 22 May and 5 June 1936; Somersetshire Quarter Sessions, Licensing Committee, Minute Book, Somersetshire Record Office, QS/LIC/1/3, 26 March 1936; McMinnies, *Signpost* (3rd ed., London: Simpkin Marshall, 1937), 311.
10 Barclay, Perkins & Co. Minute Book, Meetings of the Jt. Committee, London Metropolitan Archives, Acc. 2305/7/8, 15 June 1934 and 12 June 1935, 183; *Caterer and Hotel-Keeper*, 11 March 1933.
11 *Brewer and Wine Merchant*, March 1931.
12 *Luncheon and Tea Room Journal*, July 1935; McMinnies, *Signpost* (1935), 149.
13 Ewer, *Roadhouse*, 27.
14 *Dover Express*, 19 March 1943.
15 McMinnies, *Signpost* (2nd and 3rd eds., 1935–37).
16 Interview with George Hersey, 'It Grew – and Grew – and Grew!' *Hotel and Catering Weekly*, 6 October 1933.
17 *Caterer and Hotel-Keeper*, 17 February 1934.
18 McMinnies, *Signpost* (1935), 179.
19 *Times*, 20 July 1934.
20 *Luncheon and Tea Room Journal*, March 1938.
21 S. Marella, 'The Modern Road House: Success Depends on the Site', *Caterer and Hotel-Keeper*, 30 November 1934.
22 *Hotel Review*, October 1934; *Caterer and Hotel-Keeper*, 5 August 1933; Long, *English Inns and Road-Houses*, 179.
23 John Piper, 'Fully Licensed', *Architectural Review*, March 1940, 100.
24 S. Marella, 'The Modern Road House: Building and Planning the New Premises', *Caterer and Hotel-Keeper*, 7 December 1934, and 'What a Swimming Pool Needs', 1 February 1935.
25 Marella, 'The Modern Road House'.
26 Ewer, *Roadhouse*, 18–19.
27 'Road-Houses: Food and Recreation for Motorists', *Manchester Guardian*, 15 November 1933.
28 McMinnies, *Signpost* (1935), 159.

29 Similar establishments outside London's orbit were the Mile 3 Roadhouse, near Bristol, and Askers Roadhouse, near Bridport (McMinnies, *Signpost* [3rd ed., 1937], 338).
30 McMinnies, *Signpost* (1935), 150–51; *Herts Advertiser*, 29 March 1935.
31 McMinnies, *Signpost* (3rd ed., 1937), 338; Long, *English Inns and Road-Houses*, 178–79; Clive Aslet, 'Beer and Skittles in the Improved Public House', *Thirties Society Journal* 4 (1984): 4; Hersey Interview, 'It Grew'.
32 Hersey Interview, 'It Grew'.
33 *Evening Telegraph*, 1 June 1939; *Western Daily Press*, 7 February 1936; Robson, *Motoring in the '30s*, 51.
34 *Evening Telegraph*, 1 June 1939; *Western Daily Press*, 7 February 1936; Williams, 'The Roadhouse in Winter', *Hotel and Catering Weekly*, 10 November 1933.
35 Long, *English Inns and Road-Houses*, 178–79.
36 Ibid.
37 McMinnies, *Signpost* (1935), 178 and (3rd ed., 1937), 338.
38 *Anchor Magazine* 17 (July 1937): 154; Charles Porte, 'The Planning of Public Houses', *Journal of the Institute of Brewing* 40 (1934): 33; *Hotel and Catering Weekly*, 4 August 1933; *Herne Bay Press*, 15 February 1938.
39 *Kelly's Directory of Hertfordshire for 1937*, 23; McMinnies, *Signpost* (1935), 144; (3rd ed., 1937), 335; 4th ed. (1938), 329; Williams, 'Roadhouse in Winter'.
40 *Luncheon and Tea Room Journal*, December 1935.
41 McMinnies, *Signpost* (1935), 167.
42 Commander A. Tomlinson, *Tales from a Roadhouse*, 3rd ed. (St. Leonards-on-Sea: King Brothers & Potts, [1935] 1954), 60–61.
43 *Hotel and Catering Weekly*, 4 August 1933; McMinnies, *Signpost* (3rd ed., 1937), 304; also see Robson, *Motoring in the '30s*, 51.
44 Tomlinson, *Tales from a Roadhouse*; Bennetts, 'Why Roadhouse?'; *Hotel and Catering Weekly*, 4 August 1933; Robson, *Motoring in the '30s*, 51.
45 Sydney O. Nevile, *Seventy Rolling Years* (London: Faber & Faber, 1958), 217–19.
46 René Cutforth, *Later than We Thought: A Portrait of the Thirties* (Newton Abbot: David & Charles, 1976), 28; *Hotel and Catering Weekly*, 4 August 1933.
47 *Hotel and Catering Weekly*, 7 June 1935.
48 *Evening Telegraph*, 1 June 1939; *Western Daily Press*, 7 February 1936; Williams, 'Roadhouse in Winter'.
49 *Daily Mail*, 26 June 1931; also see *Daily Mail*, 1 August 1933.
50 Cutforth, *Later than We Thought*, 28; *Evening News*, 19 August 1932.
51 *Evening News*, 26 July 1933.
52 Lady Pamela Smith, 'Home Notes', *Essex Newsman*, 11 November 1933.
53 Bennetts, 'Why Roadhouse?' *Times*, 14 October 1933.
54 *Times*, 14 October 1933.

55 Marella, 'The Modern Road House'.
56 Long, *English Inns and Road-Houses*, 178.
57 *Caterer and Hotel-Keeper*, 2 August 1935; *West Herts and Watford Observer*, 27 July 1935; also see the *Hotel Review*, May 1935.
58 *Hotel Review*, January 1933; McMinnies, *Signpost* (1935), 118–19, 125; Anon., *Road Houses and Clubs of the Home Counties*, 25; 'Romford Now & Then' website, www.romford.org (accessed 8 February 2013).
59 McMinnies, *Signpost* (1935), 166; Long, *English Inns and Road-Houses*, 182.
60 The southwest (8), midlands (6), north (4), Scotland (4) and Wales (1) were the geographic areas.
61 McMinnies, *Signpost* (1935), 178, 180 and (3rd ed., 1937), 333.
62 *Caterer and Hotel-Keeper*, 12 June 1936; Long, *English Inns and Road-Houses*, 184.
63 McMinnies, *Signpost* (1935), 174.
64 *Caterer and Hotel-Keeper*, 21 August 1936.
65 McMinnies, *Signpost* (1935), 140–41. Gutzke, *Pubs and Progressives*, 212. Another newspaper story put the Barn's cost at £30,000, though expensive changes were later made (*Hotel and Catering Weekly*, 4 August 1933).
66 *Caterer and Hotel-Keeper*, 4 August 1933; McMinnies, *Signpost* (1935), 140–41.
67 *Hotel and Boarding House*, June 1934.
68 McMinnies, *Signpost* (4th ed., 1938), 153.
69 *Caterer and Hotel-Keeper*, 4 October 1935.
70 *Caterer and Hotel-Keeper*, 11 October 1935.
71 Barclay, Perkins & Co. Minute Book, Meetings of the Jt. Committee, 183; Gutzke, *Pubs and Progressives*, 215–27, 249–51.
72 *Caterer and Hotel-Keeper*, 12 June 1936; Long, *English Inns and Road-Houses*, 184.
73 McMinnies, *Signpost* (1935), 135; *Caterer and Hotel-Keeper*, 12 June 1936.
74 *Times*, 21 November 1936.
75 *Times*, 3 September 1941. Pity Me, a roadhouse in County Durham, had originally cost some £50,000 (*Western Daily Press*, 26 March 1947).
76 *Builder*, 3 September 1937; *Caterer and Hotel-Keeper*, 3 May and 19 July 1935.
77 *Herne Bay Press*, 5 February 1938.
78 *Hotel Review*, September 1935.
79 *Times*, 10 March 1936, 16 September 1937 and 6 December 1938.
80 *Luncheon and Tea Room Journal*, March 1938.
81 *Times*, 19–20 July 1934, 10 and 25 February and 8 July 1937; *Observer*, 31 March 1935.
82 *Times*, 2 January 1934, 31 May 1935, 31 August 1936, and 10 February and 8 July 1937, 7 and 20 October 1938; Dundas, 'I Run a Roadhouse'.
83 *Caterer and Hotel-Keeper*, 6 January 1939; Gutzke, *Pubs and Progressives*, 212.
84 *Daily Mail*, 10 September 1932; McMinnies, *Signpost* (1935), 160–61.
85 Long, *English Inns and Road-Houses*, 182.

86 Williams, 'Roadhouse in Winter'; *Gloucestershire Echo*, 25 March 1936; Dundas, 'I Run a Roadhouse'.
87 Barbara Worsley-Gough, 'The Road House Age', *Spectator*, 24 August 1934, 252; McMinnies, *Signpost* (3rd ed., 1937), 340.
88 Worsley-Gough, 'Road House Age', 252; McMinnies, *Signpost* (1935), 173 and (3rd ed., 1937), 335; Long, *English Inns and Road-Houses*, 181.
89 Worsley-Gough, 'Road House Age', 252.
90 McMinnies, *Signpost* (1935), 141, and (3rd ed., 1937), 318.
91 'Here Is the Road-House Owner Who Runs a Rolls Royce', *Hotel and Catering Management*, April 1937.

Chapter 6

1 Robert W. Rydell and Rob Kroes, *Buffalo Bill in Bologna: The Americanization of the World, 1869–1922* (Chicago: University of Chicago Press, 2005).
2 Mark Glancy, *Hollywood and the Americanization of Britain: From the 1920s to the Present* (London: I. B. Tauris, 2014).
3 J. B. Priestley, *English Journey* (London: Heinemann, 1934), 401.
4 Burke, *London in My Time*, 36, 199.
5 Rawdon Hoare, *This Our Country: An Impression After Fourteen Years Abroad* (London: John Murray, 1935), 35.
6 Hoare, *This Our Country*, 36.
7 Malcolm Muggeridge, *The Thirties* (London: Hamish Hamilton, 1940), 16
8 Matless, *Landscape and Englishness*.
9 Long, *English Inns and Road-Houses*, 181–82.
10 This was satirised by Osbert Lancaster, *Pillar to Post* (London: John Murray, 1939).
11 *The Private Life of Henry VIII*, [film] Dir. A. Korda, UK: London Film Productions, 1933.
12 Andrew Saint (ed.), *London Suburbs* (London: Merrell Holberton in association with English Heritage, 1999).
13 McMinnies, *Signpost* (1935), 159.
14 Ibid., 160.
15 Ibid.; *Luncheon and Tea Room Journal*, December 1935.
16 *Caterer and Hotel-Keeper*, 4 October 1935.
17 M. Bagueley, 'Better and Brighter Bars', *Bartender*, 2 November 1935; Advertisement, *Bartender*, 4 March 1938.
18 Hersey Interview, 'It Grew'; Williams-Ellis, 'Roadhouse', 43.
19 'The Ace of Spades Club by E. B. Musman', *Architectural Review*, May 1933, 186–87, Cellulose [*sic*] (in fact celluloid) was an early plastic with a glass-like appearance.

20 Charlotte Benton, Tim Benton and Ghislaine Wood (eds), *Art Deco 1910–1939* (London: V&A Publications, 2003), 238.
21 See Chapter 7, 107.
22 *Herne Bay Press*, 5 February 1938.
23 *Daily Mail*, 10 September 1932; McMinnies, *Signpost* (3rd ed., 1937), 311; *Signpost* (4th ed., 1938), 153, 329.
24 McMinnies, *Signpost*, 140.
25 *Anchor Magazine* 17 (1937): 151.
26 J. Fitzpatrick, 'One of the Brigade', *Bartender*, 4 January 1938.
27 *Hotel and Catering Weekly*, 6 October 1933.
28 *Bartender*, 2 November 1935; *Fellowship*, 5 October 1925, 225; Richard Hough, *Ace of Clubs* (London: Deutsch, 1986), 101; *Hotel Review*, October 1934.
29 https://books.google.com/ngrams (accessed 15 March 2014).
30 Raymond Postgate, 'English Drinking Habits', *Holiday* 33 (February 1963): 87–88, 92.
31 *Caterer and Hotel-Keeper*, 14 June 1935; H. Caplan, 'Half a Century of Change', *Wine and Spirit Trade Review*, 1 January 1965; Lord Kinross [John Patrick Douglas Balfour], *The Kindred Spirit: A History of Gin and of the House of Booth* (London: Newman Neame, 1959), 63, 65; *Licensed Victuallers' Gazette*, 9 February 1934; Francesco Adinolfi, *Mondo Exotica: Sounds, Visions, Obsessions of the Cocktail Generation* (Durham: Duke University Press, 2008), 78–79; Judith S. Baughman (ed.), *American Decades, 1920–29* (New York: A Manley Inc., 1996), 155; Patrick Balfour, *Society Racket* (London: J. Long, 1933), 138–39.
32 McMinnies, *Signpost* (1935), 119, 130 and (1938), 153; Eileen Whiteing, *Anyone for Tennis? Growing-Up in Wallington Between the Wars* (London: London Borough of Sutton Libraries & Arts Services, 1979), 58.
33 *Herne Bay Press*, 5 February 1938.
34 *Cutty Sark: The Making of a Whisky Brand* (Edinburgh: Birlinn, 2011), 128.
35 *Hastings and St. Leonard's Observer*, 8 June 1935; *Bartender*, 4 March 1938: inside back cover.
36 M. Baguley, 'The Art of Increasing Bar Trade', *Bartender*, 2 October 1935; *Caterer and Hotel-Keeper*, 23 April 1937; *Illustrated London News*, 9 July 1932.
37 McMinnies, *Signpost* (4th ed., 1938), 153.
38 Catherine Horwood, '"Girls Who Arouse Dangerous Passions": Women and Bathing, 1900–39', *Women's History Review* 9 (2000): 653–73; Patricia Cunningham, 'Swimwear in the Thirties: The BVD Company in a Decade of Innovation', *Dress* 12 (1986): 11–27.
39 Matless, *Landscape and Englishness*.
40 Charles Graves, 'The Bathing Boom', *Nash's Pall Mall Gazette*, August 1934, 20; *Daily Mail*, 1 August 1933.
41 Graves, 'The Bathing Boom', 20, 76.

42 Clough Williams-Ellis, 'The Future of Swimming Pools', *Hotel Review*, January 1935; Ernest M. Porter, 'Swimming Pools Are "Booming" – Are You Profiting by It?', *Caterer and Hotel-Keeper*, 28 June 1935.
43 George Orwell, *The Lion and the Unicorn* (London: Secker and Warburg, 1941).
44 Worsley-Gough, 'Road House Age', 252.
45 Long, *English Inns and Road-Houses*, 180.
46 McMinnies, *Signpost* (1935), 141.
47 Clunn, *The Face of the Home Counties*, 456.
48 *Road Houses and Clubs of the Home Counties*, 23.
49 McMinnies, *Signpost* (1935), 1, 16, 145, 166, 172.
50 Anon., *Road Houses and Clubs of the Home Counties*, 23.
51 *Hotel Review*, May 1935; *Road Houses and Clubs of the Home Counties*, inside back cover; McMinnies, *Signpost* (1935), 137.
52 McMinnies, *Signpost* (1935), 144–45.
53 McMinnies, *Signpost* (1937), 304; *Road Houses and Clubs of the Home Counties*, back cover; Hannah Andrassy, 'Spinning a Golden Thread: The Introduction of Elastic into Swimwear', *Things* 5 (1996–97): 75–76; *Evening News*, 26 July 1933.
54 *Hotel*, October 1936; *Daily Mail*, 24 June 1935; Graves, 'The Bathing Boom', 20; *Daily Mail*, 24 June 1935.
55 *Caterer and Hotel-Keeper*, 23 April 1937.
56 *Daily Mail*, 22 June 1938; *Manchester Guardian*, 14 May 1936.
57 Clough Williams-Ellis, 'The Future of Swimming Pools', 42; McMinnies, *Signpost* (1935), 158.
58 Williams-Ellis, 'The Future of Swimming Pools'; Marella, 'The Modern Road House: Success Depends on the Site'.
59 *London's Famous Clubs and Cabarets – The Ace of Spades Club*; *Outer London Clubs and Cabarets – The Ace of Spades*, [film] Dir. unknown, UK: Pathé, 7 August, 1933, reel 1086.02; *Outer London Clubs and Cabarets – The Bell*, [film] Dir. unknown, UK: Pathé, 17 July 1933, reel 1076.07; *Outer London Clubs and Cabarets – The Showboat*; *Roadhouse Nights*, [film] Dir. unknown, UK: Pathé, 18 July 1932, reel 1058.14; reel 1100.12; *The Water Cabaret*, [film] Dir. unknown, UK: Pathé 16 July 1934. Each of these newsreels can be seen by the reader at www.britishpathe.com.
60 Marella, 'The Modern Road House: Building and Planning the New Premises', 'Choosing Your Colour Schemes', and 'Managers Must Be "Salesmen"', *Caterer and Hotel-Keeper*, 7 December 1934, 11 January and 15 February 1935; Balfour, *Society Racket*, 120.
61 *Melody Maker*, 27 April 1935; *Daily Express*, 17 September 1936; *Daily Mail*, 1 August 1933; *Gloucestershire Echo*, 16 May 1934; *London News*, 9 July 1932.
62 Hersey Interview, 'It Grew'; McMinnies, *Signpost* (1935), 178.
63 Lancaster, *Progress at Pelvis Bay*, 67.

64 McMinnies, *Signpost* (1935), 126.
65 As shown in a photograph from the opening night, Sasha/Getty Images, July 1931, #3367962.
66 McMinnies, *Signpost* (1935), 126; *Gloucestershire Echo*, 16 October 1934; Ewer, *Roadhouse*, 10, 19; *Scotsman*, 13 September 1934; *Daily Mail*, 1 August 1932.
67 S. Marella, 'The Modern Road House: Managers Must Be "Salesmen"', *Caterer and Hotel-Keeper*, 15 February 1935; McMinnies, *Signpost* (1935), 143–44, 159.
68 Alan Warwick, 'Roadhouse', *Pearson's Magazine*, October 1933, 428.
69 McMinnies, *Signpost* (1935), 172.
70 James J. Nott, *Music for the People: Popular Music and Dance in Interwar Britain* (Oxford: Oxford University Press, 2002).
71 *This Is the Life*, [film] Dir. Albert de Courville; UK: British Lion, 1933; Warwick, 'Roadhouse', 428.
72 *Outer London Clubs and Cabarets – 'The Bell'*.
73 Law, *The Experience of Suburban Modernity*.

Chapter 7

1 See Bibliography section 'Roadhouse novels'.
2 Graham Greene, *Collected Essays* (Harmondsworth: Penguin, 1969), 226.
3 David Glover, 'Wallace, (Richard Horatio) Edgar (1875–1932)', in *Oxford Dictionary of National Biography* (Oxford: Oxford University Press, 2004).
4 Robert James, *Popular Culture and Working-Class Taste in Britain, 1930–39* (Manchester: Manchester University Press, 2010), Appendix I.
5 David Glover, 'Looking for Edgar Wallace: The Author as Consumer', *History Workshop* 37, 1 (1994): 143–64; Margaret Lane, *Edgar Wallace: The Biography of a Phenomenon* (London: Book Club, 1938); Wheeler W. Dixon, 'The Colonial Vision of Edgar Wallace', *Journal of Popular Culture* 32, 1 (1998): 121–39.
6 Glover, 'Wallace', 155.
7 Edgar Wallace, *My Hollywood Diary* (London: Hutchinson and Co., 1932).
8 Edgar Wallace, *Coat of Arms* (London: Hutchinson and Co., 1932).
9 Ibid., 47.
10 Ibid., 9.
11 Ibid., 33.
12 Ibid., 82.
13 Peter Cheyney, whom some consider to be the natural successor to Wallace, wrote a number of thriller novels which were strongly Americanized and often featured roadhouses; see, for example, Peter Cheyney, *Never a Dull Moment* (London: Collins, 1942).

14 Greene, *The Confidential Agent*, 21-23.
15 Ibid., 89. 'Caste' was elite, imperial interwar slang for class.
16 Anthony Skene, *The Roadhouse Murder* (London: The Sexton Blake Library, 1933).
17 Kelly Boyd, *Manliness and the Boys' Story Paper, 1855-1940* (Basingstoke: Palgrave, 2002), 92.
18 Not to be confused with his exact namesake, a prolific TV scriptwriter, born in 1924.
19 Skene, *The Roadhouse Murder*, 8.
20 Cutforth, *Later than We Thought*, 28.
21 Much American thriller fiction of this period concentrated on the attempts to control gangsterism brought about by prohibition.
22 Skene, *The Roadhouse Murder*, 10.
23 Ibid., 9.
24 Ibid., 11.
25 The Great West Road was home to the original Ace of Spades roadhouse, so this is perhaps an allusion to that establishment.
26 Desmond Reid, *Roadhouse Girl* (London: The Sexton Blake Library, 1957), 61.
27 Ewer, *Roadhouse*; *Home Notes*, 4 August 1934.
28 W. B. Owen, 'Thompson, William Marcus (1857-1907)'. Rev. Matthew Lee, in *Oxford Dictionary of National Biography* (Oxford: Oxford University Press, 2004).
29 *Times*, 24 November 1964.
30 For example, Oxford did not admit women as full members of the university until 1920, http://www.ox.ac.uk/about/oxford-people/women-at-oxford (accessed 22 December 2015).
31 Kenneth Morgan, *Bolshevism and the British Left* (London: Lawrence & Wishart, 2006), 49.
32 Margaret Cole, *The Life of GDH Cole* (London: Macmillan, 1971), 89.
33 Clive Barker and Maggie B. Gale (eds), *British Theatre Between the Wars, 1918-1939* (Cambridge: Cambridge University Press, 2000), 176.
34 Monica Ewer, *Insecurity* (London: R. Hale & Co., 1930).
35 *Times*, 24 November 1964.
36 John Tosh, *The Pursuit of History* (Harlow: Longman, 2002), 64.
37 Rachel Anderson, *The Purple Heart Throbs: The Sub-literature of Love* (London: Hodder and Stoughton, 1974), 205.
38 Light, *Forever England*, 1991.
39 Ros Ballaster, *Women's Worlds: Ideology, Femininity and the Woman's Magazine* (London: Macmillan, 1991), 94.
40 Nicola Beauman identifies these libraries as the most likely source for women's romantic fiction in the 1930s. Nicola Beauman, *A Very Great Profession: The Woman's Novel 1914-1939* (London: Persephone, 1983).

41 Advertisement for *Roadhouse* in *Sunday Times*, 7 April 1935.
42 Ewer, *Roadhouse*, 2.
43 Ibid.
44 Claude-General Neon Lights Ltd to Oliver Hill, 9 November 1937, RIBA archive, Hio/55/6.
45 Kate Caffrey, '*37–'39: Last Look Round* (London: Gordon & Cremonesi, 1978), 13.
46 Ewer, *Roadhouse*, 2.
47 Ibid., 18.
48 See *Road Houses and Clubs of the Home Counties*.
49 Ewer, *Roadhouse*, 60, 76, 114.
50 See Chapter 5, 115.
51 Group Services Ltd to Oliver Hill, 29 December 1936, RIBA archive, Hio/55/6.
52 See Bernhard Rieger, *Technology and the Culture of Modernity in Britain and Germany, 1890–1945* (Cambridge: Cambridge University Press, 2005).
53 Ewer, *Roadhouse*, 2.
54 Ibid., 1.
55 Ibid., 34.
56 John Betjeman, 'Harrow on the Hill' in *The Best of Betjeman* (London: John Murray, 1978).
57 Gilbert and Hancock, 'New York City and the Transatlantic Imagination', 77–107.
58 Geoffrey Clayton, *Rally Round Rosalind* (London: G. G. Harrap & Co., 1938), 22.
59 Winifred Frances Peck, *They Come, They Go: The Story of an English Rectory* (London: Faber & Faber, 1937), 294.
60 Rex Warner, *The Aerodrome: A Love Story* (Harmondsworth: Penguin, 1941).
61 Ewer, *Roadhouse*, 1.
62 Ibid., 18.
63 See Marshall Berman, *All That Is Solid Melts into Air: The Experience of Modernity* (New York: Simon and Schuster, 1983).
64 Ewer, *Roadhouse*, 25.
65 O'Connell, *The Car and British Society*; Law, 'The Car Indispensable', 424–33.
66 Ewer, *Roadhouse*, 34.
67 Ibid.
68 Ibid., 207.
69 Marc Augé, *Non-places: Introduction to an Anthropology of Supermodernity* (London: Verso, 1995).
70 Ewer, *Roadhouse*, 29.
71 Ibid., 19.
72 Michael Shelden, 'Greene (Henry) Graham (1904–1991)' in *Oxford Dictionary of National Biography* (Oxford: Oxford University Press, 2004).
73 Ewer, *Roadhouse*, 78.
74 *Outer London Clubs and Cabarets – The Bell*.

75 Ewer, *Roadhouse*, 12.
76 Ibid., 34.
77 John Carey, *The Intellectuals and the Masses: Pride and Prejudice Among the Literary Intelligentsia, 1880–1939* (London: Faber, 1992).
78 Ewer, *Roadhouse*, 19.
79 Ibid., 27.
80 *Outer London Clubs and Cabarets – The Showboat.*
81 Hoare, *This Our Country*, 36.
82 Ewer, *Roadhouse*, 125.

Chapter 8

1 *Hotel and Catering Weekly*, 23 June 1933; Burke, *London in My Time*, 199.
2 Thomas Burke, *English Night-Life* (London: B. T. Batsford, 1941), 141.
3 *Caterer and Hotel-Keeper*, 5 October 1934.
4 *Luncheon & Tea Room Journal*, December 1935.
5 Ewer, *Roadhouse*, 136.
6 *Times*, 24 June 1932, 28 August, 4 and 19 September 1934, and 26 February and 5 March 1935.
7 Elsa Dundas, 'I Run a Roadhouse', *Daily Mirror*, 22 May 1935.
8 *Evening News*, 26 July 1933.
9 *Times*, 25 February 1937 and 17 August 1938.
10 *Road Houses and Clubs of the Home Counties*, 3. Another unspecified roadhouse in the south-east opened in May 1936, and within months changed hands with lower prices advertised (*Kent & Sussex Courier*, 21 August 1936).
11 *Observer*, 31 March 1935; *Road Houses and Clubs of the Home Counties*, 4, 26; McMinnies, *Signpost* (1935), 142–43.
12 This sounds like one pub visiting another. For a history of London's *jeunesse d'orée*, see Taylor, *Bright Young People*.
13 *Surrey Comet*, 28 October 1933.
14 Cutforth, *Later than We Thought.*
15 Light, *Forever England.*
16 Cyril James, 'If I had been a Cad', *Daily Mirror*, 2 December 1936.
17 Priestley, *English Journey* 401.
18 *Caterer and Hotel-Keeper*, 7 July 1939; 'Jack Isow, (Joseph Aaron Isowitzky), the Thatched Barn', *Gazette*, 21 April 1939.
19 *Caterer and Hotel-Keeper*, 7 July 1939; McMinnies, *Signpost*, 3rd ed. (1937), 333; Barclay, Perkins & Co., Minute Books of the Board of Directors, Acc. 2307/7/1, 1937, London Metropolitan Archives; *Anchor Magazine* 17 (July 1937): 151–52, 154.

20 McMinnies, *Signpost* (1935), 137; Marella, 'The Modern Road House: What a Swimming Pool Needs', *Evening News*, 26 July 1933; George Long, *English Inns and Road-Houses* (London: Werner Laurie, 1937), 181; *Hotel & Catering Weekly*, 5 and 12 July 1935; also see *Times*, 25 June and 2 July 1935, and 11 and 15 February 1937.
21 *Times*, 11 and 15 February 1937; also see *Times*, 25 June and 2 July 1935; *Chelmsford Chronicle*, 19 August 1938.
22 *Times*, 11 and 15 February 1937.
23 Margery Allingham, *The Fashion in Shrouds* (London: Heinemann, 1938), 17.
24 *Caterer and Hotel-Keeper*, 15 November 1935.
25 Ibid., 13 August 1937.
26 Ibid., 10 September 1937; *Times*, 11 February 1937.
27 Ewer, *Roadhouse*, 125, 173.
28 McMinnies, *Signpost* (1935), 172, and 3rd ed. (1937), 332; *Brewer & Wine Merchant*, May 1938.
29 *Times*, 4 May and 24 August 1938, and 16 March 1939; *Aberdeen Press and Journal*, 26 January 1938.
30 *Road Houses of the Home Counties*, 36–37; *Anchor Magazine* 19 (1939): 84–85, 197; Style & Winch, Estates Ledger, AE/E/1, Heineken UK Archives, 14 June 1938.
31 *Anchor Magazine* 16 (April 1936): 98; Barclay, Perkins & Co., Estate Reports Books, Heineken UK Archives, AI/E/15, 6 June 1935.
32 *Caterer and Hotel-Keeper*, 17 June 1938; Barclay, Perkins & Co., Estate Reports Books, AI/E/16, 2 November 1936.
33 *A Monthly Bulletin* 28 (January 1957): 4–5.
34 Gutzke, *Pubs and Progressives*.
35 *Caterer and Hotel-Keeper*, 9 September 1933 and 30 October 1936; Clive Aslet, 'Refueling', 21; *Pennant*, April 1932, 14; *Hotel Review*, February 1937.
36 McMinnies, *Signpost* (1935); Long, *English Inns*, 183–84; Porter, 'Swimming Pools Are "Booming" – Are You Profiting By It?'.
37 McMinnies, *Signpost* (1935), 136–82; 4th ed. (1938).
38 *Scotsman*, 5 July 1945. Two well-known roadhouses had already disappeared forever. The White Rabbit, opened in 1935 in Surrey, declared bankruptcy in 1943. More surprisingly, in that same year, the Nautical William, a palatial Shropshire roadhouse, apparently had no takers for its £30,000 original premises, and so went to auction.
39 It later became a button factory, and remains in light commercial use today.
40 Fredric Boyce, *SOE: The Scientific Secrets* (Stroud: The History Press Ltd, 2003), 22.
41 Francis Walley, 'Prestressing', in R. J. M. Sutherland, Dawn Humm and Mike Chrimes (eds), *Historic Concrete: Background to Appraisal* (London: Thomas Telford Publishing, 2001), 191–210.
42 The National Archives, Letter from Board of Trade to Ministry of Works, 26 September 1949, WORK 17/266.
43 Bennetts, 'Why Roadhouse?'.

44 Greene, *The Confidential Agent*, 12, 14.
45 Marella, 'The Modern Road House: Managers Must Be "Salesmen"'.
46 McKibbin, *Classes and Cultures*, 2.
47 Ibid., 23–24, 29, 33, 42–3.
48 Marella, 'The Modern Road House: Managers Must Be "Salesmen"'.
49 In *Thrones, Dominations,* Lord Peter is already by 1936 a careful and attentive property developer, a change that must have come as a surprise to the ghost of Dorothy Sayers (Dorothy L. Sayers and Jill Paton Walsh, *Thrones, Dominations* (New York: St. Martin's, 1998)).
50 We are grateful to Trevor Lloyd for these insights.
51 McMinnies, *Signpost*, 1st ed. (1935), 159; *Western Daily Press*, 11 October 1947; *Times*, 16 September 1937.
52 *Daily Mail*, 11 June 1945.
53 *Times*, 6 January 1948 and 22 August 1967.
54 Ibid., 26 August 1960.
55 Ibid., 13 September 1941.
56 McMinnies, *Signpost* (4th ed., 1938), 329.
57 *Times*, Advertisements, 1941–67.
58 *Dundee Courier Advertiser*, 12 June 1950.
59 *Daily Mail*, 9 July 1949.
60 Ibid.
61 www.bbc.co.uk/history/domesday/dblock/GB-512000-195000/page/6 (accessed 15 December 2015).
62 McMinnies, *Signpost,* 2nd ed. (1936), 243, and *Signpost*, 12th ed. (1951).
63 Gutzke, *Women Drinking Out in Britain Since the Early Twentieth Century*, 70, 278.
64 Ibid.
65 John Burnett, *Liquid Pleasures: A Social History of Drinks in Modern Britain* (London: Routledge, 1999), 89, 91.
66 Ibid., 72; Gutzke, *Women Drinking Out*, 132–33; Harry Hopkins, *The New Look: A Social History of the Forties and Fifties in Britain* (New York: Houghton Mifflin, 1969), 459, 461.
67 Kate Bradley, 'Rational Recreation in the Age of Affluence: The Café and Working-Class Youth in London, c.1939–65', in Erika Rappaport, Sandra Trudgen Dawson and Mark J. Crowley (eds), *Consuming Behaviours: Identity, Politics and Pleasure in Twentieth-Century Britain* (London: Bloomsbury Academic, 2015), 73, 75–76.
68 Diana Dors was, in the early 1950s, a buxom British film starlet, platinum blond and Americanized in appearance, who had recently married Denis Hamilton. Paraphrased from www.surbiton.com/forum/ace-spades-history, 2012, (accessed 11 January 2016).
69 Ewer, *Roadhouse*, 125, 173.
70 Bennetts, 'Why Roadhouse?'.

Chapter 9

1. Anon., *Road Houses and Clubs of the Home Counties*.
2. McMinnies, *Signpost* (1935), 142–43.
3. Gutzke, *Pubs and Progressives*, 168. Brewers had begun building superpubs along major by pass and trunk roads since the mid-1920s (Gutzke, *Pubs and Progressives*, appendix 3).
4. *Western Morning News*, 18 May 1936. Isow had been rebuffed in the presence of his wife, 'a Society girl' (*Western Daily Press*, 9 August 1934).
5. *Times*, 12 January and 1 November 1937; Benskin's Watford Brewery, Minutes of General Meetings, Punch Taverns, C/V/188; Aslet, 'Refuelling the Body, the Soul and the Morris Road Houses of the 1920s and 1930s', 24.
6. Gutzke, *Pubs and Progressives*, 210–11.
7. Ewer, *Roadhouse*, 125, 173.
8. Save for Jack Isow at the Thatched Barn, who was a leading Soho figure.

Appendix

1. *Hotel and Boarding House*, June 1934.
2. *Caterer and Hotel-Keeper*, 23 April 1937.
3. *Western Daily Press*, 26 March 1947.
4. McMinnies, *Signpost* (1935), 141.
5. *Aberdeen Journal*, 26 January 1938.
6. *Caterer and Hotel-Keeper*, 4 October 1935.
7. *Hotel Review*, September 1935; McMinnies, *Signpost* (1935), 140.
8. *Caterer and Hotel-Keeper*, 19 July 1935.
9. *Caterer and Hotel-Keeper*, 30 October 1936.
10. *Caterer and Hotel-Keeper*, 12 June 1936.
11. *Caterer and Hotel-Keeper*, 6 January 1939.
12. *Herne Bay Press*, 5 February 1938.

Bibliography

Primary sources

Archives

British Film Institute.
Heineken UK Archives.
Hertfordshire Record Office.
London Metropolitan Archives.
Parliamentary Archives.
RIBA Archive.
Somersetshire Record Office.
The National Archives.
The National Archives.
The National Archives.
V&A RIBA Drawings Collection.

Articles published before 1960

Baguley, M. 'The Art of Increasing Bar Trade', *Bartender*, 2 (October 1935).
Baguley, M. 'Better and Brighter Bars', *Bartender*, 2 (November 1935).
Bennetts, Arthur E. 'Why Roadhouse?' *Luncheon and Tea Room Journal* (November 1935): 300–1.
Binford, Jessie F. 'Cook County (Illinois) Roadhouses', *Journal of Hygiene*, 16 (1930): 257–64.
Binford, Jessie F. 'May We Present the Road House? A Survey of Existing Conditions in Cook County', *Welfare Magazine*, 18 (1927): 872–80.
Clarke, W.R. 'The "Popular" Road and Guest House, Leigh-on-Sea', *Luncheon and Tea Room Journal* (December 1935): 325.
Dundas, Elsa. 'I Run a Roadhouse', *Daily Mirror* (22 May 1935).
Fairfax, Beatrice. 'Advice to the Lovelorn', *Lebanon Daily News* (27 December 1926).
Fitzpatrick, J. 'One of the Brigade', *Bartender*, 4 (January 1938).
Graves, Charles. 'The Bathing Boom', *Nash's Pall Mall Gazette* (August 1934).
Hapgood, Hutchins. 'McSorley's Saloon', *Harper's Weekly*, 58 (25 October 1913): 15–17.
Hill, Joseph. 'Licensed Houses – The Inn and the Road House', *Architectural Association Journal* (April 1937): 413–21.

Lezard, Adele. 'There is Big Money in Tea Gardens', *Hotel & Catering Weekly* (26 April 1935).

Marella, S. 'The Modern Road House: Building and Planning the New Premises', *Caterer and Hotel-Keeper* (7 December 1934).

Marella, S. 'The Modern Roadhouse: Choosing your Colour Schemes', *Caterer and Hotel-Keeper* (11 January 1935).

Marella, S. 'The Modern Roadhouse: Managers Must Be "Salesmen"', *Caterer and Hotel-Keeper* (15 February 1935).

Marella, S. 'The Modern Roadhouse: Success Depends on the Site', *Caterer and Hotel-Keeper* (30 November 1934).

Marella, S. 'What a Swimming Pool Needs', *Caterer and Hotel-Keeper* (1 February 1935).

Mayo, Earl. 'The Americanization of England', *Forum*, 32 (January 1902): 566–72.

Money, Mary Hermione, 'A Successful Venture: John and Mary's Road House, Black Corner, Crawley, Sussex', *Luncheon and Tea Room Journal* (May 1936): 146.

Myers, Garry C. 'Roadhouse Menace to Young Folk', *Hammond Times* (8 October 1935).

Pemberton, Sir Max. 'The Road House – What of It?', *True Temperance Quarterly* (8 November 1934): 5.

Piper, John. 'Fully Licensed', *Architectural Review* (March 1940): 87–100.

Porte, Charles. 'The Planning of Public Houses', *Journal of the Institute of Brewing*, 40 (1934): 32–5.

Porter, Ernest M. 'Swimming Pools are "Booming" – Are You Profiting By It?' *Caterer and Hotel-Keeper* (28 June 1935).

Smith, Lady Pamela. 'Home Notes', *Essex Newsman* (11 November 1933).

Warren, Maud Radford. 'The House of Youth', *Burlington Hawk-Eye* (7 December 1924).

Williams, J. 'The Roadhouse in Winter', *Hotel and Catering Weekly* (19 November 1933).

Williams-Ellis, Clough. 'The Future of Swimming Pools', *Hotel Review* (January 1935): 41–3.

Worsley-Gough, Barbara. 'The Road House Age' *Spectator* (24 August 1934): 252

Books published before 1960

Abercrombie, Patrick. *Greater London Plan 1944*. London: HMSO, 1945.

Anon. *Road Houses and Clubs of the Home Counties*. London: Sylvan Publications, 1934.

Architecture Club. *Recent English Architecture, 1920–1940*. London: Country Life, 1947.

Balfour, Patrick. *Society Racket*. London: J. Long, 1933.

Brown, Ivor. *The Heart of England*. London: B. T. Batsford, 1935.

Burke, Thomas. *English Night-Life*. London: B. T. Batsford, 1941.

Burke, Thomas. *London in My Time*. London: Rich & Cowan, 1934.

Clunn, Harold P. *The Face of the Home Counties*. London: Simpkin Marshall, 1936.

Cressey, Paul G. *The Taxi-Dance Hall: A Sociological Study in Commercialized Recreation and City Life*. Chicago: University of Chicago Press, 1932.
Grahame, Kenneth. *The Wind in the Willows*. London: Methuen, 1908.
Graves, Robert and Hodge, Alan. *The Long Week-End: A Social History of Great Britain 1918–1939*. London: Faber and Faber, 1941.
Hoare, Rawden. *This Our Country: An Impression After Fourteen Years Abroad*. London: John Murray, 1935.
Jeffreys, Rees. *The King's Highway*. London: Batchworth Press, 1949.
Kelly's Directory of the County of Hertfordshire for 1937. London: Kelly's Directories Limited, 1937.
Lancaster, Osbert. *Pillar to Post*. London: John Murray, 1939.
Lancaster, Osbert. *Progress at Pelvis Bay*. London: John Murray, 1936.
Lane, Margaret. *Edgar Wallace: The Biography of a Phenomenon*. London: The Book Club, 1938.
Long, George. *English Inns and Road-Houses*. London: Werner Laurie, 1937.
McMinnies, W. G. *Signpost: An Independent Guide to Pleasant Ports of Call*, 2nd–16th eds. (London: Simpkin, Marshall, 1936–55).
McMinnies, W. G. *Signpost to the Road Houses, Country Clubs and Better and Brighter Inns and Hotels of England*. London: Simpkin Marshall, 1935.
Meyrick, Eve. *Secrets of the 43*. London: John Long, 1933.
Morton, H. V. *In Search of England*. London: Methuen, 1927.
Muggeridge, Malcolm. *The Thirties*. London: Hamish Hamilton, 1940.
Oliver, Basil. *The Renaissance of the English Public House*. London: Faber and Faber, 1947.
Orwell, George. *The Lion and the Unicorn*. London: Secker and Warburg, 1941.
Priestley, J. B. *English Journey*. London: Heinemann, 1934.
Prioleau, John. *Motoring for Women*. London: Geoffrey Bles, 1925.
Rhondda, Viscountess. *Leisured Women*. London: The Hogarth Press, 1928.
RIBA. *Rebuilding Britain*. London: Lund Humphries, 1943.
Society of Motor Manufacturers and Traders. *The Motor Industry of Great Britain 1937*. London: SMMT, 1937.
Society of Motor Manufacturers and Traders. *The Motor Industry of Great Britain 1939*. London: SMMT, 1939.
Tomlinson, Commander A. *Tales from a Roadhouse*. St. Leonards-on-Sea: King Brothers & Potts, [1937] 1954.
Unwin, Raymond. 'Memorandum No. 2', *Greater London Planning Committee Report*. London: HMSO, 1929.
Vecchi, Joseph. *The Tavern Is My Drum*. London: Odhams Press, 1948.
Wallace, Edgar. *My Hollywood Diary*. London: Hutchinson and Co., 1932.
Waugh, Evelyn. *Vile Bodies*. London: Chapman & Hall, 1930.
Williams, Ernest Edwin. *The New Public-House*. London: Chapman and Hall, 1924.
Williams-Ellis, Clough. *England and the Octopus*. London: Geoffrey Bles, 1928.

Williams-Ellis, Clough and Keynes, John Maynard. *Britain and the Beast*. London: Dent, 1937.
Williams-Ellis, Clough and Summerson, John N. *Architecture Here and Now*. London: Thomas Nelson & Sons, 1934.
Wyndham, Horace. *Nights in London*. London: John Lane, 1926.

Memoirs

Cutforth, René. *Later than We Thought: A Portrait of the Thirties*. Newton Abbot: David & Charles, 1976.
Whiteing, Eileen. *Anyone for Tennis? Growing-Up in Wallington Between the Wars*. London: London Borough of Sutton Libraries & Arts Services, 1979.

Roadhouse novels and short stories

Allingham, Margery. *The Case of the Late Pig*. London: Penguin, [1937] 1983.
Allingham, Margery. *The Fashion in Shrouds*. London: Heinemann, 1938.
Arlen, Michael. *The Green Hat*. London: Collins, 1924.
Blake, Nicholas. *Thou Shell of Death*. New York: Harper & Row, [1936] 1977.
Cheyney, Peter. *Never a Dull Moment*. London: Collins, 1942.
Clarke, T. E. B. *Jeremy's England*. London: John Long, 1934.
Clayton, Geoffrey. *Rally Round Rosalind*. London: G. G. Harrap & Co., 1938.
Cole, G. D. H. *Counterpoint Murder*. London: Collins, 1940.
Early, Eleanor. *Whirlwind*. Chicago: White House, 1928.
Ewer, Monica. *Insecurity*. London: R. Hale & Co., 1930.
Ewer, Monica. *Roadhouse*. London: Sampson Low & Co., 1935.
Fitzgerald, F. Scott. *This Side of Paradise*. New York: Scribners, 1920.
Greene, Graham. *Brighton Rock*. Harmondsworth: Penguin, [1938] 1970.
Greene, Graham. *The Confidential Agent*. London: Heinemann, 1939.
Hamilton, Patrick. *The Siege of Pleasure*. London: Constable, 1932.
Hammett, Dashiell. *Red Harvest*. New York: Alfred A. Knopt, [1929] 2000.
Moore, Margery. *Unsteady Flame*. London: Mills and Boon, 1937.
Peck, Winifred Frances. *They Come, They Go: The Story of an English Rectory*. London: Faber & Faber, 1937.
Powell, Anthony. *Hearing Secret Harmonies*. London: Arrow, [1977] 2005.
Priestley, J. B. *Let the People Sing*. London: Heinemann, 1939.
Reid, Desmond. *Roadhouse Girl*. London: The Sexton Blake Library, 1957.
Skene, Anthony. *The Roadhouse Murder*. London: The Sexton Blake Library, 1933.
Wallace, Edgar. *The Coat of Arms*. London: Hutchinson and Co., 1932.
Warner, Rex. *The Aerodrome: A Love Story*. Harmondsworth: Penguin, 1941.
Williams, Valentine. 'The Dot-and-Carry Case', in *The Curiosity of Mr. Treadgold*. Boston: Houghton Mifflin Co., 1937.

Roadhouse plays

Furber, Douglas. *Wild Oats*, 1938.
Hackett, Walter. *Road House: A Play in Three Acts*. London: Samuel French, 1934.
Rhode, John. *What Happened at 8:20?*, BBC Radio, 1938.
Williams, Emlyn. *Night Must Fall*, 1934.

Roadhouse movies (not necessarily consulted)

Band Waggon. [film], Dir. Marcel Varnel; UK: Gainsborough Studios, 1940.
Confession. [film], Dir. Ken Hughes; UK: Anglo Guild Productions, 1955.
Hot Water. [film], Dir. Frank R. Strayer; USA: Twentieth Century Fox, 1937.
Mad Hour. [film], Dir. Joseph C. Boyle; USA: First National Pictures, 1928.
Marilyn (*Roadhouse Girl*, in the United States). [film], Dir. Wolf Rilla; UK: Nettlefold Films, 1953.
Money Means Nothing. [film], Dir. Christy Cabanne; USA: Monogram Pictures, 1934.
Road House. [film], Dir. Richard Rosson; USA: Fox Film Corporation, 1928.
Roadhouse. [film], Dir. Jean Negulesco; USA: Twentieth Century Fox, 1948.
Roadhouse. [film], Dir. Maurice Elvey; UK: Gainsborough Studios, 1934.
Roadhouse Nights. [film], Dir. Hobart Henley; USA: Paramount Studios, 1930.
Roadhouse Queen. [film], Dir. Lesley Pearce; USA: Mack Sennett Comedies, 1933.
Rolled Stockings. [film], Dir. Richard Rosson; USA: Paramount Famous Lasky Corporation, 1927.
San Antonio Rose. [film], Dir. Charles Lamont; USA: Universal Pictures, 1941.
The Delicious Little Devil. [film], USA, Dir. Robert Z. Leonard; Universal Film Manufacturing Company, 1919.
The Road to Ruin. [film], Dir. Dorothy Davenport; USA: Cliff Broughton Productions, 1928.
The Roadhouse Murder. [film], Dir. J. Walter Ruben; USA: RKO Radio Pictures, 1932.
The Secluded Roadhouse. [film], Dir. unknown; USA: Fred Balshofer Productions, 1926.
The Wild Party. [film], Dir. Dorothy Arzner; USA: Paramount Studios, 1929.
This Is the Life. [film], Dir. Albert de Courville; UK: British Lion, 1933.
Why Be Good? [film], Dir. William A. Seiter; USA: Warner Brothers, 1929.
Youth Runs Wild. [film], Dir. Mark Robson; USA: RKO Radio Pictures, 1944.

Roadhouse newsreels

London's Famous Clubs and Cabarets – The Ace of Spades Club, [film] Dir. unknown, UK: Pathé, 24 April 1933, reel 1072.14.
Outer London Clubs and Cabarets – The Ace of Spades, [film] Dir. unknown, UK: Pathé, 7 August 1933, reel 1086.02.
Outer London Clubs and Cabarets – The Bell, [film] Dir. unknown, UK: Pathé, 17 July 1933, reel 1076.07.

Outer London Clubs and Cabarets – The Hungaria River Club – Maidenhead, [film] Dir. unknown, UK: Pathé (1933), reel 1088.05.
Outer London Clubs and Cabarets – The Showboat, [film] Dir. unknown, UK: Pathé, 18 September 1933, reel 1088.18.
Roadhouse Nights, [film] Dir. unknown, UK: Pathé, 18 July 1932, reel 1058.14.
The Order of the Bath, [film] Dir. unknown, UK: Pathé, 8 August 1938, reel 1174.06.
The Water Cabaret, [film] Dir. unknown, UK: Pathé, 16 July 1934, reel 1100.12.

Other films and television programmes

The Girl Who Was Death, [film] Dir. David Tomblin, UK: ITC Entertainment, 18 January 1968.
The Private Life of Henry VIII, [film] Dir. A. Korda, UK: London Film Productions, 1933.

Magazines and journals

Anchor Magazine.
Architectural Review.
Autocar.
Bartender.
Brewer and Wine Merchant.
Builder.
Caterer and Hotel-Keeper.
Design for Today.
English Review.
Fellowship.
Flight.
Forum.
Harper's Weekly.
Holiday.
Hotel and Boarding House.
Hotel & Catering Weekly.
Hotel Review.
Licensed Victuallers' Gazette.
Luncheon and Tea Room Journal.
Melody Maker.
Motor Trader.
Pearson's Magazine.
Pennant.
RIBA Journal.

Smart Set: True Stories from Real Life.
Spectator.
True Temperance Quarterly.
Welfare Magazine.
Wine and Spirit Trade Review.

Newspapers

Aberdeen Journal.
Albuquerque Journal.
Atlanta Constitution.
Atlantic News–Telegraph.
Burlington Hawk-Eye.
Capital Times.
Charleston Gazette.
Chelmsford Chronicle.
Daily Mail.
Daily Mirror.
Dover Express.
Dundee Courier Advertiser.
Edwardsville Intelligencer.
Essex Newsman.
Evening Independent.
Evening News.
Evening Telegraph.
Gettysburg Times.
Gleaner.
Gloucestershire Echo.
Hammond Times.
Hastings & St. Leonard's Observer.
Herne Bay Press.
Herts Advertiser.
Indianapolis (Indiana) Star.
Kingsport Times.
Lebanon Daily News.
Lima News.
London Gazette.
Lowell Sun.
Maidenhead Advertiser.
Manchester Guardian.
Montana Standard.
Nash's Pall Mall Gazette.

New Castle News.
New York Times.
Newport Mercury and Weekly News.
Nottingham Evening Post.
Observer.
Odgen Standard-Examiner.
Olean Times.
Oshkosh Daily Northwestern.
Oxnard Daily Courier.
Roswell Daily Record.
Salt Lake Tribune.
Scotsman.
Sheboygan Press.
Surrey Comet.
Syracuse Herald.
Times.
Titusville Herald.
Washington Times.
Waterloo Daily Courier.
Wells Journal and Somerset and West of England Advertiser.
West Herts & Watford Observer.
Western Daily Press.
Yorkshire Evening Post.

Theses from the period

Russell, Daniel. 'The Roadhouse: A Study of Commercialized Amusements in the Environs of Chicago'. Unpublished Master's dissertation, University of Chicago, 1931.

Secondary sources

Journal articles

Andrassy, Hannah. 'Spinning a Golden Thread: The Introduction of Elastic into Swimwear', *Things*, 5 (1996–97): 75–76.

Brassard, Genevieve. 'Fast and Loose in Interwar London: Mobility and Sexuality in Elizabeth Bowen's to the North', *Women: A Cultural Review*, 18, 3 (2007): 282–302.

Bryant, Rebecca A. 'Shaking Things Up: Popularizing the Shimmy in America', *American Music*, 20 (2002): 168–87.

Cunningham, Patricia. 'Swimwear in the Thirties: The BVD Company in a Decade of Innovation', *Dress*, 12 (1986): 11–27.

Davies, Andrew. 'The Scottish Chicago?: From "Hooligans" to "Gangsters" in Inter-War Glasgow', *Cultural and Social History*, 4, 4 (2007): 511–27.

Dixon, Wheeler W. 'The Colonial Vision of Edgar Wallace', *The Journal of Popular Culture*, 32, 1 (1998): 121–39.

Gilbert, David and Hancock, Claire. 'New York City and the Transatlantic Imagination: French and English Tourism and the Spectacle of the Modern Metropolis, 1893–1939', *Journal of Urban History*, 33, 1 (2006): 77–107.

Glover, David. 'Looking for Edgar Wallace: The Author as Consumer', *History Workshop*, 37, 1 (1994): 143–64.

Gutzke, David W. 'Gender, Class, and Public Drinking in Britain During the First World War', *Historie Sociale/Social History*, 27 (1994): 367–91.

Gutzke, David W. 'Progressivism and the History of the Public House, 1850–1950', *Cultural and Social History*, 4 (2007): 235–59.

Gutzke, David W. 'Sydney Nevile: Squire in the Slums or Progressive Brewer?' *Business History* 53 (2011): 960–69.

Horwood, Catherine. '"Girls Who Arouse Dangerous Passions": Women and Bathing, 1900–39', *Women's History Review*, 9 (2000): 653–73.

Law, Michael John. '"The Car Indispensable": The Hidden Influence of the Car in Interwar Suburban London', *Journal of Historical Geography*, 38, 4 (2013): 424–33.

Law, Michael John. 'Speed and Blood on the Bypass: The New Automobilities of Interwar London', *Urban History*, 39, 3 (2012): 490–509.

Law, Michael John. '"Stopping to Dream": The Beautification and Vandalism of London's Interwar Arterial Roads', *London Journal*, 35, 1 (2010): 58–84.

Law, Michael John. 'Turning Night into Day: Transgression and Americanization at the English Interwar Roadhouse', *Journal of Historical Geography*, 35, 3 (2009): 473–94.

Ling, Peter. 'Sex and the Automobile in the Jazz Age', *History Today*, 39, November (1989): 18–20.

McGovern, James R. 'The American Woman's Pre-World War I, Freedom in Manners and Morals', *Journal of American History*, 55 (1968): 315–33.

Murphy, Mary. 'Bootlegging Mothers and Drinking Daughters: Gender and Prohibition in Butte, Montana', *American Quarterly*, 46 (1994): 174–94.

Nieuwenhuis, Paul and Wells, Peter. 'The All-Steel Body as a Cornerstone to the Foundations of the Mass Production Car Industry', *Industrial and Corporate Change*, 16, 2 (2007): 183–211.

Postgate, Raymond. 'English Drinking Habits', *Holiday*, 33 (February 1963): 87–88.

Settle, Louise. 'The Kosmo Club Case: Clandestine Prostitution During the Interwar Period', *Twentieth-Century British History*, 25, 4 (2014): 562–84.

Shore, Heather. '"Constable Dances with Instructress": The Police and the Queen of Nightclubs in Interwar London', *Social History*, 38 (2013): 183–202.

Urry, John. *Automobility, Car Culture and Weightless Travel: A Discussion Paper*, Lancaster: Lancaster University, 1999, unpaginated.
Waters, Chris. 'Beyond "Americanization": Rethinking Anglo-American Cultural Exchange Between the Wars', *Cultural and Social History*, 4, 4 (2007): 451–59.

Books

Adinolfi, Francesco. *Mondo Exotica: Sounds, Visions, Obsessions of the Cocktail Generation*. Durham: Duke University Press, 2008.
Anderson, Rachel. *The Purple Heart Throbs: The Sub-Literature of Love*. London: Hodder and Stoughton, 1974.
Atwell, David. *Cathedrals of the Movies: A History of British Cinemas and Their Audiences*. London: Architectural Press, 1980.
Augé, Marc. *Non-places: Introduction to an Anthropology of Supermodernity*. London: Verso, 1995.
Ballaster, Ros. *Women's Worlds: Ideology, Femininity and the Woman's Magazine*. London: Macmillan, 1991.
Barker, Clive and Gale, Maggie B. (eds) *British Theatre Between the Wars, 1918–1939*. Cambridge: Cambridge University Press, 2000.
Baughman, Judith S. (ed.) *American Decades, 1920–29*. New York: A Manley Inc., 1996.
Beauman, Nicola. *A Very Great Profession: The Woman's Novel, 1914–1939*. London: Persephone, 1983.
Beaven, Brad. *Leisure, Citizenship and Working-Class Men in Britain, 1850–1945*. Manchester: Manchester University Press, 2005.
Belasco, Warren J. *Americans on the Road: From Autocamp to Motel, 1910–1945*. Cambridge, MA: MIT Press, 1979.
Benton, Charlotte, Benton, Tim and Wood, Ghislaine (eds) *Art Deco 1910–1939*. London: V&A Publications, 2003.
Berman, Marshall. *All That Is Solid Melts into Air: The Experience of Modernity*. New York: Simon and Schuster, 1983.
Blanke, David. *Hell on Wheels: The Promise and Peril of America's Car Culture 1900–1940*. Lawrence: University Press of Kansas, 2007.
Blocker, Jack S., Fahey, David M. and Tyrrell, Ian R. (eds) *Alcohol and Temperance in Modern History: An International Encyclopedia*. Santa Barbara: ABC-CLIO, 2003.
Bolton, Paul, et al. *Agriculture: Historical Statistics Standard Note: SN/SG/3339*. London: HMSO, 2015.
Boyce, Frederic. *SOE: The Scientific Secrets*. Stroud: The History Press, 2003.
Boyd, Kelly. *Manliness and the Boys' Story Paper, 1855–1940*. Basingstoke: Palgrave, 2002.
Buchanan, Colin. *London Road Plans, 1900–1970*. London: Greater London Council, 1970.

Burnett, John. *A Social History of Housing, 1815–1985*. London: Methuen, 1986.

Caffrey, Kate. *'37-'39: Last Look Round*. London: Gordon & Cremonesi, 1978.

Campbell, Neil, Davies, Jude and McKay, George (eds) *Issues in Americanization and Culture*. Edinburgh: Edinburgh University Press, 2004.

Carey, John. *The Intellectuals and the Masses: Pride and Prejudice Among the Literary Intelligentsia, 1880–1939*. London: Faber, 1992.

Clapson, Mark. *Suburban Century: Social Change and Urban Growth in England and the United States*. Oxford: Berg, 2003.

Cole, Margaret. *The Life of GDH Cole*. London: Macmillan, 1971.

Costigliola, Frank. *Awkward Dominion: American Political, Economic, and Cultural Relations with Europe, 1919–1933*. Ithaca, NY: Cornell University Press, 1984.

De Grazia, Victoria. *Irresistible Empire: America's Advance Through Twentieth-Century Europe*. London: Belknap, 2005.

D'Emilio, John and Freedman, Estelle B. *Intimate Matters: A History of Sexuality in America*. Chicago: University of Chicago Press, 1997.

Delgado, Alan. *The Annual Outing and Other Excursions*. London: Allen and Unwin, 1977.

Duis, Perry R. *The Saloon: Public Drinking in Chicago and Boston, 1880–1920*. Urban: University of Illinois Press, 1983.

Erenberg, Lewis A. *Steppin' Out: New York Nightlife and the Transformation of American Culture, 1890–1930*. Westport, CT: Greenwood, 1981.

Gardiner, Juliet. *The Thirties: An Intimate History*. London: Harper, 2010.

Glancy, Mark. *Hollywood and the Americanization of Britain: From the 1920s to the Present*. London: I. B. Tauris, 2014.

Gloversmith, Frank. *Class, Culture and Social Change: A New View of the 1930's*. Brighton: Harvester, 1980.

Gray, Richard and Cinema Theatre Association. *Cinemas in Britain: One Hundred Years of Cinema Architecture*. London: Lund Humphries, 1996.

Greenaway, John R. *Drink and British Politics Since 1830: A Study in Policy Making*. Basingstoke: Palgrave Macmillan, 2003.

Greene, Graham. *Collected Essays*. Harmondsworth: Penguin, 1969.

Gutzke, David W. *Pubs and Progressives: Reinventing the Public House in England, 1896–1960*. DeKalb: Northern Illinois University, 2006.

Gutzke, David W. *Women Drinking Out in Britain Since the Early Twentieth Century*. Manchester: Manchester University Press, 2014.

Haslam, Richard. *Clough Williams-Ellis*. London: Academy Editions, 1996.

Henry, Ian (ed.) *Leisure in Different Worlds, vol. 1: Leisure: Modernity, Postmodernity and Lifestyles*. London: LSA, 1994.

Hern, Anthony. *The Seaside Holiday. The History of the English Seaside Resort*. London: Cresset Press, 1967.

Horn, Pamela. *Women in the 1920s*. Stroud: Alan Sutton, 1995.

Hough, Richard. *Ace of Clubs*. London: Deutsch, 1986.

Houlbrook, Matt. *Queer London: Perils and Pleasures in the Sexual Metropolis, 1918–57*. Chicago: University of Chicago Press, 2005.
Humphries, Steve. *A Secret World of Sex: Forbidden Fruit: The British Experience 1900–1950*. London: Sidgwick & Jackson, 1988.
Hutchinson, Iain. *The Flight of the Starling*. Erskine: Kea, 1992.
Jackson, Alan A. *The Middle Classes, 1900–1950*. Nairn: David St. John Thomas, 1991.
Jackson, Alan A. *Semi-Detached London: Suburban Development, Life and Transport, 1900–39*. London: Allen and Unwin, 1973.
James, Robert. *Popular Culture and Working-Class Taste in Britain, 1930–39*. Manchester: Manchester University Press, 2010.
Jensen, Joan M. and Scharf, Lois (eds) *Decades of Discontent: The Women's Movement, 1920–40*. Boston: Northeastern University Press, 1987.
Jones, Stephen G. *Workers at Play: A Social and Economic History of Leisure, 1918–1939*. London: Routledge & Kegan Paul, 1986.
Kane, Josephine. *The Architecture of Pleasure: British Amusement Parks, 1900–1939*. Farnham: Routledge, 2013.
Kinross [John Patrick Douglas Balfour]. *The Kindred Spirit: A History of Gin and of the House of Booth*. London: Newman Neame, 1959.
Kupfermann, Elias and Dixon-Smith, Carol. *Maidenhead Through Time*. Stroud: Amberley Publishing, 2014.
Laver, James. *Between the Wars*. Boston: Houghton Mifflin Co., 1961.
Law, Michael John. *The Experience of Suburban Modernity: How Private Transport Changed Interwar London*. Manchester: Manchester University Press, 2014.
Lewis, Roy and Maude, Angus. *The English Middle Classes*. London: Phoenix House, 1949.
Light, Alison. *Forever England: Femininity, Literature and Conservatism Between the Wars*. London: Routledge, 1991.
Marshall, James. *The History of the Great West Road: Its Social and Economic Influence on the Surrounding Area*. Hounslow: Heritage Publications, 1995.
Matless, David. *Landscape and Englishness*. London: Reaktion, 1998.
Mauch, Christof and Zeller, Thomas (eds) *The World Beyond the Windshield: Roads and Landscapes in the United States and Europe*. Athens: Ohio University Press, 2008.
McKay, George (ed.) *Yankee Go Home: (and take me with U): Americanization and Popular Culture*. Sheffield: Sheffield Academic Press, 1997.
McKibbin, Ross. *Classes and Cultures: England, 1918–51*. Oxford: Oxford University Press, 1998.
Montgomery, Maureen E. *'Gilded Prostitution': Status, Money and Transatlantic Marriages, 1870–1914*. London: Routledge, 1989.
Morgan, Kenneth. *Bolshevism and the British Left*. London: Lawrence & Wishart, 2006.
Morrison, Kathryn. *Carscapes: The Motor Car, Architecture and Landscape in England*. New Haven: Yale University Press, 2012.
Mort, Frank. *Capital Affairs: London and the Making of the Permissive Society*. New Haven: Yale University Press, 2010.

Napper, Lawrence. *British Cinema and Middlebrow Culture in the Interwar Years*. Exeter: University of Exeter Press, 2009.

Nevile, Sydney O. *Seventy Rolling Years*. London: Faber & Faber, 1958.

Nott, James J. *Music for the People: Popular Music and Dance in Interwar Britain*. Oxford: Oxford University Press, 2002.

O'Connell, Sean. *The Car and British Society: Class, Gender and Motoring 1896–1939*. Manchester: Manchester University Press, 1998.

Okrent, Daniel. *Last Call: The Rise and Fall of Prohibition*. New York: Scribner, 2011.

Oliver, Paul, Davis, Ian and Bentley, Ian. *Dunroamin: The Suburban Semi and Its Enemies*. London: Barrie & Jenkins, 1981.

Pegram, Thomas R. *Battling Demon Rum: The Struggle for a Dry America, 1800–1933*. Chicago: Ivan R. Dee, 1998.

Peiss, Kathy. *Cheap Amusements: Working Women and Leisure at the Turn of the Century New York*. Philadelphia: Temple University Press, 1986.

Peto, James, Loveday, Donna, and Powers, Alan (eds) *Modern Britain, 1929–1939*. London: Design Museum, 1999.

Plowden, William. *The Motor Car and Politics, 1896–1970*. London: Bodley Head, 1971.

Pringle, Margaret. *Dance Little Ladies: The Days of the Debutante*. London: Orbis, 1977.

Pugh, Martin. *'We Danced All Night': A Social History of Britain Between the Wars*. London: Bodley Head, 2008.

Rappaport, Erika, Dawson, Sandra Trudgen and Crowley, Mark J. (eds) *Consuming Behaviours: Identity, Politics and Pleasure in Twentieth-Century Britain*. London: Bloomsbury Academic, 2015.

Raub, Patricia. *Yesterday's Stories: Popular Women's Novels of the Twenties and Thirties*. Westport, CT: Greenwood, 1994.

Richards, Jeffrey. *The Age of the Dream Palace: Cinema and Society in Britain, 1930–1939*. London: Routledge, 1989.

Rieger, Bernhard. *Technology and the Culture of Modernity in Britain and Germany, 1890–1945*. Cambridge: Cambridge University Press, 2005.

Robson, Graham. *Motoring in the '30s*. Cambridge: Patrick Stephens, 1979.

Rose, Jonathan. *The Intellectual Life of the British Working Classes*. New Haven: Yale University Press, 2001.

Rosen, Marjorie. *Popcorn Venus: Women, Movies and the American Dream*. New York: Coward, McCann & Geoghegan, 1973.

Rydell, Robert W. and Kroes, Rob. *Buffalo Bill in Bologna: The Americanization of the World, 1869–1922* Chicago, IL: University of Chicago Press, 2005.

Saint, Andrew (ed.) *London Suburbs*. London: Merrell Holberton in Association with English Heritage, 1999.

Sedgwick, Michael. *Passenger Cars, 1924–1942*. London: Blandford Press, 1975.

Slater, David and Taylor, Peter J. (eds) *The American Century: Consensus and Coercion in the Projection of American Power*. Oxford: Blackwell, 1999.

Stevenson, John. *The Slump: Britain in the Great Depression*. London: Routledge, 2013.
Sweet, Matthew. *Shepperton Babylon*. London: Faber and Faber, 2006.
Taylor, David. J. *Bright Young People: The Rise and Fall of a Generation, 1918-1940*. London: Chatto & Windus, 2007.
Thorold, Peter. *The Motoring Age: The Automobile and Britain, 1896-1939*. London: Profile Books, 2003.
Tosh, John. *The Pursuit of History*. Harlow: Longman, 2002.
Vaughan, Paul. *Something in Linoleum*. London: Sinclair-Stevenson, 1994.
Walkowitz, Judith R. *Nights Out: Life in Cosmopolitan London*. New Haven: Yale University Press, 2012.
Webster, Duncan. *Looka Yonder!: The Imaginary America of Populist Culture*. London: Routledge, 1988.
Weinreb, Ben and Hibbert, Christopher. *The London Encyclopaedia*. London: Macmillan, 1987.
Wollen, Peter and Kerr, Joe. *Autopia: Cars and Culture*. London: Reaktion, 2002.

Chapters in edited collections

Aslet, Clive. 'Refuelling the Body, the Soul and the Morris Road Houses of the 1920s and 1930s'. In Marcus Binney and Emma Milne (eds) *Time Gentlemen Please!* London: SAVE Britain's Heritage and CAMRA, 1983, 20-5.
Bradley, Kate, 'Rational Recreation in the Age of Affluence: The Café and Working-Class Youth in London, c.1939-65'. In Erika Rappaport, Sandra Trudgen Dawson and Mark J. Crowley (eds) *Consuming Behaviours: Identity, Politics and Pleasure in Twentieth-Century Britain*. London: Bloomsbury Academic, 2015, 71-86.
Critoph, Gerald E. 'The Flapper and Her Critics'. In Carol V. R. George (ed.) *'Remember the Ladies': New Perspectives on Women in American History: Essays in Honor of Nelson Manfred Blake*. Syracuse: Syracuse University Press, 1975, 145-60.
Gutzke, David W. 'Progressivism in Britain and Abroad'. In David W. Gutzke (ed.) *Britain and Transnational Progressivism*. New York: Palgrave MacMillan, 2008, 23-64.
Koshar, Rudi. 'Driving Cultures and the Meaning of Roads'. In Christof Mauch and Thomas Zeller (eds) *The World Beyond the Windshield: Roads and Landscapes in the United States and Europe*. Athens: Ohio University Press, 2008, 14-34.
Kroes, Rob. 'Americanization, What Are We Talking About?' In Rob Kroes, Richard Rydell and Doeko Bosscher (eds) *Cultural Transmissions and Receptions: American Mass Culture in Europe*. Amsterdam: VU University Press, 1993, 302-20.
Nott, James J. '"The Plague Spots of London": William Joynson-Hicks, the Conservative Party, and the Campaign against London's Nightclubs, 1924-29'. In Clare V.J. Griffiths, James J. Nott and William Whyte (eds), *Classes, Cultures, and Politics: Essays on British History for Ross McKibbin*. Oxford: Oxford University Press, 2011, 227-46.
Potts, Alex. 'Constable Country Between the Wars'. In Raphael Samuel (ed.) *Patriotism: The Making and Unmaking of British National Identity*. London: Routledge, 1989, 160-86.

Powers, Madelon. 'Decay from Within: The Inevitable Doom of the American Saloon'. In Susanna Barrow and Robin Room (eds) *Drinking: Behavior and Belief in Modern History*. Berkeley: University of California, 1991, 112–31.

Ryan, Mary P. 'The Projection of a New Womanhood: The Movie Moderns in the 1920's'. In Jean E. Friedman and William G. Shade (eds) *Our American Sisters: Women in American Life and Thought*. Toronto: D.C. Heath & Co., 1982, 500–18.

Walley, Francis. 'Prestressing. In R.J.M Sutherland, Dawn Humm and Mike Chrimes (eds) *Historic Concrete: Background to Appraisal*. London: Thomas Telford Publishing, 2001, 191–210.

Theses

North, D. L. 'Middle-Class Suburban Lifestyles and Culture in England, 1919–1939'. Unpublished DPhil thesis, University of Oxford, 1989.

White, Kevin F. 'The Flapper's Boyfriend: The Revolution in Morals and the Emergence of Modern American Male Sexuality, 1910–30'. PhD thesis, Ohio State University, 1990.

Websites

A Vision of Britain Through Time, www.visionofbritain.org.uk (accessed 5 September 2013).

BBC, www.bbc.co.uk/history/domesday/dblock/GB-512000-195000/page/6 (accessed 15 December 2015).

Google Ngram Viewer, https://books.google.com/ngrams (accessed 4 August 2014).

Great Fosters Hotel, http://www.greatfosters.co.uk/hotel/history/ (accessed 12 February 2013).

Oxford Dictionary of National Biography, Oxford: Oxford University Press, 2004, online ed. http://www.oxforddnb.com (accessed 19 January 2015).

Romford Now & Then website. http://www.romford.org (accessed 17 June 2013).

Surbiton.com, www.surbiton.com/forum/ace-spades-history, 2012 (accessed 11 January 2016).

University of Houston, Digital History Project, http://www.digitalhistory.uh.edu/database/article_display.cfm?HHID=454 (accessed 2 March 2012).

University of Oxford, http://www.ox.ac.uk/about/oxford-people/women-at-oxford (accessed 22 December 2015).

Index

Note: The letter 'n' following locators refers to notes

Abercrombie, Patrick 18, 55 n.11
American drinking establishments
   cocktails 32
   courting couples 4
   desegregated public drinking 31
   disappearance of chaperones 32
   flappers 32
   impact of automobile 32
   new drinking habits 4, 31–2,124
   prohibition 3, 4, 15, 16, 31–2, 37, 39, 47, 54, 85, 87, 123–4, 129
   speakeasies, cabarets, roadhouses and nightclubs 4, 32
American roadhouses
   absence of adult supervision 36
   adolescent drinking 35
   amenities 4, 33
   bloodshed and murder 37
   brothels 34
   Chicago 33
   circuits of vice 34
   cocktails 8, 32, 36
   courting 31, 35
   crime 16, 33, 124
   dancing 15–17, 33, 35–7
   desegregated leisure 79, 123
   drugs 34
   egalitarian ambiance 32
   factors fostering rise 15
   films 36
   flappers 4, 31–3, 123
   flasks 35
   immorality 35
   interiors 33
   jazz 33, 36, 47
   juvenile and adolescent customers 34
   male escorts 33
   origins of term 15
   pejorative reputation 52
   petting 32–3, 35–6
   police 37
   premarital intercourse 36
   prostitution 4–5, 16, 34, 123
   romance in parking lots 35
   secluded car parks 35–6
   shimmy 36
   transgression and crime 5, 16, 33–4
   typology 16
   white slavery rings 34
Anglo-American exchanges 29, 45
   Americanization 38–9, 51, 81–94: fictional 95–6, 104, 108, 124; history 81; theory 2–3, 127–8
   British columnists disseminate unsavoury image 37
   British roadhouses hybrid 13
   British stereotype of US drinking norms 37
   cocktails 85
   comparison between US and British roadhouses 39, 54
   cultural imports from US 12
   differing access to the automobile 52
   drinking habits 32
   impact of US roadhouse reputations on Britain 51–2
   influencing perception of British road houses 9, 37, 124
   modernity 89, 92–5, 117
   parallels between US cities and London 37, 126
   parallels in drinking with Britain 47
   prohibition 31
   reputation of US roadhouses 9, 37, 123
anti-Semitism 51, 120, 126
Arlen, Michael 20
Automobile Association 111
automobiles. *See* driving
automobility 130

Index

Ballaster, Ros 101
brewers' improved pubs 7–8, 10, 18, 27–8, 45–6, 73, 138 n.23, 147 n.1
brewers' super pubs 76, 115
Bright Young Things
   composition 23, 39
   disdain for later roadhouses 112, 117
   press coverage 51
   river clubs 20
Butlin, Billy 116

cars. *See* driving
chauffeurs
   accommodation 19, 29, 116, 127
   choosing destinations 73
   masculinity 60
   not using them 18, 49, 130
   using them 2, 55
   violent 97
cinemas
   architectural style 26
   audiences 21
   imaginary America 3
   leisure 11
Clunn, Harold 25, 28, 57–8
countryside
   commercialization 58
   deep England 60, 88
   liminality 106–7, 128–9
   modernity 60
   motoring destination 22, 61, 79
   population movement 10

dancing
   American roadhouses 15–17, 33, 35–7
   crazes 47
   evening dress 72, 93
   flappers 31
   late night 39, 48, 74, 76, 92
   live music 25, 27–8, 33, 72, 80, 103, 113
   river clubs 21–2
   shimmy 36
   unlicensed 51
demographics 55–6
Dix, Dorothy 35
drinking
   association with United States 9, 32, 36–7, 63
   bartenders 88
   cocktails 45, 62, 64
   drinking and driving 62–4
   gendered drinking 8, 87
   improved pubs 1, 7–8, 10, 17–18, 26–9, 45–6, 65, 73, 76, 78, 115, 124, 127
   licensing 40
   limited drinking hours 63
   modern image 85–6
   progressive beliefs 7, 27
   superpubs 76
driving 31, 52–3
   car adoption rates 18, 54–5
   closed-roofed vehicles 51, 62
   drinking and driving 62–4
   driving to roadhouses 57, 112, 129–30
   modernity 130
   motor rallies 70
   picking up girls 113
   sports cars 109
   types of driving 59–61

Ewer, Monica
   background and life 99–100
   Insecurity (1930) 100
   Roadhouse (1935): artifice 85, 107; categorization 101; filmic approach 107; finances 67, 109, 111, 114, 122, 126; modernity 100–5; respectability 40
Ewer, Norman 100

Fitzgerald, F. Scott 32
flappers. *See* American roadhouses

golf 8, 11, 25, 27, 130
government, British
   arterial roads 22, 56–7
   petrol ration 116
   price controls 118
   women's drinking 7
government, local 89
Greene, Graham
   Brighton Rock (1938) 43, 53
   The Confidential Agent (1939) 97–8, 107, 117, 127
   on Edgar Wallace 96
   roadhouse novels 13

Hackett, Walter 41
Hoare, Rawdon 82

Isow, Jack
    anti-Semitism 51, 126
    Soho clubs 21
    Thatched Barn 113, 115

Jackson, Alan 11
jazz
    Americanization 128
    bands 28, 38, 47
    post-war clubs 121
    transgression 5, 36, 123

Lancaster, Osbert
    Progress at Pelvis Bay (1936) 65–6, 80, 92, 126
leisure 2–13
    architecture 80, 84–5
    driving 21
    changes in leisure time 27, 31, 39, 46, 65, 74
    gender 78–9, 88
    middle class 27–9
    post-war 120–5
    privacy 48
lidos
    public 23, 88–9, 94
    roadhouse 77, 83
Light, Alison 11, 61, 101
Long, George 17
lower-middle classes
    cinema 21
    reading habits 96, 101
    suburbanization 55
    using roadhouses 64

Mais, S. P. B. 17, 20
McKibbin, Ross 10, 117
McMinnies, W. G.
    Signpost (1935 et seq): class 9; modernity 83; movies 85; roadhouse amenities 26, 29, 70–2, 76–9, 83–92, 112; roadhouses' decline 118–20, 125–7; transgression 40, 43–8, 52, 116
Meyrick, Mrs Kate 39, 46–7
    'Queen of Nightclubs' 38
    transatlantic exchanges 38
middle classes
    drinking habits 7, 18, 62, 64, 124, 128
    driving 12, 46, 94, 125, 129
    leisure 11, 29, 60–2, 89, 130
    reading habits 101
    suburbia 2, 10–11
mobilities 2, 11, 15, 97, 104
mock-Tudor
    architecture 84, 94, 102, 107, 128
    interwar fashion 83
moderne architecture 26, 83, 89, 94, 108, 128
modernist architecture 19, 58–9, 84, 104–6
modernity
    Americanized 89, 92–5, 117
    cars 130
    roadhouses 100–5
    rural 60
    suburban 11
movies
    Americanization 81
    mock-Tudor 83
    roadhouses 36, 41
    romantic 100–1
Musman, Ernest B. 28, 84, 115

O'Connell, Sean 11, 52
outdoors
    cars 60
    interwar obsession 23, 129
    swimming 88, 124

Pegram, Thomas 32
police
    American roadhouses 37
    British roadhouses 9, 98, 113, 124, 129
    Soho 46, 129
Postgate, Raymond 31
poverty 47, 55, 100
Powell, Anthony 13
Priestley, J. B. 81, 113
Prince of Wales, Edward 9, 46, 80, 112

roadhouse
    advertising 112, 114
    amenities 59, 66, 69, 71–2, 74
    Americans, influx of 120
    appeal 79
    bands 38, 47, 72, 80, 82, 92–3, 103, 107–8, 113
    brewers 6–7, 12, 18, 27–9, 65, 67, 71, 76–7, 103, 113, 115, 126

brothels 49, 129
buildings 69, 128
cabaret shows 93
changes 9, 54, 64–5
class 10, 113
clientele 5–6, 8, 10, 24, 27, 46, 49, 62, 69, 71, 73, 80, 84, 117
clubs 79
cocktails 38, 45, 62–3, 80, 84, 87–8, 94, 103
comparison with US 4
cost 59, 77–8
courtship 8, 13
crime 95, 124, 128
crime fiction 13, 41, 43
dancing (*See separate entry*)
decline 12, 121–2
definition 17
demographics 10
desegregated leisure 6, 79, 88, 124
discount vouchers 112
disrepute 44, 49–50
down-market patrons 118
drinking (*See separate entry*)
driving 8, 10–11, 13, 15, 18, 65, 125
driving test and car trials 70
drugs 43
economic difficulties 114
Elstree film studios 85
employment of US bartenders 3
entertainment 117
family venues 122
fantasy world 85
fashionable image 85
female and male customers 78
fiction and Americanization 95
fictional working-class patrons 108
financing 29
golf 68, 71, 76, 80, 114
heightened competition 115–16, 126
homosexuality 51, 64, 129
hot summers 91
hybrid 28
illicit sex 9, 51
image 6, 84
immorality 42
impact of Second World War 116
impact of taxation 117
impact of US on British perspective 12
increased mobilities 11

lack of American investment 3
letting rooms 8, 74, 83, 119
licensed 40
lidos 77, 83
limited drinking hours 63
locations 75, 128
loss of allure 117
loss of identity 113
loss of US drinking traits 9
marketing 94
middle-class leisure 11
modernity 59, 100–5
movies 36, 41, 85
narrowing patron custom 117
new dating rituals 88
newsreels: entertainment 92–4, 102, 108–9; general 2, 27, 50, 102, 112, 125
overnight accommodation 51
period of popularity 12
petting 45
picking up women 113
playwrights 41
police 9, 98, 113, 124, 129
portable cocktail bars 64
profitability 111
property boom 119
prostitution 4–5, 43, 64, 120–1, 129
reputation 12, 40, 49–50
resiliency 118
respectability 5, 8
risqué reputations 9, 46
river clubs 17, 20–1, 130
sale at public auctions 114–15
sex in car parks 51
small pub roadhouses 17
'smart set' 5–6, 9, 12, 39, 52, 124–5
social clubs 79
social elite 72
suburbanization 10
super 5, 18, 21–2, 29, 47, 59, 92
survival strategies 118–19
swimming and swimming pools 6, 27, 75, 89, 91, 109, 113, 120
tea drinking 65
total numbers 2
transformation of leisure 5
transformed into motels 119
transgressive behaviour 5
typology 5, 17–18

widest appeal 2
youth as customers 121
Roadhouse Association 17
roadhouse establishments
    Ace of Spades (Great West Road) 22–3, 69–70, 82, 87, 89, 124
    Ace of Spades (Kingston Bypass) 9, 21–5, 48–51, 64, 68–71, 83–4, 90–3, 97, 102–3, 106–8, 112, 122, 128
    Adelphi 133
    Aldermaston Mill 48, 75, 132
    As You Like It 132
    Askers Road House 68, 76, 82, 132
    Barn 93, 112, 125, 132
    Bell House 72, 90–1, 93, 112, 114, 125, 127
    Berkeley Arms 28–9, 109, 115
    Birch Hotel 27
    Bridge House Hotel 67, 77
    Bubbling Brook 133
    Chase Hotel 27
    Chez Laurie 28, 44–8, 71, 77, 82–5, 128
    Clock 43, 70, 82–3, 112, 124–5, 128
    Comet 28, 84, 115, 126
    Crib Road House 71, 75, 93
    Croft Spa Hotel 133
    Crossways 114, 126, 133
    Crown Inn 77, 132
    Fenn Green 75, 133
    Finchdale Abbey House 44, 48, 115, 127
    Firleaze Road House 133
    Fisher's Pond 133
    Four Ways 133
    Galleon 76
    Gay Adventure 44, 55, 78, 85, 97
    George & Dragon 133
    Golden Lion 76, 133
    Great Fosters 27
    Green Plunge 131
    Havering Court 44, 76
    Hendon Way 76, 83, 132
    High Tower 114, 133
    Hilden Manor 79, 82, 84, 88
    Houseboat 44, 74–5, 77, 82, 114
    Kingfisher's Pool 87
    La Jollon 126, 133
    Larkfield 115, 127
    Laughing Water 19–20, 43, 58–9, 132
    Manor House 132
    Maybury 71, 77, 82–3, 119, 128
    MG's 78, 133
    Mill Stream 48, 133
    Moat Farm Road House 82, 132
    Monkey Puzzle 44, 48, 87, 111, 132
    Myllet Arms 48, 76, 85, 88, 115–16, 126
    Nautical William 44, 88, 91, 158
    Oatlands Park 27
    Old Barn 19, 20, 40, 66, 72, 132
    Old Mill Pool 132
    Old Water Mill 132
    Orchard Hotel 69, 133
    Pantiles 72, 75, 82, 89
    Pity Me 131
    Popular Road and Guest House 48, 68, 72, 83, 111, 133
    Pottal Pool 78, 134
    Prospect Inn 28, 102–3
    Rob Roy 68, 70, 134
    Showboat 24, 26–7, 53, 82–3, 104, 108–9, 114, 116, 126, 128
    Silver Arrow 134
    Silver Slipper 67, 134
    Spider's Web 5, 12, 40, 43, 50, 56, 67, 69–74, 78–9, 82–3, 88, 92–3, 102, 114, 119–20, 127–8
    Spinning Wheel Road House 57, 132
    Stewponey Hotel 44, 77
    Sugar Bowl 44
    Thatched Barn 5, 21, 24–6, 43–4, 51, 53, 56, 59, 69, 71, 73–9, 83–5, 92, 107, 113, 116, 126, 128
    Tudor House 40, 66, 72, 76, 79, 97, 126, 132
    Wagon Shed 134
    Water Splash 134
    Watermill 132
    White Rabbit Roadhouse 66, 68, 77, 134, 158
    Willow Barn 44, 78, 82
    Wookey Hole Caves 66–7, 75, 132
roadhouse owners/managers 6
    arrogant reputation 117
    Barclay, Perkins & Co. 113, 115
    Bester, Mrs 72–3
    Butt, Dame Clara 68
    Clarke, W.R. 68
    Collins, John 115
    Colosanti, Leonard 120
    Darnley, Lord 91
    Dundas, Elsa 65

Family Restaurant Ltd 75, 77
Fisher-Brown, Miss M.J. 66, 68
Hatherton, Lady 78
Hersey brothers 68, 70
Isow, Jack (*See separate entry*)
Kennedys 70
Lucy-Hulbert, Mrs 78
Reavenall, A.C. 67
Richardson, Humphrey L. 67
Short, Eustace 66
social class 73
Tomlinson, Commander 19, 40, 66, 72
Warrington, Thomas 45–6, 69, 71, 77
Waters, Walter and Frederick 69–70
Weymouth, Lord 67
Winwood Roadhouses Ltd 77
women 78
roads
   arterial 22, 56–8, 64, 102, 130
   country 59
   superseding rail, river 26

Sexton Blake story papers 13, 95–9
ships 74, 91, 104
slump 54, 59
Soho
   crime 4, 21, 37–9, 43, 124, 129
   espresso bars 121
   night clubs 4, 10, 46–7, 50–1, 113
Special Operations Executive 116
suburbia
   arterial roads 59
   housing 83
   modernity 11
   relative wealth 55
   roadhouse customers 88, 112

Taylor, A. J. P. 1
Taylor, David 10, 21
Taylor, Peter 2

upper classes
   roadhouse owners 78
   society 117
   Victorian and Edwardian 6

Vecchi, Joseph 21

Walkowitz, Judith 10, 38–9
Wallace, Edgar
   background and life 96
   The Coat of Arms (1931) 96–7, 124
   The Hand of Power (1927) 96
West End. *See also* Soho
   bartenders 85
   competing with roadhouses 5, 108, 112, 115, 130
   entertainment 12–13, 21, 28, 92–4
   gentlemen's clubs 9
   restaurants 73, 76, 92, 103
Williams-Ellis, Clough
   conservationism 22
   modernist 59
   roadhouse architect 18–20, 58, 91
working classes
   anonymity 31
   chauffeurs 19
   cultural consumption 21, 100, 113
   drinking 6, 29, 108
   driving 32
   leisure 11
   prostitution 34
   roadhouse ownership 111